# LAB MANUA

## *to Accompany*

FIFTH EDITION

Starting Out with

C++

*From Control Structures through Objects*

Tony Gaddis

## Dean DeFino
*Salisbury University*

## Michael Bardzell
*Salisbury University*

PEARSON

Addison
Wesley

Boston  San Francisco  New York
London  Toronto  Sydney  Tokyo  Singapore  Madrid
Mexico City  Munich  Paris  Cape Town  Hong Kong  Montreal

| | |
|---|---|
| Publisher | *Greg Tobin* |
| Executive Editor | *Michael Hirsch* |
| Editorial Assistant | *Lindsey Triebel* |
| Cover Designer | *Joyce Cosentino Wells* |
| Marketing Manager | *Michelle Brown* |
| Marketing Assistant | *Dana Lopreato* |
| Prepress and Manufacturing | *Carol Melville* |
| Supplement Coordination | *Marianne Groth* |

ISBN 0-321-43313-0
1 2 3 4 5 6 7 8 9 10—BB—09 08 07 06

# Contents

# Lab Manual Introduction

## To the Student...

A closed laboratory in computer programming is a vital activity for helping you gain valuable programming skills. Programming cannot be learned by "spectators". In other words, you cannot become a skilled programmer simply by watching others do it. You must spend numerous hours working on programs yourself. A closed laboratory experience gives you the opportunity to edit, write, compile, build, and execute programs of varying length and complexity under the guidance of your instructor. You will be able to reinforce concepts learned in class with a "hands on" approach. Throughout the course, your programming skills should steadily progress by applying knowledge learned in class to the laboratory setting.

This lab manual is divided into chapters called "Lesson Sets". At the beginning of each lesson set you will see a Purpose section which outlines the goals and expected outcomes of the lesson. This is immediately followed by a Procedure section. The first two steps of this section ask you to complete the Pre-lab Reading and Pre-lab Writing Assignments as a prerequisite to attempting the labs. It is imperative that you do both assignments before coming to your lab session. The laboratory exercises assume you have read and understood the key points of the corresponding lesson. The Pre-lab Writing Assignment usually consists of 8 – 10 very simple fill in the blank questions. Once the Pre-lab Reading is complete, you should have no trouble completing these questions. Your instructor may choose to collect this assignment at the beginning of your lab session. Although each Pre-lab Reading Assignment gives a concise overview of key concepts from the corresponding chapter in the text, it is not a substitute for reading your text. The text develops ideas in much more detail and also covers certain topics that cannot be included in a closed lab due to time constraints. Hence, this lab manual should be used as a supplement, not a replacement, for the text.

Your instructor will tell you which lab assignments should be completed during the lab session and which should be completed outside of class for homework. Although a hard copy of all code used for the lab assignments is included at the end of each lesson set, the code is also included in electronic form on the Web at www.aw.com/cssupport, under author "Gaddis." You should use this code rather than re-typing it from scratch.

## To the Instructor...

A closed laboratory in computer programming is a vital activity for helping students gain valuable programming skills under your guidance. Many different opinions concerning the content of such labs have been generated over the past few years, ranging from programming assignments to scheduled exercises using prepared materials. Although this manual emphasizes the latter approach and has pre-developed code for students to complete or edit, there are assignments that ask each student to independently create small programs which may be assigned as lab activities or as post-lab homework. These student generated code assignments are not intended as a substitute for larger programming assignments. Rather, they are small programs designed to test students on the material given in the lessons. The length of the lab activities vary from fifty minutes to two hours, depending on the particular institution. For this reason, the manual is divided into "Lesson Sets", each consisting of two fifty to sixty minute lessons of lab work. A fifty minute lab session should be able to complete an individual lesson and a one and a half to two hour session should be enough time for an entire lesson set. These times refer to "average classes". It is of course impossible to set a time frame for each student in a given lab. It is natural that some advanced students may finish a little early, while others will need more than the suggested time frame. Each Lesson Set corresponds to a chapter from Starting Out with C++: From Control Structures through Objects, Fifth Edition, by Tony Gaddis. The one exception, however, is Chapter 6. This chapter deals with functions and the corresponding laboratory exercises are broken into two lesson sets. This manual also corresponds to Tony Gaddis's Brief Version of Starting Out with C++.

The lab exercises in each lesson set are generally very simple to start and then increase in difficulty. Consequently, the student generated code assignments, which ask students to write complete programs, are given at the end of the second lesson. Most lesson sets contain three such assignments, so you have some flexibility as to how many of these programs are written during the laboratory session. A few lessons do have one somewhat sophisticated (to a beginning programmer) student generated code assignment. Other programming assignments may also be found at the end of each chapter of the text.

Each lesson set consists of the following:

**Pre-lab Reading Assignment.** This will prepare the students for material presented in the lab. This section gives a good, but brief, review of the corresponding chapter of the text. Examples and sample code are provided throughout this section, some of which are used in the subsequent labs. Students should thus be required to read this section before coming to lab.

**Pre-lab Writing Assignment.** These consist of short and easy questions on the reading material so that you may make sure students completed the pre-lab reading.

**Two Lessons of Lab Assignments.** These are done during the lab time, one lesson per hour (or fifty minute period).

**Supplements**: The following items are available at Addison-Wesley's Instructor Resource Center. Visit the Instructor Resource Center at www.aw.com/irc to register for access.

- Solutions to the lab exercises
- Teacher's Notes which consist of the following:

**Objectives for Students.** These are similar to the Purpose section given at the beginning of each lesson set in the lab manual. However, the objectives listed are geared more for the lab work whereas the Purpose section in the manual refers to the Pre-lab Reading material as well. In some lessons they are the same.

**Assumptions.** This section gives a brief list of what students should already know before attempting the corresponding lab assignment. It is generally assumed that the students have completed and understood the previous lessons (although some of the later lessons can be skipped) and that they have read and understood the Pre-lab Reading Assignment for the current lesson.

**Pre-lab Writing Assignment Solutions.** This section contains the answers to the Pre-lab Writing Assignment.

**Lab Assignments.** This section first lists the labs and then gives a more detailed description of each lab. Labs are broken into the lessons in which they are assigned.

Each instructor is encouraged to pick and choose labs based on the needs of their individual classes. The following is a suggested outline for a 14 week course that meets in a closed lab once a week for 50-60 minutes. This allows you to still cover one chapter a week for most weeks. As a general rule, a one hour lab session is enough time to complete section A of each lesson set. Assignments from section B, including the student generated code assignments, could be given as homework assignments.

| Week 1 | Lesson Set 1 | Lab 1.1 | Lab 1.2 | Lab 1.3 | Lab 1.4 (Optional Homework) |
|--------|--------------|---------|---------|---------|------------------------------|
| Week 2 | Lesson Set 2 | Lab 2.1 | Lab 2.2 | | Lab 2.4 (Optional Homework) |
| Week 3 | Lesson Set 3 | Lab 3.1 | Lab 3.2 | Lab 3.3 | Lab 3.5 (Optional Homework) |
| Week 4 | Lesson Set 4 | Lab 4.1 | Lab 4.2 | Lab 4.3 | Lab 4.4 (Optional Homework) |
| Week 5 | Lesson Set 5 | Lab 5.1 | Lab 5.2 | | Lab 5.4 (Optional Homework) |
| Week 6 | Lesson Set 6.1 | Lab 6.1 | Lab 6.2 | | Lab 6.3 (Optional Homework) |
| Week 7 | Lesson Set 6.2 | Lab 6.5 | Lab 6.6 | | Lab 6.7 (Optional Homework) |
| Week 8 | Lesson Set 7 | Lab 7.1 | Lab 7.2 | | Lab 7.3 (Optional Homework) |
| Week 9 | Lesson Set 8 | Lab 8.1 | Lab 8.2 | | Lab 8.3 (Optional Homework) |
| Week 10 | Lesson Set 9 | Lab 9.1 | Lab 9.2 | | Lab 9.3 (Optional Homework) |
| Week 11 | Lesson Set 10 | Lab 10.1 | Lab 10.2 | Lab 10.3 | Lab 10.4 (Optional Homework) |
| Week 12 | Lesson Set 11 | Lab 11.1 | Lab 11.2 | Lab 11.3 | Lab 11.4 (Optional Homework) |
| Week 13 | Lesson Set 12 | Lab 12.2 | Lab 12.3 | | Lab 12.4 (Optional Homework) |
| Week 14 | Lesson Set 13 | Lab 13.1 | Lab 13.3 | Lab 13.4 | Lab 13.2 (Optional Homework) |

For a one semester course that meets 2 hours a week in a closed lab, one lesson set per week will cover the manual in a fourteen week semester.

# 1 Introduction to Programming and the Translation Process

| | | |
|---|---|---|
| **PURPOSE** | 1. | To become familiar with the login process and the C++ environment used in the lab |
| | 2. | To understand the basics of program design and algorithm development |
| | 3. | To learn, recognize and correct the three types of computer errors: |

syntax errors
run time errors
logic errors

| | | |
|---|---|---|
| | 4. | To learn the basics of an editor and compiler and be able to compile and run existing programs |
| | 5. | To enter code and run a simple program from scratch |

| | | |
|---|---|---|
| **PROCEDURE** | 1. | Students should read the Pre-lab Reading Assignment before coming to lab. |
| | 2. | Students should complete the Pre-lab Writing Assignment before coming to lab. |
| | 3. | In the lab, students should complete Labs 1.1 through 1.4 in sequence. Your instructor will give further instructions as to grading and completion of the lab. |

| Contents | Pre-requisites | Approximate completion time | Page number | Check when done |
|---|---|---|---|---|
| Pre-lab Reading Assignment | | 20 min. | 2 | |
| Pre-lab Writing Assignment | Pre-lab reading | 10 min. | 6 | |
| **Lesson 1A** | | | | |
| Lab 1.1 Opening, Compiling and Running Your First Program | Pre-lab reading | 20 min. (Including overview of local system) | 7 | |
| Lab 1.2 Compiling a Program with a Syntax Error | Familiarity with the environment Finished Lab 1.1 | 15 min. | 7 | |

*continues*

| Lab 1.3<br>Running a Program with a<br>Run Time Error | Understanding of<br>the three types<br>of errors | 15 min. | 8 |
|---|---|---|---|
| **Lesson 1B** | | | |
| Lab 1.4<br>Working with Logic Errors | Understanding of<br>logic errors | 15 min. | 9 |
| Lab 1.5<br>Writing Your First Program | Finished Labs<br>1.1 through 1.4 | 30 min. | 11 |

## PRE-LAB READING ASSIGNMENT

### Computer Systems

A **computer system** consists of all the components (hardware and software) used to execute the desires of the computer user. **Hardware** is the electronic physical components that can retrieve, process and store data. It is generally broken down into five basic components:

| | |
|---|---|
| Central Processing Unit (C.P.U.) | This is the unit where programs are executed. It consists of the **control unit**, which oversees the overall operation of program execution and the **A.L.U.** (Arithmetic/Logic Unit), which performs the mathematical and comparison operations. |
| Main Memory | The area where programs and data are stored for use by the CPU |
| Secondary Storage | The area where programs and data are filed (stored) for use at a later time |
| Input Devices | The devices used to get programs and data into the computer (e.g., a keyboard) |
| Output Devices | The devices used to get programs and data from the computer (e.g., a printer) |

**Software** consists of a sequence of instructions given to perform some pre-defined task. These labs concentrate on the software portion of a computer system.

### Introduction to Programming

A **computer program** is a series of instructions written in some computer language that performs a particular task. Many times beginning students concentrate solely on the language code; however, quality software is accomplished only after careful design that identifies the needs, data, process and anticipated outcomes. For this reason it is critical that students learn good design techniques before attempting to produce a quality program. Design is guided by an **algorithm**, which is a plan of attacking some problem. An algorithm is used for many aspects of tasks, whether a recipe for a cake, a guide to study for an exam or the specifications of a rocket engine.

*Problem example:* Develop an algorithm to find the average of five test grades.

An algorithm usually begins with a general broad statement of the problem.

> Find the average of Five Test Grades

From here we can further refine the statement by listing commands that will accomplish our goal.

> Read in the Grades    Find the Average    Write out the Average

Each box (called a node) may or may not be refined further depending on its clarity to the user. For example: **Find the Average** may be as refined as an experienced programmer needs to accomplish the task of finding an average; however, students learning how to compute averages for the first time may need more refinement about how to accomplish the goal. This refinement process continues until we have a listing of steps understandable to the user to accomplish the task. For example, **Find the Average** may be refined into the following two nodes.

> Total=sum of 5 grades    Average=Total/5

Starting from left to right, a node that has no refinement becomes part of the algorithm. The actual algorithm (steps in solving the above program) is listed in bold.

Find the Average of Five Test Grades

**Read in the Grades**

Find the Average

**Total = sum of 5 grades**
**Average = Total / 5**

**Write Out the Average**

From this algorithm, a program can be written in C++.

## Translation Process

Computers are strange in that they only understand a sequence of 1s and 0s. The following looks like nonsense to us but, in fact, is how the computer reads and executes everything that it does:

100100011110101011100100001110001000

Because computers only use two numbers (1 and 0), this is called **binary** code. can imagine how complicated programming would be if we had to learn this very complex language. That, in fact, was how programming was done many years ago; however, today we are fortunate to have what are called **high level languages** such as C++. These languages are geared more for human understanding and thus make the task of programming much easier. However, since the computer only understands low level binary code (often called machine code), there must be a translation process to convert these high level languages to machine code. This is often done by a **compiler**, which is a software package that translates high level languages into machine code. Without it we could not run our programs. The figure below illustrates the role of the compiler.

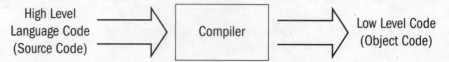

High Level Language Code (Source Code) → Compiler → Low Level Code (Object Code)

The compiler translates source code into object code. The type of code is often reflected in the extension name of the file where it is located.

*Example:* We will write source (high level language) code in C++ and all our file names will end with .cpp, such as:

```
firstprogram.cpp    secondprogram.cpp
```

When those programs are compiled, a new file (object file) will be created that ends with .obj, such as:

```
firstprogram.obj    secondprogram.obj
```

The compiler also catches grammatical errors called **syntax errors** in the source code. Just like English, all computer languages have their own set of grammar rules that have to be obeyed. If we turned in a paper with a proper name (like John) not capitalized, we would be called to task by our teacher, and probably made to correct the mistake. The compiler does the same thing. If we have something that violates the grammatical rules of the language, the compiler will give us error messages. These have to be corrected and a grammar error free program must be submitted to the compiler before it translates the source code into machine language. In C++, for example, instructions end with a semicolon. The following would indicate a syntax error:

```
cout << "Hi there" << endl
```

Since there is no semicolon at the end, the compiler would indicate an error, which must be corrected as follows:

```
cout << "Hi there" << endl;
```

After the compile process is completed, the computer must do one more thing before we have a copy of the machine code that is ready to be executed. Most programs are not entirely complete in and of themselves. They need other modules previously written that perform certain operations such as data input and output. Our programs need these attachments in order to run. This is the function of the **linking process**. Suppose you are writing a term paper on whales and would like a few library articles attached to your report. You would go to the library, get a copy of the articles (assuming it would be legal to do so), and attach them to your paper before turning it in. The **linker** does this to your program. It goes to a "software library" of programs and attaches the appropriate code to your program. This produces what is called the executable code, generated in a file that often ends with .exe.

*Example:* firstprogram.exe    secondprogram.exe

The following figure summarizes the translation process:

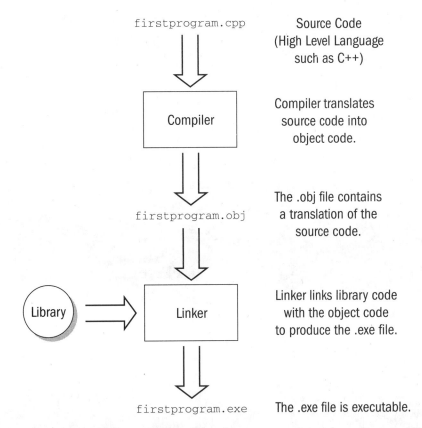

Once we have the executable code, the program is ready to be run. Hopefully it will run correctly and everything will be fine; however that is not always the case. During "run time", we may encounter a second kind of error called a **run time error**. This error occurs when we ask the computer to do something it cannot do. Look at the following sentence:

You are required to swim from Naples, Italy to New York in five minutes.

Although this statement is grammatically correct, it is asking someone to do the impossible. Just as we cannot break the laws of nature, the computer cannot violate the laws of mathematics and other binding restrictions. Asking the computer to divide by 0 is an example of a run time error. We get executable code; however, when the program tries to execute the command to divide by 0, the program will stop with a run time error. Run time errors, particularly in C++, are usually more challenging to find than syntax errors.

Once we run our program and get neither syntax nor run time errors, are we free to rejoice? Not exactly. Unfortunately, it is now that we may encounter the worst type of error: the dreaded **Logic error**. Whenever we ask the computer to do something, but mean for it to do something else, we have a logic error. Just as there needs to be a "meeting of the minds" between two people for meaningful communication to take place, there must be precise and clear instructions that generate our intentions to the computer. The computer only does what we ask it to do. It does not read our minds or our intentions! If we ask a group of people to cut down the tree when we really meant for them to trim the bush, we have a communication problem. They will do what we ask, but what we asked and what we wanted are two different things. The same is true for the computer. Asking it to multiply by 3 when we want something doubled is an example of a logic error. Logic errors are the most difficult to find and correct because there are no error messages to help us locate the problem. A great deal of programming time is spent on solving logic errors.

## Integrated Environments

An integrated development environment (IDE) is a software package that bundles an editor (used to write programs), a compiler (that translates programs) and a run time component into one system. For example, the figure below shows a screen from the Microsoft Visual C++ integrated environment.

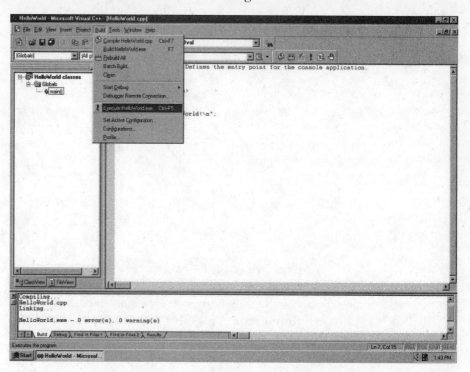

Other systems may have these components separate which makes the process of running a program a little more difficult. You should also be aware of which Operating System you are using. An **Operating System** is the most important software on your computer. It is the "grand master" of programs that interfaces the computer with your requests. Your instructor will explain your particular system and C++ environment so that you will be able to develop, compile and run C++ programs on it.

# PRE-LAB WRITING ASSIGNMENT

## Fill-in-the-Blank Questions

1. Compilers detect _____ errors.

2. Usually the most difficult errors to correct are the _____ errors, since they are not detected in the compilation process.

3. Attaching other pre-written routines to your program is done by the _____ process.

4. _____ code is the machine code consisting of ones and zeroes that is read by the computer.

5. Dividing by zero is an example of a _____ error.

**Learn the Environment That You Are Working In**

The following information may be obtained from your instructor.

1. What operating system are you using?

2. What C++ environment are you working in?

3. If you are not working in an integrated environment, what are the compile, run and edit commands that you will need?

## LESSON 1A

Your instructor may assign either Appendix A or Appendix B depending on your environment. Appendix A is for labs using Visual C++ and Appendix B is for labs using UNIX. If you are using an environment other than these two, your instructor will give you instructions for this first lesson and ask you to complete Lab 1.1 below.

**LAB 1.1    Opening, Compiling and Running Your First Program**

*Exercise 1:* Logon to your system based on your professor's instructions.

*Exercise 2:* Bring in the `firstprog.cpp` program from the Lab 1 folder.

*Exercise 3:* Compile the program.

*Exercise 4:* Run the program and write what is printed on the screen.

The code of `firstprog.cpp` is as follows:

```
// This is the first program that just writes out a simple message
// Place your name here

#include <iostream>              // needed to perform C++ I/O
using namespace std;

int main ()

{

    cout << "Now is the time for all good men" <<  endl;
    cout << "To come to the aid of their party" <<  endl;

    return 0;

}
```

**LAB 1.2    Compiling a Program with a Syntax Error**

*Exercise 1:* Bring in program `semiprob.cpp` from the Lab 1 folder.

*Exercise 2:* Compile the program. Here we have our first example of the many syntax errors that you no doubt will encounter in this course. The error message you receive may be different depending on the system you are using, but the compiler insists that a semicolon is missing somewhere. Unfortunately, where the message indicates that the problem exists, and where the problem actually occurs may be two different places. To correct the problem place a semicolon after the line `cout << "Today is a great day for Lab"`.

Most syntax errors are not as easy to spot and correct as this one.

*Exercise 3:* Re-compile the program and when you have no syntax errors, run the program and input 9 when asked. Record the output.

*Exercise 4:* Try running it with different numbers. Record your output.

Do you feel you are getting valid output?

The code of `semiprob.cpp` is as follows:

```cpp
// This program demonstrates a compile error.

// Place your name here

#include <iostream>
using namespace std;

int main()

{
    int number;
    float total;


    cout << "Today is a great day for Lab"
    cout << endl << "Let's start off by typing a number of your choice" << endl;
    cin  >> number;

    total = number * 2;
    cout << total << " is twice the number you typed" << endl;

    return 0;

}
```

## LAB 1.3  Running a Program with a Run Time Error

*Exercise 1:* Bring in program `runprob.cpp` from the Lab 1 folder.

*Exercise 2:* Compile the program. You should get no syntax errors.

*Exercise 3:* Run the program. You should now see the first of several run time errors. There was no syntax or grammatical error in the program; however, just like commanding someone to break a law of nature, the program is asking the computer to break a law of math by dividing by zero. It cannot be done. On some installations, you may see this as output that looks very strange. Correct this program by having the code divide by 2 instead of 0.

*Exercise 4:* Re-compile and run the program. Type 9 when asked for input. Record what is printed.

*Exercise 5:* Run the program using different values. Record the output. Do you feel that you are getting valid output?

The code of `runprob.cpp` is as follows:

```cpp
// This program will take a number and divide it by 2.

// Place your name here


#include <iostream>
using namespace std;

int main()

{

    float number;
    int divider;

    divider = 0;

    cout << "Hi there" << endl;
    cout << "Please input a number and then hit return" << endl;
    cin  >> number;

    number = number / divider;

    cout << "Half of your number is " << number << endl;

    return 0;
}
```

## LESSON 1B

### LAB 1.4    Working with Logic Errors

*Exercise 1:* Bring in program `logicprob.cpp` from the Lab 1 folder. The code follows.

```cpp
// This program takes two values from the user and then swaps them
// before printing the values.  The user will be prompted to enter
// both numbers.

// Place your name here

#include <iostream>
using namespace std;
```

*continues*

```
int main()

{

    float firstNumber;
    float secondNumber;

    // Prompt user to enter the first number.

    cout << "Enter the first number" << endl;
    cout << "Then hit enter" << endl;
    cin  >> firstNumber;

    // Prompt user to enter the second number.

    cout << "Enter the second number" << endl;
    cout << "Then hit enter" << endl;
    cin  >> secondNumber;

    // Echo print the input.

    cout << endl << "You input the numbers as " << firstNumber
         << " and " << secondNumber << endl;

      // Now we will swap the values.

    firstNumber = secondNumber;
    secondNumber = firstNumber;

    // Output the values.

    cout  << "After swapping, the values of the two numbers are "
          << firstNumber << " and " << secondNumber << endl;

    return 0;

}
```

*Exercise 2:* Compile this program. You should get no syntax errors.

*Exercise 3:* Run the program. What is printed?

*Exercise 4:* This program has no syntax or run time errors, but it certainly has a logic error. This logic error may not be easy to find. Most logic errors create a challenge for the programmer. Your instructor may ask you not to worry about finding and correcting the problem at this time.

## LAB 1.5    Writing Your First Program (Optional)

*Exercise 1:* Develop a design that leads to an algorithm and a program that will read in a number that represents the number of kilometers traveled. The output will convert this number to miles. 1 kilometer = 0.621 miles. Call this program `kilotomiles.cpp`.

*Exercise 2:* Compile the program. If you get compile errors, try to fix them and re-compile until your program is free of syntax errors.

*Exercise 3:* Run the program. Is your output what you expect from the input you gave? If not, try to find and correct the logic error and run the program again. Continue this process until you have a program that produces the correct result.

# 2 Introduction to the C++ Programming Language

| | |
|---|---|
| **PURPOSE** | 1. To briefly introduce the C++ programming language |
| | 2. To show the use of memory in programming |
| | 3. To introduce variables and named constants |
| | 4. To introduce various data types: |
| |     a. Integer |
| |     b. Character |
| |     c. Floating point |
| |     d. Boolean |
| |     e. String |
| | 5. To introduce the assignment and `cout` statements |
| | 6. To demonstrate the use of arithmetic operators |

| | |
|---|---|
| **PROCEDURE** | 1. Students should read the Pre-lab Reading Assignment before coming to lab. |
| | 2. Students should complete the Pre-lab Writing Assignment before coming to lab. |
| | 3. In the lab, students should complete Labs 2.1 through 2.4 in sequence. Your instructor will give further instructions as to grading and completion of the lab. |

| Contents | Prerequisites | Approximate completion time | Page number | Check when done |
|---|---|---|---|---|
| Pre-lab Reading Assignment | | 20 min. | 14 | |
| Pre-lab Writing Assignment | Pre-lab reading | 10 min. | 19 | |
| **Lesson 2A** | | | | |
| Lab 2.1 Working with the `cout` Statement | Pre-lab reading | 20 min. | 20 | |
| Lab 2.2 Working with Constants, Variables, and Arithmetic Operators | Understanding of variables and operators | 30 min. | 21 | |

*continues*

| **Lesson 2B** | | | |
| --- | --- | --- | --- |
| **Lab 2.3**<br>Rectangle Area and Perimeter | Understanding of<br>basic components<br>of a program | 30 min. | 22 |
| **Lab 2.4**<br>Working with Characters<br>and Strings | Completion of<br>labs 2.1-2.3 | 30 min. | 22 |

# PRE-LAB READING ASSIGNMENT

## The C++ Programming Language

Computer programming courses generally concentrate on program design that can be applied to any number of programming languages on the market. It is imperative, however, to apply that design to a particular language. This course uses C++, a popular object-oriented language, for that purpose.

For now, we can think of a C++ program as consisting of two general divisions: header and main. The **header**, or **global section**, gives preliminary instructions to the compiler. It consists of comments that describe the purpose of the program, as well as information on which library routines will be used by the program.

```
// This program prints to the screen the words:
// PI = 3.14
// Radius = 4
// Circumference = 25.12

#include <iostream>
using namespace std;

const double PI  = 3.14;

int main()
{
    float radius;
    radius = 4.0;

    cout << "PI = " << PI << endl;
    cout << "Radius = " << radius << endl;
    cout << "Circumference = " << 2 * PI * radius << endl;

    return 0;
}
```

Everything in bold (everything above the int main() statement) is considered the header or global section. Everything else is the main section.

**Comments** are included in every program to document what a program does and how it operates. These statements are ignored by the computer but are most valuable to the programmers who must update or fix the program. In C++, comments begin with `//` which is an indication to the compiler to ignore everything from the `//` to the end of the line. Comments can also cross line boundaries by beginning with `/*` and ending with `*/`. Notice that the first three lines of the previous program all begin with `//` and thus are comments. Those same lines could also have been written as the following:

```
/*   This program prints to the screen the words:
     PI = 3.14
     Radius = 4
     Circumference = 25.12
*/
```

The next statement, the `#include` statement, indicates which library will be needed by the program.

```
#include <iostream>
```

Recall from Lesson Set 1, that every program needs other modules attached so that it may execute properly. Your instructor will generally tell you which libraries are needed for each particular programming assignment; however, in time you will learn this task for yourself.

Every C++ program has a **main** function which indicates the start of the executable instructions. Every `main` must begin with a left brace `{` and end with a right brace `}`. The statements inside those braces will be explained as we progress through this lesson.

## Memory

Memory storage is the collection of locations where instructions and data that are used by the program are temporarily stored. Recall from Lesson Set 1 that a computer only understands a sequence of 1s and 0s. These are binary digits or **bits (BInary digiTs)**. Eight of these brought together are called a **byte**, which is the most common unit of storage. These chunks of memory can be thought of as hotel mailboxes at the registration desk. The size of each of those boxes indicates the type of mail that can be stored there. A very small mailbox can only hold notes or postcards. Larger mailboxes can hold letters, while even larger ones can hold packages. Each mailbox is identified by a number or name of an occupant. We have identified two very important attributes of these mailboxes: the name or number, which indicates the mailbox that is being referenced, and the size, which indicates what type of "data" can be placed there.

*Example:* **postcards Jim** is an indication that the mailbox called Jim can only hold postcards, while the statement **packages Mary** indicates that the mailbox called Mary can hold large packages. Memory locations in a computer are identified by the same two attributes: data type and name.

Much of programming is getting data to and from memory locations and thus it is imperative that the programmer tell the computer the name and data type of each memory location that he or she intends to use. In the sample program the statement **float radius** does just that. `float` is a data type that indicates what kind of data can be stored and `radius` is the name for that particular memory location.

## Variables and Constants

The ability to change or not change the data stored can be a third attribute of these memory locations. Components of memory in which data values stored can change during the execution of the program are called **variables**. These usually should not be defined in the header or global section of the program. In our sample program, radius is defined in the main function. Components of memory in which data values stored are initialized once and never changed during the execution of the program are called **constants**. They are often defined in the global section and are preceded (in C++) by the word **const**. PI, in the sample program, is an example of a named constant.

## Identifiers in C++

Identifiers are used to name variables, constants and many other components of a program. They consist exclusively of letters, digits and the underscore _ character. They cannot begin with a digit and cannot duplicate reserved words used in C++ such as **int** or **if**. All characters in C++ are case sensitive; thus memory locations called simple, Simple, and SIMPLE are three distinct locations. It has become standard practice among programmers to make constants all uppercase and variables predominantly lowercase characters.

The statement **const double PI = 3.14;** in our sample program is contained in the global section. It defines a memory location called PI to be a constant holding a double (a data type discussed shortly) value equal to 3.14 which will *not* change during the execution of the program.

The statement **float radius;** in the sample program is contained in the main section. It defines a variable memory location called radius that holds a floating point data type (type discussed shortly) which can be changed during the execution of the program.

Both of these statements are called **definitions**. They reserve by name enough memory to hold the data type specified.

Variables, like constants, can be given an initial value when they are defined, but that value is not permanent and can be altered. For example:

```
int count = 7;       // Defines a variable memory location called count that
                     // initially has the value of 7
count = count + 1;   // count is now altered
```

## Data Types

As noted earlier, computer memory is composed of locations identified by a data type and a name (like the room number of a hotel mailbox). The data type indicates what kind of data can be stored, thus setting the size of that location.

## Integer Data Type

Integers are real numbers that do not contain any fractional component. They take up less memory than numbers with fractional components. C++ has three data types that are integers: **short**, **int** and **long**. The difference is strictly in the amount of memory (bytes) they reserve: short reserving the least and long reserving the most. Larger integers may need the long data type.

The following three statements define integer variables in C++:

```
short count;
int sum;
long total;
```

## Floating Point Data Type

In computer science 3 = 3.0 is not a true statement. The number on the left is an integer and the number on the right is a real, or floating point, number (a number that has a fractional component). Although mathematically the two are equal, the computer stores them as different data types. C++ uses both **float** and **double** to indicate floating point numbers, with double using more memory than float.

The following two statements define floating point variables in C++.

```
float average;
double nationaldebt;
```

## Character Data Type

Character data includes the letters of the alphabet (upper and lower cases), the digits 0–9 and special characters such as ! ? . , *. All these symbols combined are called **alphanumeric**. Each character data is enclosed with single quotes to distinguish it from other data types. Thus '8' is different than 8. The first is a character while the second is an integer. The following statement defines a C++ character variable initialized to 'a'.

```
char letter = 'a';
```

## Boolean Data Type

The Boolean data type, named after the mathematician George Boole, allows only two values: true or false, which are internally represented as 0 and non-zero, respectively. The following statement defines a Boolean variable initialized to false.

```
bool found = false;
```

String Type: A variable defined to be character data can store only one character in its memory location, which is not very useful for storing names. The **string class** has become part of standard C++ and, although not a primitive type defined by the language, it can be used as a type for storing several characters in a memory location. We must "include" the string library (#include <string>) in the program header. The following statement defines a string initialized to "Daniel": string name = "Daniel"; Note that a string is enclosed in double (not single) quotes. Thus the string "a" is not the same as the character 'a'.

## Assignment Operator

The = symbol in C++ is called the **assignment operator** and is read "is assigned the value of." It assigns the variable on its left the value on its right. Although this symbol looks like an equal sign, do not confuse it with equality. The left hand side must always be a variable. For example, count = 8; is a legitimate statement in C++, however 8 = count; generates a syntax error.

## Fundamental Instructions

Most programming languages, including C++, consist of five fundamental instructions from which all code can be generated.

1. **Assignment Statements**: These statements place values in memory locations. The left side of an assignment statement consists of one and only one variable. The right side consists of an **expression**. An expression can be any manipulation of **literal** numbers (actual numbers such as 7 or 38, etc.), or the contents of constants and/or variables, that will "boil down" to one value. That value is placed in the memory location of the variable on the left. C++ uses = as the separator between the left and right side of the assignment statement. Those new to programming often get this confused with equality; however = in C++ is not equality but rather the symbol to indicate assignment. The = in C++ is read as "is assigned the value of".

*Example:*

```
int count;

int total;

total = 10;        // 10 is a literal that is placed in the memory
                   // location called total

count = 3 + 4;     // The right hand side of the statement is evaluated to
                   // 7. count is assigned the value of 7.

total = total + count; // The right hand side is evaluated 10 + 7,
                       // and 17 is placed in the memory location called
                       // total.
```

This last statement may seem a bit confusing. Starting with the right side, it says to get the value that is in `total` (10 in this case), add it to the value that is in `count` (7 in this case), and then store that combined sum (17) in the memory location called `total`. Notice that `total`, which was initially 10, gets changed to 17.

2. **Output Statements**: These instructions send information from the computer to the outside world. This information may be sent to the screen or to some file. In C++ the **cout** **<<** statement sends information to the screen. The `#include <iostream>` directive must be in the header for `cout` to be used.

```
cout << total;
```

The above statement sends whatever value is stored in the variable `total` to the screen. C++ uses the semicolon as a statement terminator.

We can output literal strings (such as "Hello") by inclosing them in double quotes.

The << operator acts as a separator for multiple outputs.

```
cout << "The value of total is " << total << endl;
```

The `endl` statement causes the cursor to be moved to the beginning of the next line.

The remaining three fundamental instructions will be explained in future labs.

3. **Input Statements**: These statements bring in data to the computer. (Lesson Set 3)

4. **Conditional Statements**: These instructions test conditions to determine which path of instructions to execute. (Lesson Set 4)

5. **Loops**: These instructions indicate a repetition of a series of instructions. (Lesson Set 5)

## Arithmetic Operators

Programming has the traditional arithmetic operators:

| Operation | C++ Symbol |
|---|---|
| addition | + |
| subtraction | - |
| multiplication | * |
| division | / |
| modulus | % |

**Integer division** occurs when both the numerator and denominator of a divide operation are integers (or numbers stored in variables defined to be integers). The result is always an integer because the decimal part is truncated or "chopped" from the number. Thus 9/2 will give the answer 4 not 4.5! For this reason there are two division operations for integer numbers. The modulus operator, (%) used only with integers, gives the remainder of a division operation. 9/2 gives 4 while 9 % 2 gives 1 (the remainder of the division).

*Example:*
```
int count = 9;
int div = 2;
int remainder;
int quotient;

quotient = count / div;        // quotient is assigned a 4
remainder = count % div;       // remainder is assigned a 1
```

You should go back and review the sample program on the first page of the Pre-lab Reading Assignment. By now you should understand most of the statements.

# PRE-LAB WRITING ASSIGNMENT

## Fill-in-the-Blank Questions

1. A _____ is a memory location whose value cannot change during the execution of the program.

2. _____ is a data type that only holds numbers with no fractional component.

3. _____ is a data type that holds numbers with fractional components.

4. _____ is an arithmetic operator that gives the remainder of a division problem.

5. cout << is an example of the _____ fundamental instruction.

6. _____ data types only have two values: true and false.

7. One byte consists of _____ bits.

8. // or /* in C++ indicates the start of a _____.

9. A _____ is a memory location whose value can change during the execution of the program.

10. A _____ can hold a sequence of characters such as a name.

# LESSON 2A

## LAB 2.1   Working with the cout Statement

*Exercise 1:* Retrieve program name.cpp from the Lab 2 folder.
Fill in the code so that the program will do the following:

Write your first and last name on one line.
Write your address on the next line (recall the function of the endl statement).
Write your city, state and zip on the next line.
Write your telephone number on the next line.
Remember that to output a literal, such as "Hello", you must use quotes.
Compile and run the program.

*Example:*   Deano Beano
123 Markadella Lane
Fruitland, Md. 55503
489-555-5555

The code for name.cpp is as follows:

```
//  This program will write the name, address and telephone
//  number of the programmer.

// PLACE YOUR NAME HERE

#include <iostream>
using namespace std;

int main()
{

    // Fill in this space to write your first and last name
    // Fill in this space to write your address (on new line)
    // Fill in this space to write you city, state and zip (on new line)
    // Fill in this space to write your telephone number (on new line)

    return 0;

}
```

*Exercise 2:* Change the program so that three blank lines separate the telephone number from the address. Compile and run the program.

*Exercise 3:* Change the program so that the following (but with your name and address) is printed. Try to get the spacing just like the example. Compile and run the program.

```
************
       Programmer: Deano Beano
                   123 Markadella Lane
                   Fruitland, Md. 55503

       Telephone: 489-555-5555

************
```

## LAB 2.2    Working with Constants, Variables and Arithmetic Operators

*Exercise 1:* Bring in the file `circlearea.cpp` from the Lab 2 folder.

The code of `circlearea.cpp` is as follows:

```cpp
// This program will output the circumference and area
// of the circle with a given radius.

// PLACE YOUR NAME HERE

#include <iostream>
using namespace std;

const  double PI = 3.14;
const  double RADIUS = 5.4;

int main()

{

       _____area              // definition of area of circle

       float  circumference;          // definition of circumference

       circumference = 2 * PI * RADIUS; // computes circumference

       area =_____;             // computes area

// Fill in the code for the cout statement that will output (with description)
// the circumference

// Fill in the code for the cout statement that will output (with description)
// the area of the circle

       return 0;
}
```

*Exercise 2:* Fill in the blanks and the cout statements so that the output will produce the following:

**The circumference of the circle is 33.912**
**The area of the circle is 91.5624**

*Exercise 3:* Change the data type of circumference from float to int. Run the program and record the results.

The circumference of the circle is _____.

The area of the circle is _____.

Explain what happened to get the above results.

# LESSON 2B

## LAB 2.3  Rectangle Area and Perimeter

*Exercise 1:* Using Lab 2.2 as an example, develop a program that will determine the area and perimeter of a rectangle. The length and width can be given as constants. (LENGTH=8 WIDTH=3)

*Exercise 2:* Compile and run your program. Continue to work on it until you get the following output.

**The area of the rectangle is 24**
**The perimeter of the rectangle is 22**

## LAB 2.4  Working with Characters and Strings

*Exercise 1:* Retrieve program stringchar.cpp from the Lab 2 folder. This program illustrates the use of characters and strings. The char data type allows only one character to be stored in its memory location. The string data type (actually a class and not a true data type built into the language) allows a sequence of characters to be stored in one memory location. The code follows:

```cpp
// This program demonstrates the use of characters and strings

// PLACE YOUR NAME HERE

#include <iostream>
#include <string>
using namespace std;

// Definition of constants
const string FAVORITESODA = "Dr. Dolittle";  // use double quotes for strings
const char BESTRATING = 'A';                  // use single quotes for characters


int main()

{
```

```
char rating;            // 2nd highest product rating
string favoriteSnack;   // most preferred snack
int numberOfPeople;     // the number of people in the survey
int topChoiceTotal;     // the number of people who prefer the top choice


//  Fill in the code to do the following:
//  Assign the value of "crackers" to favoriteSnack
//  Assign a grade of 'B' to rating
//  Assign the number 250 to the numberOfPeople
//  Assign the number 148 to the topChoiceTotal


// Fill in the blanks of the following:
cout << "The preferred soda is " <<_____<< endl;
cout << "The preferred snack is " <<_____<< endl;
cout << "Out of " <<_____<< " people "
     <<_____  << " chose these items!" << endl;
cout << "Each of these products were given a rating of " <<_____;
cout << " from our expert tasters" << endl;
cout << "The other products were rated no higher than a " << rating
     << endl;


return 0;


}
```

*Exercise 2:* Fill in the indicated code, then compile and run the program. Continue to work on the program until you have no syntax, run-time, or logic errors.

The output should look similar to the following:

    The preferred soda is Dr. Dolittle

    The preferred snack is crackers

    Out of 250 people 148 chose these items!

    Each of these products were given a rating of A from our expert tasters

    The other products were rated no higher than a B

*Exercise 3:* Is it possible to change the choice of FAVORITESODA by adding code within the main module of the program? Why or why not?

*Exercise 4:* Is it possible to change the choice of favoriteSnack by adding code within the program? Why or why not?

# 3

# Expressions, Input, Output and Data Type Conversions

**PURPOSE**

1. To learn input and formatted output statements
2. To learn data type conversions (coercion and casting)
3. To work with constants and mathematical functions
4. To briefly introduce the concept of files

**PROCEDURE**

1. Students should read the Pre-lab Reading Assignment before coming to lab.
2. Students should complete the Pre-lab Writing Assignment before coming to lab.

| Contents | Pre-requisites | Approximate completion time | Page number | Check when done |
|---|---|---|---|---|
| Pre-lab Reading Assignment | | 20 min. | 26 | |
| Pre-lab Writing Assignment | Pre-lab reading | 10 min. | 32 | |
| **LESSON 3A** | | | | |
| Lab 3.1 Working with the `cin` Statement | Confidence in use of data types | 15 min. | 33 | |
| Lab 3.2 Formatting Output | Basic understanding of `cout` and formatted output | 15 min. | 35 | |
| Lab 3.3 Arithmetic Operations and Math Functions | Understanding of pre-defined functions `pow` and `sqrt` | 20 min. | 36 | |
| **LESSON 3B** | | | | |
| Lab 3.4 Working with Type Casting | Understanding of type casting (implicit and explicit data conversion) | 20 min. | 37 | |

*continues*

| Lab 3.5 | | | |
|---|---|---|---|
| Reading and Writing to a File | Basic understanding of reading and writing files | 15 min. | 38 |
| Lab 3.6 | | | |
| Student Generated Code Assignments | Understanding of all concepts (except files) covered in this section. | 30 min. | 39 |

# PRE-LAB READING ASSIGNMENT

## Review of the cout Statement

The **cout** statement invokes an output stream, which is a sequence of characters to be displayed to the screen.

*Example:* cout << "Hi there";

The **insertion operator** << inserts the string of characters Hi there into the output stream that goes to the screen. The cout statement can be thought of as an **ostream** (output stream) data type.

## Input Instructions

Just as the cout statement transfers data from the computer to the "outside" world, the **cin** statement transfers data into the computer from the keyboard.

*Example:* cin >> grade;

The **extraction operator** >> extracts an item from the input stream. In this case, since grade is an integer, this instruction will wait for an integer to be entered at the keyboard and then will place that number in the memory location called grade.

Just as cout is of type ostream, cin is considered to be an **istream** (input stream) data type. In order to use cin and cout in a C++ program, the #include <iostream> directive should be included in the header. The >> extraction operator also serves as a separator between input variables, allowing more than one memory location to be loaded with a single cin instruction. The values read must be the same data type as their corresponding variables, although a floating point variable could receive an integer since the conversion will be made automatically. Conversion is discussed later in this lesson.

*Example:*
```
float rate;
float hours;

cin >> rate >> hours;
```

The cin statement will wait for two floating point numbers (separated by at least one blank space) to be input from the keyboard. The first will be stored in rate and the second in hours.

There is one problem with the example above; it does not indicate to the user for what data the `cin` statement is waiting. Remember that the `cin` statement is expecting data from the user at the keyboard. For this reason, every `cin` statement should be preceded by a `cout` statement that indicates to the user the data to be input. Such a `cout` statement is called a **prompt**.

*Example:*
```
float rate, hours;
                            // More than one variable can be defined
                            // in a statement. Multiple variables are
                            // separated by a comma.
float grosspay;

cout << "Please input the pay rate per hour"
     << " and then the number of hours worked" << endl;
cin >> rate >> hours;

grosspay = rate * hours;        // finds the grosspay

cout << endl << "The rate is = " << rate << endl;
cout << "The number of hours = " << hours << endl;
cout << "The gross pay =  " << grosspay << endl;
```

When `cin` is reading numeric data, whitespace (blank spaces or unseen control characters) preceding the number are ignored and the read continues until a non-numeric character is encountered.

## Strings

It is often useful to store a string, such as a name, in a variable. Since the `char` data type holds only a single character, we must define a variable that is able to hold a whole sequence of characters. One way to do this is through an **array** of characters, often referred to as a **C-string** in C++. When using this method to define a string, the programmer must indicate how many characters it can hold. The last character must be reserved for the end-of-string character `'\0'` which marks the end of the string. In Example 2 below, the variable `name` can hold up to 11 characters even though the size of the array indicates 12. The extra character is reserved for the end-of-string marker. Arrays of characters are discussed in a later chapter. For now we can define a variable to be a **string object**: Example 1 below.

*Example 1 (using a string object)*
```
string name;
cout << "What is your name";
cin  >> name;
cout << "Hi " << name << endl;
```

*Example 2 (using a C-string)*
```
char name[12]
cout << "What is your name";
cin >> name;
cout << "Hi " << name << endl;
```

Although Example 1 will work, we often do not use `cin >>` to read in strings. This is because of the way it handles **whitespace** (blank spaces, tabs, line breaks, etc.). When `cin >>` is reading numeric data, leading whitespace is ignored and the read continues until a non-numeric character is encountered. As one might expect, `cin >>` is a logical choice for reading numeric data. However, when `cin >>` is reading into a variable defined as a string, it skips leading whitespaces but stops if a blank space is encountered within the string. Names that have a space in it such as Mary Lou, would not be read into one variable using `cin >>`. We can get around this restriction by using special functions for reading whole lines of input. The `getline` function allows us to input characters into a string object. In Example 1 above we could read a name like Mary Lou into the `name` variable with the statement

```
getline(cin, name);
```

The first word in the parentheses is an indication of "where" the data is coming from. In this case it is coming from the keyboard so we use `cin`. Data could come from other sources such as files (discussed later in this chapter) in which case the name of the file would be used instead of `cin`. The second word in parentheses is the name of the variable that will "receive" the string (`name` in this case).

When using C-strings, we can read whole lines of input using `cin.getline (string_name, length)`, where length specifies the number of characters the C-string can hold. In Example 2 above, we could read a name like Mary Lou into the `name` variable with the statement

```
cin.getline(name,12);
```

This allows a maximum of 11 characters to be read in and stored in `name`, reserving a space for the '\0' end-of-string character.

## Summary of storing and inputting strings

| | |
|---|---|
| `cin >> name;` | Skips leading whitespaces <br> Stops at the first trailing whitespace which is not consumed (ie. the whitespace is not placed in name) |
| `cin.getline(name,12);` | Does not skip leading whitespaces <br> Stops when either 11 characters are read or when an end-of-line '\n' character is encountered (which is not consumed) |

## Formatted Output

C++ has special instructions that allow the user to control output attributes such as spacing, decimal point precision, data formatting and other features.

*Example:*

```
cout << fixed          // This displays the output in decimal
                       // format rather than scientific notation.

cout << showpoint;     // This forces all floating-point output to
                       // show a decimal point, even if the values
                       // are whole numbers

cout << setprecision(2);   // This rounds all floating-point numbers
                           // to 2 decimal places
```

The order in which these **stream manipulators** appear does not matter. In fact, the above statements could have been written as one instruction:

```
cout << setprecision(2) << fixed << showpoint;
```

Spacing is handled by an indication of the width of the field that the number, character, or string is to be placed. It can be done with the `cout.width(n);` where n is the width size. However it is more commonly done by the `setw(n)` within a `cout` statement. The `#include <iomanip>` directive must be included in the header (global section) for features such as `setprecision()` and `setw()`.

*Example:*
```
float price = 9.5;

float rate = 8.76;
cout << setw(10) << price << setw(7) << rate;
```

The above statements will print the following:

```
    9.5    8.76
```

There are seven blank spaces before 9.5 and three blank spaces between the numbers. The numbers are right justified. The computer memory stores this as follows:

| | | | | | | | 9 | . | 5 | | | | 8 | . | 7 | 6 |
|---|---|---|---|---|---|---|---|---|---|---|---|---|---|---|---|---|

Note: So far we have used `endl` for a new line of output. `'\n'` is an escape sequence which can be used as a character in a string to accomplish the same thing.

*Example:* Both of the following will do the same thing.

```
cout << "Hi there\n";              cout << "Hi there" << endl;
```

## Expressions

Recall from Lesson Set 2 that the assignment statement consists of two parts: a variable on the left and an expression on the right. The expression is converted to one value that is placed in the memory location corresponding to the variable on the left. These expressions can consist of variables, constants and literals combined with various operators. It is important to remember the mathematical precedence rules which are applied when solving these expressions.

## Precedence Rules of Arithmetic Operators

1. Anything grouped in parentheses is top priority
2. Unary negation (example: –8)
3. Multiplication, Division and Modulus * / %
4. Addition and Subtraction + –

*Example:*
```
( 8 * 4/2 + 9 - 4/2 + 6 * (4+3) )
( 8 * 4/2 + 9 - 4/2 + 6 * 7 )
( 32 /2   + 9 - 4/2 + 6 * 7 )
(   16    + 9 - 4/2 + 6 * 7 )
(   16    + 9 - 2   + 6 * 7 )
(   16    + 9 - 2   + 42 )
(       25      - 2 + 42 )
(            23     + 42 ) =    65
```

## Converting Algebraic Expressions to C++

One of the challenges of learning a new computer language is the task of changing algebraic expressions to their equivalent computer instructions.

*Example:* `4y(3-2)y+7`

How would this algebraic expression be implemented in C++?

`4 * y * (3-2) * y + 7`

Other expressions are a bit more challenging. Consider the quadratic formula:

$$\frac{-b \pm \sqrt{b^2 - 4ac}}{2a}$$

We need to know how C++ handles functions such as the square root and squaring functions.

There are several predefined math library routines that are contained in the `cmath` library. In order to use these we must have the `#include <cmath>` directive in the header.

Exponents in C++ are handled by the `pow(number,exp)` function, where `number` indicates the base and `exp` is the exponent. For example,

$2^3$ would be written as `pow(2,3)`

$5^9$ would be written as `pow(5,9)`

Square roots are handled by `sqrt(n)`. For example,

$\sqrt{9}$ would be written as `sqrt(9)`

Look at the following C++ statements and try to determine what they are doing.

```
formula1 = ( -b + sqrt(pow(b,2) -(4 * a * c))) / (2 * a);
formula2 = ( -b - sqrt(pow(b,2) -(4 * a * c))) / (2 * a);
```

(These are the roots from the quadratic formula in C++ format.)

## Data Type Conversions

Recall the discussion of data types from Lesson Set 2. Whenever an integer and a floating point variable or constant are mixed in an operation, the integer is changed temporarily to its equivalent floating point. This automatic conversion is called **implicit type coercion**.

Consider the following:

```
int count;
count = 7.8;
```

We are trying to put a floating point number into an integer memory location. This is like trying to stuff a package into a mailbox that is only large enough to contain letters. Something has to give. In C++ the floating point is **truncated** (the entire fractional component is cut off) and, thus, we have loss of information.

Type conversions can be made explicit (by the programmer) by using the following general format: static_cast<DataType>(Value). This is called **type casting** or **type conversion**.

*Example:*

```
int count;
float sum;

count = 10.89;                      // Float to integer  This is Type coercion
                                    // 10 is stored in count

count = static_cast<int>(10.89);    // Also float to integer; however this is
                                    // type casting
```

If two integers are divided, the result is an integer that is truncated. This can create unexpected results.

*Example:*
```
int num_As = 10;
int totalgrade = 50;
float percent_As;

percent_As = num_As / totalgrade;
```

In this problem we would expect `percent_As` to be .20 since 10/50 is .20. However since both `num_As` and `totalgrade` are integers, the result is integer division which gives a truncated number. In this case it is 0. Whenever a smaller integer value is divided by a larger integer value the result will always be 0. We can correct this problem by type casting.

```
percent_As = static_cast<float>(num_As)/totalgrade;
```

Although the variable `num_As` itself remains an integer, the type cast causes the divide operation to use a copy of the `num_As` value which has been converted to a float. A float is thus being divided by the integer `totalGrade` and the result (through type coercion) will be a floating-point number.

## Files

So far all our input has come from the keyboard and our output has gone to the monitor. Input, however, can come from files and output can go to files. To do either of these things we should add the `#include <fstream>` directive in the header to allow files to be created and accessed. A file containing data to be input to the computer should be defined as an `ifstream` data type and an output file should be defined as `ofstream`.

*Sample Program 3.1*

Suppose we have a data file called `grades.dat` that contains three grades, and we want to take those grades and output them to a file that we will call `finalgrade.out`. The following code shows how this can be done in C++.

```
#include <fstream>                  // This statement is needed to use files
using namespace std;


int main()
{
    float grade1, grade2, grade3;   // This defines 3 float variables
```

*continues*

```
ifstream dataFile;              // This defines an input file stream.
                                // dataFile is the "internal" name that is
                                // used in the program for accessing the
                                // data file.


ofstream outFile;               // This defines an output file stream.
                                // outFile is the "internal" name that is
                                // used in the program for accessing the
                                // output file.


outFile << fixed << showpoint;  // These can be used with output files as
                                // well as with cout.


dataFile.open("grades.dat");    // This ties the internal name, dataFile,
                                // to the actual file, grades.dat.


outFile.open("finalgrade.out"); // This ties the internal name, outFile, to
                                // the actual file, finalgrade.out.


dataFile >> grade1 >> grade2    // This reads the values from the input file
        >> grade3;              // into the 3 variables.


outFile << grade1 << endl;      // These 3 lines write the values stored in
outFile << grade2 << endl;      // the 3 variables to the output file
outFile << grade3 << endl;


return 0;
}
```

## PRE-LAB WRITING ASSIGNMENT

### Fill-in-the-Blank Questions

1. What is the final value (in C++) of the following expression?

   `(5 - 16 / 2 * 3 + (3 + 2 / 2) - 5)` _____

2. How would the following expression be written in C++?

   $2x + 3^4$

   _____

3. Implicit conversion is also known as data type _____.
4. Explicit type conversion is also known as type _____.
5. List the preprocessor directive that must be included for `cin` and `cout` to be used in a C++ program. _____
6. List the preprocessor directive that is used to allow data and output files to be used in the program. _____
7. Blank spaces or unseen control characters in a data file are referred to as _____.
8. The `<<` in a `cout` statement is called the _____ operator.
9. The `#include<`_____`>` is needed for formatted output.
10. The `'\n'` is a special character that _____.

# LESSON 3A

## LAB 3.1    Working with the `cin` Statement

Bring in the program `bill.cpp` from the Lab 3 folder. The code is listed below:

```cpp
// This program will read in the quantity of a particular item and its price.
// It will then print out the total price.
// The input will come from the keyboard and the output will go to
// the screen.

//   PLACE YOUR NAME HERE

#include <iostream>
#include <iomanip>
using namespace std;


int main()

{
        int    quantity;      // contains the amount of items purchased
        float itemPrice;      // contains the price of each item
        float totalBill;      // contains the total bill.


        cout << setprecision(2) << fixed << showpoint;   // formatted output

        cout << "Please input the number of items bought" << endl;

        // Fill in the input statement to bring in the quantity.

        // Fill in the prompt to ask for the price.

        // Fill in the input statement to bring in the price of each item.

        // Fill in the assignment statement to determine the total bill.

        // Fill in the output statement to print total bill,
        // with a label to the screen.

        return 0;
}
```

*Exercise 1:* Complete the program so that a sample run inputting 22 for the number of items bought and 10.98 for the price of each item will produce the results below.

Sample run of the program.

**Please input the number of items bought**
22

```
Please input the price of each item
10.98


The total bill is $241.56
```

*Exercise 2:* Once you have the program working, change the instruction:

```
cout << setprecision (2) << fixed << showpoint;
```

to

```
cout << setprecision(2) << showpoint;
```

Rerun the program with the same data given in Exercise 1 above and record your results. What do you think the fixed attribute in the cout statement does?

*Exercise 3:* Now put the fixed attribute back in and change the instruction to make the precision 4. Rerun the program with the same data given in Exercise 1 and record your results. What do you think the setprecision( ) attribute in the cout statement does?

The attribute showpoint forces all floating point output to show a decimal point even if the values are whole numbers. In some environments this is done automatically.

(optional)

Exercise 4: Add the following directive to the program: #include <string> in the header. Alter the program so that the program first asks for the name of the product (which can be read into a string object) so that the following sample run of the program will appear.

**Please input the name of the item**
Milk
**Please input the number of items bought**
4

**Please input the price of each item**
1.97

**The item that you bought is Milk**
**The total bill is $7.88**


Now altar the program, if you have not already done so, so that the name of an item could include a space within its string.

**Please input the name of the item**
Chocolate Ice Cream

**Please input the number of items bought**
4

**Please input the price of each item**
1.97

**The item that you bought is Chocolate Ice Cream**
**The total bill is $7.88**

## LAB 3.2    Formatting Output

Look at the following table:

```
          PRICE    QUANTITY

           1.95    8
          10.89    9
```

Assume that from the left margin, the price takes up fifteen spaces. We could say that the numbers are right justified in a 15-width space. Starting where the price ends, the next field (quantity) takes up twelve spaces. We can use the formatted output from Lab 3.1 and the statement setw(n) where n is some integer to indicate the width to produce such tables.

Bring in the program tabledata.cpp from the Lab 3 folder. The code is as follows:

```cpp
//  This program will bring in two prices and two quantities of items
//  from the keyboard and print those numbers in a formatted chart.


//PLACE YOUR NAME HERE

#include <iostream>
#include _____    // Fill in the code to bring in the library for
                          // formatted output.
using namespace std;

int main()

{
    float price1, price2;       // The price of 2 items
    int   quantity1, quantity2; // The quantity of 2 items


    cout << setprecision(2) << fixed << showpoint;
    cout << "Please input the price and quantity of the first item" << endl;

    // Fill in the input statement that reads in price1 and
    // quantity1 from the keyboard.

    // Fill in the prompt for the second price and quantity.

    // Fill in the input statement that reads in price2 and
    // quantity2 from the keyboard.

    cout << setw(15) << "PRICE" << setw(12) << "QUANTITY\n\n";

    // Fill in the output statement that prints the first price
    // and quantity. Be sure to use setw() statements.

    // Fill in the output statement that prints the second price
    // and quantity.

    return 0;

}
```

*Exercise 1:* Finish the code above by filling in the blanks and the instructions necessary to execute the following sample run. Note that two or more data items can be input at one time by having at least one blank space between them before hitting the enter key.

**Please input the price and quantity of the first item**
1.95 8

**Please input the price and quantity of the second item**
10.89 9

| PRICE | QUANTITY |
|-------|----------|
| 1.95  | 8        |
| 10.89 | 9        |

## LAB 3.3   Arithmetic Operations and Math Functions

Bring in the program `righttrig.cpp` from the Lab 3 folder. The code is as follows:

```
// This program will input the value of two sides of a right triangle and then
// determine the size of the hypotenuse.

// PLACE YOUR NAME HERE

#include <iostream>
#include <cmath>          // needed for math functions like sqrt()
using namespace std;


int main()

{

      float a,b;          // the smaller two sides of the triangle
      float hyp;          // the hypotenuse calculated by the program

      cout << "Please input the value of the two sides" << endl;
      cin >> a >> b;


      // Fill in the assignment statement that determines the hypotenuse

      cout << "The sides of the right triangle are " << a << " and " << b << endl;

      cout << "The hypotenuse is " << hyp << endl;

      return 0;

}
```

The formula for finding the hypotenuse is $hyp = \sqrt{a^2 + b^2}$.

How can this be implemented in C++? Hint: You will use two pre-defined math functions (one of them twice) learned in this lesson. One of them will be "inside" the other.

*Exercise 1:* Fill in the missing statement so that the following sample run is implemented:

```
Please input the value of the two sides
9 3
The sides of the right triangle are 9 and 3
The hypotenuse is 9.48683
```

*Exercise 2:* Alter the program so that the sample run now looks like the following:

```
Please input the value of the two sides
9 3
The sides of the right triangle are 9 and 3
The hypotenuse is 9.49
```

Note: This is not a trivial change. You must include another directive as well as use the formatted features discussed in the earlier labs of this lesson. Notice that the change is made only to the value of the hypotenuse and not to the values of 9 and 3.

# LESSON 3B

## LAB 3.4   Working with Type Casting

Bring in the program `batavg.cpp` from the Lab 3 folder. The code follows.

```
// This program will determine the batting average of a player.
// The number of hits and at bats are set internally in the program.

// PLACE YOUR NAME HERE

#include <iostream>
using namespace std;


const int AT_BAT = 421;
const int HITS = 123;

int main()
{
    int batAvg;

    batAvg = HITS / AT_BAT                              // an assignment statement
    cout << "The batting average is " << batAvg << endl;   // output the result

    return 0;
}
```

*Exercise 1:* Run this program and record the results. The batting average is _____.

*Exercise 2:* There is a logic error in this program centering around data types. Does changing the data type of batavg from int to float solve the problem? Make that change and run the program again and record the result.

The batting average is _____.

*Exercise 3:* Continue to work with this program until you get the correct result. The correct result should be 0.292162. Do not change the data type of the two named constants. Instead, use a typecast to solve the problem.

## LAB 3.5   Reading and Writing to a File

Bring in billfile.cpp from the Lab 3 folder. The code is as follows:

```
// This program will read in the quantity of a particular item and its price.
// It will then print out the total price.
// The input will come from a data file and the output will go to
// an output file.

// PLACE YOUR NAME HERE

#include <fstream>
#include <iomanip>
using namespace std;

int main()
{
        ifstream dataIn;        // defines an input stream for a data file
        ofstream dataOut;       // defines an output stream for an output file
        int quantity;           // contains the amount of items purchased
        float itemPrice;        // contains the price of each item
        float  totalBill;       // contains the total bill, i.e. the price of all items

        dataIn.open("transaction.dat");        // This opens the file.
        dataOut.open("bill.out");

        // Fill in the appropriate code in the blank below
        _____<< setprecision(2) << fixed << showpoint;  // formatted output


        // Fill in the input statement that brings in the
        // quantity and price of the item

        // Fill in the assignment statement that determines the total bill.

        // Fill in the output statement that prints the total bill, with a label,
        // to an output file


        return 0;
}
```

*Exercise 1:* Notice that this is an altered version of Lab 3.1. This program gets the information from a file and places the output to a file. You must create the data file. Your instructor will tell you how to create the data file and where to put it. Create a data file called `transaction.dat` that has the following information:

> 22
>
> 10.98

*Exercise 2:* Fill in the blank and the statements that will read the data from the file and print the following to `bill.out`:

**The total bill is $241.56**

## LAB 3.6   Student Generated Code Assignments

*Option 1:* Write a program that will read in 3 grades from the keyboard and will print the average (to 2 decimal places) of those grades to the screen. It should include good prompts and labeled output. Use the examples from the earlier labs to help you. You will want to begin with a design. The Lesson Set 1 Pre-lab Reading Assignment gave an introduction for a design similar to this problem. Notice in the sample run that the answer is stored in fixed point notation with two decimal points of precision.

*Sample run:*

**Please input the first grade**
97

**Please input the second grade**
98.3

**Please input the third grade**
95

**The average of the three grades is 96.77**

*Option 2:* The Woody furniture company sells the following three styles of chairs:

| Style | Price Per Chair |
|---|---|
| American Colonial | $ 85.00 |
| Modern | $ 57.50 |
| French Classical | $127.75 |

Write a program that will input the amount of chairs sold for each style. It will print the total dollar sales of each style as well as the total sales of all chairs in fixed point notation with two decimal places.

*Sample run:*

**Please input the number of American Colonial chairs sold**
20
**Please input the number of Modern chairs sold**
15
**Please input the number of French Classical chairs sold**
5

**The total sales of American Colonial chairs $1700.00**
**The total sales of Modern chairs $862.50**
**The total sales of French Classical chairs $638.75**
**The total sales of all chairs $3201.25**

*Option 3:* Write a program that will input total sales (sales plus tax) that a business generates for a particular month. The program will also input the state and local sales tax percentage. It will output the total sales plus the state tax and local tax to be paid. The output should be in fixed notation with 2 decimal places.

*Sample run:*

**Please input the total sales for the month**
1080
**Please input the state tax percentage in decimal form (.02 for 2%)**
.06
**Please input the local tax percentage in decimal form (.02 for 2%)**
.02

**The total sales for the month is $1080.00**
**The state tax for the month is $64.80**
**The local tax for the month is $21.60**

# 4 Conditional Statements

**PURPOSE**

1. To work with relational operators
2. To work with conditional statements
3. To learn and use nested `if` statements
4. To learn and use logical operators
5. To learn and use the `switch` statement

**PROCEDURE**

1. Students should read the Pre-lab Reading Assignment before coming to lab.
2. Students should complete the Pre-lab Writing Assignment before coming to lab.

| Contents | Pre-requisites | Approximate completion time | Page number | Check when done |
|---|---|---|---|---|
| Pre-lab Reading Assignment | | 20 min. | 42 | |
| Pre-lab Writing Assignment | Pre-lab reading | 10 min. | 48 | |
| **LESSON 4A** | | | | |
| Lab 4.1 Relational Operators and the `if` Statement | Basic understanding of relational operators and the simple `if` statement | 15 min. | 48 | |
| Lab 4.2 `if/else` and Nested `if` Statements | Basic understanding of nested `if` statements | 20 min. | 49 | |
| Lab 4.3 Logical Operators | Basic understanding of logical operators | 15 min. | 50 | |
| **LESSON 4B** | | | | |
| Lab 4.4 The `switch` Statement | Understanding of the `switch` statement | 25 min. | 51 | |
| Lab 4.5 Student Generated Code Assignments | Basic understanding of conditional statements | 30 min. | 52 | |

## PRE-LAB READING ASSIGNMENT

### Relational Operators

You have already seen that the statement `total = 5` is an assignment statement; that is, the integer 5 is placed in the variable called `total`. Nothing relevant to our everyday understanding of equality is present here. So how do we deal with equality in a program? How about greater than or less than? C++ allows the programmer to compare numeric values using **relational operators**. They are the following:

| | |
|---|---|
| > | Greater than |
| < | Less than |
| > = | Greater than or equal to |
| < = | Less than or equal to |
| = = | Equal to |
| ! - | Not equal to |

An expression of the form `num1 > num2` is called a **relational expression**. Note that it does *not* assert that `num1` is greater than `num2`. It actually tests to see if this is true. So relational expressions are boolean. Their value must be either *true* or *false*. The statement `cost!=9` is false if `cost` has value 9 and true otherwise. Consider the following code:

```
int years;
years = 6;   // assignment statement years is assigned the value of 6
years == 5; // relational expression, not an assignment statement
years = years - 1; // assignment statement
years == 5; // relational expression
```

In this sequence the first occurrence of `years == 5` is a false statement whereas the second occurrence is true. Can you see why?

### The `if` Statement

Sometimes we may only want a portion of code executed under certain conditions. To do so, we use **conditional statements**. For example, if you are writing a payroll program to compute wages, then the program should only compute overtime pay *if* the employee worked more than 40 hours in a given week. Otherwise, when the program is executed the overtime portion of the code should be bypassed. An **if statement** is one kind of conditional statement.
Consider the following program:

*Sample Program 4.1:*

```
// This program prints "You Pass" if a student's average is 60 or higher and prints
// "You Fail" otherwise

#include <iostream>
using namespace std:

int main()
{
    float average;
```

```
cout << "Input your average" << endl;
cin >> average;

if (average >= 60)  // note the use of a relational operator
    cout << "You Pass" << endl;

if (average < 60)
    cout << "You Fail" << endl;

return 0;
}
```

Note that it is not possible for this program to print out both "You Pass" and "You Fail". Only one of the if statements will be executed. Later we will see a way to write this program without using 2 if statements.

If you want to conditionally execute several statements using if, the following syntax is required:

```
if (expression)
{
    statement_1;
    statement_2;
        :
    statement_n;
}
```

Note the curly braces surrounding the set of statements to be conditionally executed.

## The if/else Statement

In Sample Program 4.1 we used two if statements. A more elegant approach would be to use the **if/else statement** as follows:

```
if (average >= 60)
    cout << "You Pass" << endl;

else
    cout << "You Fail" << endl;
```

In every if/else statement the program can take only one of two possible paths. Multiple statements can be handled using curly braces in the same way as the if statement.

## The if/else if Statement

The if/else statement works well if there are only two possible paths to follow. However, what if there are more than two possibilities? For example, suppose we need to decide what kind of vacation to take based on a yearly work bonus:

if the bonus is less than $1,000, we set up a tent and eat hot dogs in the back yard

if the bonus is less than $10,000 and greater than or equal to $1,000, we go to Disney World

if the bonus is $10,000, we go to Hawaii

We could code this using the **if/else if** statement as follows:

```
float bonus;

cout << "Please input the amount of your yearly bonus" << endl;
cin >> bonus;

if (bonus < 1000)
    cout << "Another vacation eating hot dogs on the lawn" << endl;

else if (bonus < 10000)
    cout << "Off to Disney World!" << endl;

else if (bonus == 10000)
    cout << "Lets go to Hawaii!" << endl;
```

Can you explain why the first else if conditional statement does not require a greater than or equal to 1000 condition?

In general we can use as many else if expressions as needed to solve a given problem.

## The Trailing else

What happens in the code above if the bonus entered is greater than $10,000? Actually, nothing will happen since none of the conditional expressions are true in this case. Sometimes it is advantageous to add a final or **trailing else** at the end of a chain of if/else if statements to handle "all other cases." For example, we could modify the code to read:

```
if (bonus < 1000)
    cout << "Another vacation on the lawn" << endl;
else if (bonus < 10000)
    cout << "Off to Disney World!" << endl;
else if (bonus == 10000)
    cout << "Lets go to Hawaii!" << endl;
else
{
    cout << bonus << " is not a valid bonus" << endl;
    cout << "Please run the program again with valid data" << endl;
}   // Note the necessary use of the curly brackets here
```

Of course, few would complain about a bonus greater than $10,000 and the Hawaii trip could still be done on this budget. However, if the maximum possible bonus is $10,000, then the trailing else will let the user know that an illegal value has been entered.

## Nested if Statements

Often programmers use an if statement within another if statement. For example, suppose a software engineering company wants to screen applicants first for experienced programmers and second for C++ programmers specifically. One possible program is the following:

*Sample Program 4.2:*

```cpp
#include <iostream>
using namespace std;

int main()
{
    char programmer, cPlusPlus;

    cout << "Before we consider your application, answer the following"
         << endl;
    cout << " yes ( enter Y ) or no ( enter N )" << endl;
    cout << "Are you a computer programmer?" << endl;

    cin >> programmer;

    if (programmer == 'Y')
    {
        cout << "Do you program in C++?" << endl;
        cin >> cPlusPlus;

        if (cPlusPlus == 'Y')
            cout << " You look like a promising candidate for employment"
                 << endl;
        else if (cPlusPlus == 'N')
            cout << " You need to learn C++ before further consideration"
                 << endl;
        else
            cout << " You must enter Y or N" << endl;
    }

    else if (programmer == 'N')
        cout << " You are not currently qualified for employment" << endl;

    else
        cout <<  " You must enter Y or N" << endl;
    return 0;
}
```

Note how C++ programmers are identified using a nested `if` statement. Also note how the trailing `else` is used to detect invalid input.

## Logical Operators

By using relational operators C++ programmers can create relational expressions. Programmers can also combine truth values into a single expression by using **logical operators**. For example, instead of a statement such as "if it is sunny, then we will go outside," one may use a statement such as "if it is sunny and it is warm, then we will go outside." Note that this statement has two smaller statements "it is sunny" and "it is warm" joined by the **AND** logical operator. To evaluate to `true`, both the sunny and warm requirements must be met.

The **NOT** operator negates a single statement. For example, "it is sunny" can be negated by "it is not sunny."

The **OR** operator is similar to the AND in that it connects two statements. However, there is an ambiguity about the meaning of the word *or* in English. In the statement "tonight at 8:00 I will go to the concert in the park or I will go to the stadium to see the ball game," the word **or** is *exclusive*. That is, I can go to the concert or to the game, but not both. However, in the statement "I need to draw an ace or a king to have a good poker hand," the word **or** is *inclusive*. In other words, I can draw a king, an ace, or even both, and I will have a good hand. So we have a choice to make. Let A and B be two statements. A OR B could mean A or B but not both. It could also mean A or B or both. In computer science we use the second meaning of the word *or*. For example, in the statement "if it is sunny or it is warm, then I will go outside," there are three scenarios where I will go outside: if it is sunny but not warm, if it is warm but not sunny, or if it is sunny and warm.

The syntax used by C++ for logical operators is the following:

```
AND     &&
OR      ||
NOT     !
```

Consider the following:

```
if (dollars <= 0 || !(accountActive) )
    cout << " You may not withdraw money from the bank";
```

It is good programming practice to enclose the operand after the (!) operator in parentheses. Unexpected things can happen in complicated expressions if you do not. When will this code execute the `cout` statement? What type of variable do you think `accountActive` is?

## The `switch` Statement

We have already seen how `if` statements can affect the branching of a program during execution. Another way to do this is using the **switch statement**. It is also a conditional statement. The `switch` statement uses the value of an integer expression to determine which group of statements to branch through. The sample program below illustrates the syntax.

*Sample Program 4.3:*

```
#include <iostream>
using namespace std;

int main()
{
    char grade;

    cout << "What grade did you earn in Programming I?" << endl;
    cin >> grade;

    switch( grade )     // This is where the switch statement begins
      {
        case 'A':cout << "an A - excellent work!" << endl;
            break;
```

```
        case 'B':cout << "you got a B - good job" << endl;
              break;
        case 'C':cout << "earning a C is satisfactory" << endl;
              break;
        case 'D':cout << "while D is passing, there is a problem" << endl;
              break;
        case 'F':cout << "you failed - better luck next time" << endl;
              break;
        default:cout << "You did not enter an A, B, C, D, or F" << endl;
    }

    return 0;

}
```

Note the use of the curly braces that enclose the cases and the use of break; after each case. Also, consider the variable grade. It is defined as a character data type and the case statements have character arguments such as 'B'. This seems to contradict what we said above, namely that the switch statement uses the value of integer expressions to determine branching. However, this apparent contradiction is resolved by the compiler automatically converting character data into the integer data type. Finally, notice the role of the default statement. The default branch is followed if none of the case expressions match the given switch expression.

## Character & string comparisons

So far, relational operators have been used to compare numeric constants and variables. Characters and string objects can also be compared with the same operators. For example:

```
char letter = 'F';
string word = "passed";



switch(letter)
{
    case 'A': cout << "Your grade is A." << endl;
        break;
    case 'B': cout << "Your grade is B." << endl;
        break;
    case 'C: cout << "Your grade is C." << endl;
        break;
    case 'D': cout << "Your grade is D." << endl;
        break;
    case 'F':   word = "failed";
        break;
    default: cout << "You did not enter an A,B,C,D or F" << endl;
}

if (word == "passed")
    cout << "You passed" << endl;
else
    cout << "You failed" << endl;
```

What is printed ?

## PRE-LAB WRITING ASSIGNMENT

### Fill-in-the-Blank Questions

1. The two possible values for a relational expression are _____ and _____. . .

2. C++ uses the _____ symbol to represent the AND operator.

3. The `switch` statement and `if` statements are examples of _____ statements.

4. In C++ is the meaning of the OR logical operator inclusive or exclusive? _____

5. C++ uses the _____ symbol to represent the OR operator.

6. It is good programming practice to do what to the operand after the NOT operator? _____

7. The `switch` statement uses the value of a(n) _____ expression to determine which group of statements to branch through.

8. In a `switch` statement the _____ branch is followed if none of the case expressions match the given `switch` expression.

9. C++ allows the programmer to compare numeric values using _____.

10. The C++ symbol for equality is _____.

## LESSON 4A

### LAB 4.1 Relational Operators and the `if` Statement

*Exercise 1:* Bring in the file `initialize.cpp` from the Lab 4 folder. The code follows:

```cpp
// This program tests whether or not an initialized value
// is equal to a value input by the user

// PLACE YOUR NAME HERE

#include <iostream>
using namespace std;

int main( )
{
    int num1,                  // num1 is not initialized
        num2 = 5;              // num2 has been initialized to 5

    cout << "Please enter an integer" << endl;
    cin >> num1;


    cout << "num1 = " << num1 << " and num2 = " << num2 << endl;

    if (num1 = num2)
            cout << "Hey, that's a coincidence!" << endl;
```

```
if (num1 != num2)
        cout << "The values are not the same" << endl;


return 0;

}
```

*Exercise 1:* Run the program several times using a different input each time. Does the program do what you expect? Is so, explain what it is doing. If not, locate the error and fix it.

*Exercise 2:* Modify the program so that the user inputs both values to be tested for equality. Make sure you have a prompt for each input. Test the program with pairs of values that are the same and that are different.

*Exercise 3:* Modify the program so that when the numbers are the same it prints the following lines:
> **The values are the same.**
> **Hey that's a coincidence!**

*Exercise 4:* Modify the revised Exercise 3 program by replacing the two `if` statements with a single `if/else` statement. Run the program again to test the results.

## LAB 4.2 `if/else if` Statements

Bring in the file `grades.cpp` from the Lab 4 folder. The code follows:

```
//  This program prints "You Pass" if a student's average is
//  60 or higher and prints "You Fail" otherwise

// PLACE YOUR NAME HERE
#include <iostream>
using namespace std;

int main()
{

    float average;     // holds the grade average

    cout << "Input your average:" << endl;
    cin >> average;

    if (average > 60)
       cout << "You Pass" << endl;

    if (average < 60)
       cout << "You Fail" << endl;

    return 0;

}
```

*Exercise 1:* Run the program three times using 80, 55 and 60 for the average. What happens when you input 60 as the average? Modify the first if statement so that the program will also print "You Pass" if the average equals 60.

*Exercise 2:* Modify the program so that it uses an if/else statement rather than two if statements.

*Exercise 3:* Modify the program from Exercise 2 to allow the following categories: Invalid data (data above 100), 'A' category (90–100), 'B' category (80–89), "You Pass" category (60–79), "You Fail" category (0–59).
What will happen to your program if you enter a negative value such as -12?

## Lab 4.3    Logical Operators

Retrieve LogicalOp.cpp from the Lab 4 folder. The code is as follows:

```cpp
// This program illustrates the use of logical operators

// PLACE YOUR NAME HERE

#include <iostream>
using namespace std;

int main()
{
    char year;
    float gpa;

    cout << "What year student are you ?" << endl;
    cout << "Enter 1 (freshman), 2 (sophomore), 3 (junior), or 4 (senior)"
         << endl << endl;
    cin >> year;

    cout << "Now enter your GPA" << endl;
    cin >> gpa;

    if (gpa >= 2.0 && year == '4')
       cout << "It is time to graduate soon" << endl;

    else if (year != '4'|| gpa <2.0)
       cout << "You need more schooling" << endl;

    return 0;
}
```

*Exercise 1:* How could you rewrite gpa >= 2.0 in the first if statement using the NOT operator?

*Exercise 2:* Could you replace year !='4' in the else if statement with year < 4 or year <= 3? Why or why not?

*Exercise 3:* If you replace

```
if ( gpa >= 2.0 && year == '4')
```

with

```
if ( gpa >= 2.0 || year == '4')
```

and replace

```
else if ( year != '4'|| gpa < 2.0)
```

with

```
else if ( year != '4' && gpa < 2.0)
```

which students will graduate and which will not graduate according to this new program?

Does this handle all cases (i.e., all combinations of year and gpa)?

*Exercise 4:* Could you replace else if ( year != '4'|| gpa < 2.0) with the single word else?

# LESSON 4B

## LAB 4.4   The switch Statement

*Exercise 1:* Bring in the file switch.cpp from the Lab 4 folder. This is Sample Program 4.3 from the Pre-lab Reading Assignment. The code is shown below. Remove the break statements from each of the cases. What is the effect on the execution of the program?

```cpp
// This program illustrates the use of the switch statement.

// PLACE YOUR NAME HERE

#include <iostream>
using namespace std;


int main()
{
    char grade;

    cout << "What grade did you earn in Programming I ?" << endl;
    cin >> grade;

    switch( grade )              // This is where the switch statement begins
    {
      case 'A': cout << "an A - excellent work !" << endl;
            break;
      case 'B': cout << "you got a B - good job" << endl;
            break;
      case 'C': cout << "earning a C is satisfactory" << endl;
            break;
      case 'D': cout << "while  D is passing, there is a problem" << endl;
            break;
```

```
        case 'F': cout << "you failed - better luck next time" << endl
                  break;
        default:  cout << "You did not enter an A, B, C, D, or F" << endl;
        }


    return 0;

}
```

---

*Exercise 2:* Add an additional `switch` statement that allows for a Passing option for a grade of D or better. Use the sample run given below to model your output.

*Sample Run:*

**What grade did you earn in Programming I ?**
**A**
**YOU PASSED!**
**an A - excellent work!**

*Exercise 3:* Rewrite the program `switch.cpp` using `if` and `else if` statements rather than a `switch` statement. Did you use a trailing `else` in your new version? If so, what did it correspond to in the original program with the `switch` statement?

## LAB 4.5 Student Generated Code Assignments

*Option 1:* Write a program that prompts the user for their quarterly water bill for the last four *quarters*. The program should find and output their average *monthly* water bill. If the average bill exceeds $75, the output should include a message indicating that too much water is being used. If the average bill is at least $25 but no more than $75, the output should indicate that a typical amount of water is being used. Finally, if the average bill is less than $25, the output should contain a message praising the user for conserving water. Use the sample run below as a model for your output.

*Sample Run 1:*

**Please input your water bill for quarter 1:**
**300**

**Please input your water bill for quarter 2:**
**200**

**Please input your water bill for quarter 3:**
**225**

**Please input your water bill for quarter 4:**
**275**

**Your average monthly bill is $83.33. You are using excessive amounts of water**

*Sample Run 2:*

**Please input your water bill for quarter 1:**
100

**Please input your water bill for quarter 2:**
150

**Please input your water bill for quarter 3:**
75

**Please input your water bill for quarter 4:**
125

**Your average monthly bill is $37.50. You are using a typical amount of water**

*Option 2:* The local t-shirt shop sells shirts that retail for $12. Quantity discounts are given as follow:

| Number of Shirts | Discount |
| --- | --- |
| 5–10 | 10% |
| 11–20 | 15% |
| 21–30 | 20% |
| 31 or more | 25% |

Write a program that prompts the user for the number of shirts required and then computes the total price. Make sure the program accepts only nonnegative input.

Use the following sample runs to guide you:

*Sample Run 1:*

**How many shirts would you like ?**
4

**The cost per shirt is $12 and the total cost is $48**

*Sample Run 2:*

**How many shirts would you like ?**
0

**The cost per shirt is $12 and the total cost is $0**

*Sample Run 3:*

**How many shirts would you like ?**
8

**The cost per shirt is $10.80 and the total cost is $86.40**

*Sample Run 4:*

**How many shirts would you like ?**
-2

**Invalid Input: Please enter a nonnegative integer**

*Option 3:* The University of Guiness charges $3000 per semester for in-state tuition and $4500 per semester for out-of-state tuition. In addition, room and board is $2500 per semester for in-state students and $3500 per semester for out-of-state students. Write a program that prompts the user for their residential status (i.e., in-state or out-of-state) and whether they require room and board (Y or N). The program should then compute and output their bill for that semester.

Use the sample output below:

*Sample Run 1:*

**Please input "I" if you are in-state or "0" if you are out-of-state:**
I

**Please input "Y" if you require room and board and "N" if you do not:**
N

**Your total bill for this semester is $3000**

*Sample Run 2:*

**Please input "I" if you are in-state or "0" if you are out-of-state:**
0

**Please input "Y" if you require room and board and "N" if you do not:**
Y

**Your total bill for this semester is $8000**

# 5 Looping Statements

**PURPOSE**

1. To introduce counter and event controlled loops
2. To work with the `while` loop
3. To introduce the `do-while` loop
4. To work with the `for` loop
5. To work with nested loops

**PROCEDURE**

1. Students should read the Pre-lab Reading Assignment before coming to lab.
2. Students should complete the Pre-lab Writing Assignment before coming to lab.
3. In the lab, students should complete labs assigned to them by the instructor.

| Contents | Pre-requisites | Approximate completion time | Page number | Check when done |
|---|---|---|---|---|
| Pre-lab Reading Assignment | | 20 min. | 56 | |
| Pre-lab Writing Assignment | Pre-lab reading | 10 min. | 64 | |
| **LESSON 5A** | | | | |
| Lab 5.1 Working with the `while` Loop | Basic understanding of the `while` loop | 25 min. | 64 | |
| Lab 5.2 Working with the `do-while` Loop | Basic understanding of `do-while` loop | 25 min. | 66 | |
| **LESSON 5B** | | | | |
| Lab 5.3 Working with the `for` Loop | Understanding of `for` loops | 15 min. | 68 | |
| Lab 5.4 Nested Loops | Understanding of nested `for` loops | 15 min | 69 | |
| Lab 5.5 Student Generated Code Assignments | Basic understanding of loop control structures | 30 min. | 71 | |

# PRE-LAB READING ASSIGNMENT

## Increment and Decrement Operator

To execute many algorithms we need to be able to add or subtract 1 from a given integer quantity. For example:

```
count = count + 1;      // what would happen if we used ==
                        // instead of = ?
count += 1;
```

Both of these statements **increment** the value of count by 1. If we replace "+" with "-" in the above code, then both statements **decrement** the value of count by 1. C++ also provides an **increment operator** ++ and a **decrement operator** -- to perform these tasks. There are two modes that can be used:

```
count++;        // increment operator in the postfix mode
count--;        // decrement operator in the postfix mode

++count;        // increment operator in the prefix mode
--count;        // decrement operator in the prefix mode
```

The two increment statements both execute exactly the same. So do the decrement operators. What is the purpose of having postfix and prefix modes? To answer this, consider the following code:

```
int age = 49;
if (age++ > 49)
    cout << "Congratulations - You have made it to the half-century"
         << " mark !" << endl;
```

In this code, the cout statement will not execute. The reason is that in the postfix mode the comparison between age and 49 is made *first*. Then the value of age is incremented by one. Since 49 is not greater than 49, the if conditional is false. Things are much different if we replace the postfix operator with the prefix operator:

```
int age = 49;
if (++age > 49)
    cout << " Congratulations - You have made it to the half-century"
         << " mark !" << endl;
```

In this code age is incremented first. So its value is 50 when the comparison is made. The conditional statement is true and the cout statement is executed.

## The while Loop

Often in programming one needs a statement or block of statements to repeat during execution. This can be accomplished using a **loop**. A loop is a control structure that causes repetition of code within a program. C++ has three types of loops. The first we will consider is the **while loop**. The syntax is the following:

```
while (expression)
{
    statement_1;
    statement_2;
        :
    statement_n;
}
```

If there is only one statement, then the curly braces can be omitted. When a `while` loop is encountered during execution, the expression is tested to see if it is true or false. The block of statements is repeated as long as the expression is true. Consider the following:

*Sample Program 5.1:*

```cpp
#include <iostream>
using namespace std;

int main()
{
    int num = 5;
    int numFac = 1;

    while (num > 0)
    {
        numFac = numFac * num;
        num--;          // note the use of the decrement operator
    }

    cout << " 5! = " << numFac << endl;

    return 0;
}
```

This program computes 5! = 5 * 4 * 3 * 2 * 1 and then prints the result to the screen. Note how the `while` loop controls the execution. Since `num = 5` when the while loop is first encountered, the block of statements in the body of the loop is executed at least once. In fact, the block is executed 5 times because of the decrement operator which forces the value of `num` to decrease by one every time the block is executed. During the fifth **iteration** of the loop `num` becomes 0, so the next time the expression is tested `num > 0` is false and the loop is exited. Then the `cout` statement is executed.

What do you think will happen if we eliminated the decrement operator `num--` in the above code? The value of `num` is always 5. This means that the expression `num > 0` is always true! If we try to execute the modified program, the result is an **infinite loop**, i.e., a block of code that will repeat forever. One must be very cautious when using loops to ensure that the loop will terminate. Here is another example where the user may have trouble with termination.

*Sample Program 5.2:*

```cpp
#include <iostream>
using namespace std;

int main()
{
    char letter = 'a';

    while (letter != 'x')
```

*continues*

```
            {
                cout << "Please enter a letter"  << endl;
                cin >> letter;
                cout << "The letter your entered is " << letter << endl;
            }
        return 0;
}
```

Note that this program requires input from the user during execution. Infinite loops can be avoided, but it would help if the user knew that the 'x' character terminates the execution. Without this knowledge the user could continually enter characters other than 'x' and never realize how to terminate the program. In the lab assignments you will be asked to modify this program to make it more user friendly.

## Counters

Often a programmer needs to control the number of times a particular loop is repeated. One common way to accomplish this is by using a **counter**. For example, suppose we want to find the average of five test scores. We must first input and add the five scores. This can be done with a **counter-controlled** loop as shown in Sample Program 5.3. Notice how the variable named test works as a counter. Also notice the use of a constant for the number of tests. This is done so that the number of tests can easily be changed if we want a different number of tests to be averaged.

*Sample Program 5.3:*

```
#include <iostream>
using namespace std;

const int NUMBEROFTESTS = 5;

int main()

{
        int score ;                   // the individual score read in
        float total = 0.0;            //  the total of the scores
        float average;                //  the average of the scores
        int test = 1;                 //  counter that controls the loop

        while (test <= NUMBEROFTESTS)  //  Note that test is 1 the first time
                                       //  the expression is tested
        {
         cout << "Enter your score on test " << test << ": " << endl;
         cin >> score;

         total = total + score;
         test++;
        }


        average = total / NUMBEROFTESTS;
```

```
cout  << "Your average based on " << NUMBEROFTESTS
        << " test scores is " << average << endl;


    return 0;

}
```

Sample Program 5.3 can be made more flexible by adding an integer variable called numScores that would allow the user to input the number of tests to be processed.

## Sentinel Values

We can also control the execution of a loop by using a **sentinel value** which is a special value that marks the end of a list of values. In a variation of the previous program example, if we do not know exactly how many test scores there are, we can input scores which are added to total until the sentinel value is input. Sample Program 5.4 revises Sample Program 5.3 to control the loop with a sentinel value. The sentinel in this case is -1 since it is an invalid test score. It does not make sense to use a sentinel between 0 and 100 since this is the range of valid test scores. Notice that a counter is still used to keep track of the number of test scores entered, although it does not control the loop. What happens if the first value the user enters is a -1?

*Sample Program 5.4:*

```
#include <iostream>
using namespace std;



int main()

{
        int score ;            //  the individual score read in
        float total = 0.0;     //  the total of the scores
        float average;         //  the average of the scores
        int test = 1;          //  counter that controls the loop



        cout << "Enter your score on test " << test
            << " (or -1 to exit): " << endl;
        cin >> score;          // Read the 1st score

        while (score != -1)    // While we have not entered the sentinel
                               // (ending) value, do the loop

        {


        total = total + score;
        test++;

        cout << "Enter your score on test " << test
            << " (or -1 to exit): " << endl;
        cin >> score;          // Read the next score
```

*continues*

```
        }

        if (test > 1)                 // If test = 1, no scores were entered
        {
         average = total / (test - 1);

         cout << "Your average based on " << (test - 1)
              << " test scores is " << average << endl;
        }


        return 0;
}
```

Notice that the program asks for input just before the while loop begins and again as the last instruction in the while loop. This is done so that the while loop can test for sentinel data. Often this is called **priming the read** and is frequently implemented when sentinel data is used to end a loop.

## Data Validation

One nice application of the while loop is data validation. The user can input data (from the keyboard or a file) and then a while loop tests to see if the value(s) is valid. The loop is skipped for all valid input but for invalid input the loop is executed and prompts the user to enter new (valid) input. The following is an example of data validation.

```
cout << "Please input your choice of drink "
     << "(a number from 1 to 4 or 0 to quit)" << endl;
cout << " 1  -  Coffee" << endl
     << " 2  -  Tea" << endl
     << " 3  -  Coke" << endl
     << " 4  -  Orange Juice" << endl << endl
     << " 0  -  QUIT" << endl << endl;
cin >> beverage;

while (beverage < 0 || beverage > 4)
{
 cout << "Valid choices are 0 - 4.  Please re-enter: ";
 cin >> beverage;
}
```

What type of invalid data does this code test for? If beverage is an integer variable, what happens if the user enters the character '$' or the float 2.9?

## The do-while Loop

The while loop is a **pre-test** or **top test** loop. Since we test the expression before entering the loop, if the test expression in the while loop is initially false, then no iterations of the loop will be executed. If the programmer wants the loop to be executed at least once, then a **post-test** or **bottom test** loop should be used. C++ provides the **do-while loop** for this purpose. A do-while loop is similar to a while loop except that the statements inside the loop body are executed *before* the expression is tested. The format for a single statement in the loop body is the following:

```
do
    statement;
while (expression);
```

Note that the statement must be executed once even if the expression is false. To see the difference between these two loops consider the code

```
int num1 = 5;
int num2 = 7;

while (num2 < num1)
{
      num1 = num1 + 1;
      num2 = num2 - 1;
}
```

Here the statements `num1 = num1 + 1` and `num2 = num2 - 1` are never executed since the test expression `num2 < num1` is initially false. However, we get a different result using a `do-while` loop:

```
int num1 = 5;
int num2 = 7;

do
{
      num1 = num1 + 1;
      num2 = num2 - 1;
} while (num2 < num1);
```

In this code the statements `num1 = num1 + 1` and `num2 = num2 - 1` are executed exactly once. At this point `num1 = 6` and `num2 = 6` so the expression `num2 < num1` is false. Consequently, the program exits the loop and moves to the next section of code. Also note that since we need a block of statements in the loop body, curly braces must be placed around the statements. In Lab 5.2 you will see how `do-while` loops can be useful for programs that involve a repeating menu.

## The `for` Loop

The **`for` loop** is often used for applications that require a counter. For example, suppose we want to find the average (mean) of the first $n$ positive integers. By definition, this means that we need to add $1 + 2 + 3 + \ldots + n$ and then divide by $n$. Note this should just give us the value in the "middle" of the list $1, 2, \ldots, n$. Since we know exactly how many times we are performing a sum, the `for` loop is the natural choice.

The syntax for the `for` loop is the following:

```
for (initialization; test; update)
{
      statement_1;
      statement_2;
          :
      statement_n;
}
```

Notice that there are three expressions inside the parentheses of the `for` statement, separated by semicolons.

1. The **initialization expression** is typically used to initialize a counter that must have a starting value. This is the first action performed by the loop and is done only once.

2. The **test expression**, as with the `while` and `do-while` loops, is used to control the execution of the loop. As long as the test expression is true, the body of the `for` loop repeats. The `for` loop is a pre-test loop which means that the test expression is evaluated before each iteration.

3. The **update expression** is executed at the end of each iteration. It typically increments or decrements the counter.

Now we are ready to add the first *n* positive integers and find their mean value.

*Sample Program 5.5:*

```cpp
#include <iostream>
using namespace std;

int main()
{
    int value;
    int total = 0;
    int number;
    float mean;

    cout << "Please enter a positive integer" << endl;
    cin >> value;

    if (value > 0)
    {
        for (number = 1; number <= value; number++)
        {
            total = total + number;
        }                                    // curly braces are optional since
                                             // there is only one statement

        mean = static_cast<float>(total) / value; // note the use of the typecast
                                                   // operator

        cout << "The mean average of the first " << value
            << " positive integers is " << mean << endl;
    }
    else
        cout << "Invalid input - integer must be positive" << endl;
    return 0;
}
```

Note that the counter in the `for` loop of Sample Program 5.5 is `number`. It increments from 1 to `value` during execution. There are several other features of this code that also need to be addressed. First of all, why is the typecast operator needed to compute the mean? What do you think will happen if it is removed?

Finally, what would happen if we entered a float such as 2.99 instead of an integer? Lab 5.3 will demonstrate what happens in these cases.

## Nested Loops

Often programmers need to use a loop within a loop, or **nested loops**. Sample Program 5.6 below provides a simple example of a nested loop. This program finds the average number of hours per day spent programming by each student over a three-day weekend. The outer loop controls the number of students and the inner loop allows the user to enter the number of hours worked each of the three days for a given student. Note that the inner loop is executed three times for each iteration of the outer loop.

*Sample Program 5.6:*

```cpp
// This program finds the average time spent programming by a student each
// day over a three day period.

#include <iostream>
using namespace std;

int main()
{
    int numStudents;
    float numHours, total, average;
    int count1 = 0, count2 = 0;     // these are the counters for the loops

    cout << "This program will find the average number of hours a day"
        << " that each given student spent programming over a long weekend"
        << endl << endl;

    cout << "How many students are there ?" << endl << endl;
    cin >> numStudents;

    for (count1 = 1; count1 <= numStudents; count1++)
    {
        total = 0;
        for (count2 = 1; count2 <= 3; count2++)
        {
            cout << "Please enter the number of hours worked by student "
                << count1 << " on day " << count2 << "." << endl;
            cin >> numHours;

            total = total + numHours;
        }
        average = total / 3;

        cout << endl;
        cout << "The average number of hours per day spent programming by"
            << " student " << count1 <<" is " << average
            << endl << endl << endl;
    }
    return 0.
}
```

In Lab 5.4 you will be asked to modify this program to make it more flexible.

# PRE-LAB WRITING ASSIGNMENT

## Fill-in-the-Blank Questions

1. A block of code that repeats forever is called _____.

2. To keep track of the number of times a particular loop is repeated, one can use a(n) _____.

3. An event controlled loop that is always executed at least once is the _____.

4. An event controlled loop that is not guaranteed to execute at least once is the _____.

5. In the conditional if(++number < 9), the comparison number < 9 is made _____ and number is incremented _____. (Choose first or second for each blank.)

6. In the conditional if(number++ < 9), the comparison number < 9 is made _____ and number is incremented _____. (Choose first or second for each blank.)

7. A loop within a loop is called a _____.

8. To write out the first 12 positive integers and their cubes, one should use a(n) _____ loop.

9. A(n) _____ value is used to indicate the end of a list of values. It can be used to control a while loop.

10. In a nested loop the _____ loop goes through all of its iterations for each iteration of the _____ loop. (Choose inner or outer for each blank.)

# LESSON 5A

## LAB 5.1   Working with the `while` Loop

Bring in program `while.cpp` from the Lab 5 folder. (This is Sample Program 5.2 from the Pre-lab Reading Assignment). The code is shown below:

```cpp
// PLACE YOUR NAME HERE

#include <iostream>
using namespace std;

int main()
{
    char letter = 'a';

    while (letter != 'x')
    {
        cout << "Please enter a letter" << endl;
        cin >> letter;
        cout << "The letter you entered is " << letter << endl;
    }

    return 0;
}
```

*Exercise 1:* This program is not user friendly. Run it a few times and explain why.

*Exercise 2:* Add to the code so that the program is more user friendly.

*Exercise 3:* How would this code affect the execution of the program if the while loop is replaced by a do-while loop? Try it and see.

Bring in program sentinel.cpp from the Lab 5 Folder. The code is shown below:

```
// This program illustrates the use of a sentinel in a while loop.
// The user is asked for monthly rainfall totals until a sentinel
// value of -1 is entered. Then the total rainfall is displayed.

// PLACE YOUR NAME HERE

#include <iostream>
using namespace std;

int main()
{
    // Fill in the code to define and initialize to 1 the variable month
    float total = 0, rain;

    cout << "Enter the total rainfall for month " << month << endl;
    cout << "Enter -1 when you are finished" << endl;
    // Fill in the code to read in the value for rain


    // Fill in the code to start a while loop that iterates
    // while rain does not equal -1
    {
        // Fill in the code to update total by adding it to rain
        // Fill in the code to increment month by one

        cout << "Enter the total rainfall in inches for month "
            << month << endl;
        cout << "Enter -1 when you are finished" << endl;
        // Fill in the code to read in the value for rain

    }

    if (month == 1)
        cout << "No data has been entered" << endl;

    else
        cout << "The total rainfall for the " << month-1
```

*continues*

```
                    << " months is "<< total << " inches." << endl;


            return 0;
}
```

*Exercise 4:* Complete the program above by filling in the code described in the statements in bold so that it will perform the indicated task.

*Exercise 5:* Run the program several times with various input. Record your results. Are they correct? What happens if you enter –1 first? What happens if you enter only values of 0 for one or more months? Is there any numerical data that you should not enter?

*Exercise 6:* What is the purpose of the following code in the program above?

```
if (month == 1)
        cout << "No data has been entered" << endl;
```

## LAB 5.2   Working with the `do-while` Loop

Bring in the program `dowhile.cpp` from the Lab 5 folder. The code is shown below:

```
// This program displays a hot beverage menu and prompts the user to
// make a selection. A switch statement determines which item the user
// has chosen. A do-while loop repeats until the user selects item E
// from the menu.

// PLACE YOUR NAME HERE

#include <iostream>
#include <iomanip>
using namespace std;

int main()
{
    // Fill in the code to define an integer variable called number,
    // a floating point variable called cost,
    // and a character variable called beverage

    bool validBeverage;

    cout << fixed << showpoint << setprecision(2);


    do
    {
        cout << endl << endl;
        cout << "Hot Beverage Menu" << endl << endl;
        cout << "A: Coffee         $1.00" << endl;
        cout << "B: Tea            $ .75" << endl;
        cout << "C: Hot Chocolate  $1.25" << endl;
        cout << "D: Cappuccino     $2.50" << endl << endl << endl;
```

```cpp
cout << "Enter the beverage A,B,C, or D you desire" << endl;
cout << "Enter E to exit the program" << endl << endl;
// Fill in the code to read in beverage

switch(beverage)
{
case 'a':
case 'A':
case 'b':
case 'B':
case 'c':
case 'C':
case 'd':
case 'D':  validBeverage = true;
           break;
default:   validBeverage = false;
}

if (validBeverage == true)
{
     cout << "How many cups would you like?" << endl;
     // Fill in the code to read in number
}

// Fill in the code to begin a switch statement
// that is controlled by beverage
{
case 'a':
case 'A': cost = number * 1.0;
       cout << "The total cost is $ " << cost << endl;
       break;
// Fill in the code to give the case for hot chocolate ($1.25 a cup)
// Fill in the code to give the case for tea ( $0.75 a cup)
// Fill in the code to give the case for cappuccino ($2.50 a cup)


case 'e':
case 'E': cout << " Please come again" << endl;
           break;
default:cout << // Fill in the code to write a message
                // indicating an invalid selection.
             cout << " Try again please" << endl;
}


} // Fill in the code to finish the do-while statement with the
  // condition that beverage does not equal E or e.

  // Fill in the appropriate return statement
}
```

*Exercise 1:* Fill in the indicated code to complete the above program. Then compile and run the program several times with various inputs. Try all the possible relevant cases and record your results.

*Exercise 2:* What do you think will happen if you do not enter A, B, C, D or E? Try running the program and inputting another letter.

*Exercise 3:* Replace the line

```
if (validBeverage == true)
```

with the line

```
if (validBeverage)
```

and run the program again. Are there any differences in the execution of the program? Why or why not?

# LESSON 5B

## LAB 5.3   Working with the `for` Loop

Bring in program `for.cpp` from the Lab 5 folder (this is Sample Program 5.5 from the Pre-lab Reading Assignment). This program has the user input a number *n* and then finds the mean of the first *n* positive integers. The code is shown below:

```cpp
// This program has the user input a number n and then finds the
// mean of the first n positive integers

// PLACE YOUR NAME HERE

#include <iostream>
using namespace std;


int main()
{
    int value;       // value is some positive number n
    int total = 0;   // total holds the sum of the first n positive numbers
    int number;      // the amount of numbers
    float mean;      // the average of the first n positive numbers

    cout << "Please enter a positive integer" << endl;
    cin >> value;

    if (value > 0)
    {
        for (number = 1; number <= value; number++)
        {
            total = total + number;
        }  // curly braces are optional since there is only one statement

        mean = static_cast<float>(total) / value; // note the use of the typecast
                                                   // operator here
        cout << "The mean average of the first " << value
             << " positive integers is " << mean << endl;
```

```
      }
   else
      cout << "Invalid input - integer must be positive" << endl;

   return 0;
}
```

*Exercise 1:* Why is the typecast operator needed to compute the mean in the statement `mean = static_cast(float)(total)/value;`? What do you think will happen if it is removed? Modify the code and try it. Record what happens. Make sure that you try both even and odd cases. Now put `static_cast<float> total` back in the program.

*Exercise 2:* What happens if you enter a float such as 2.99 instead of an integer for `value`? Try it and record the results.

*Exercise 3:* Modify the code so that it computes the mean of the consecutive positive integers *n, n+1, n+2, . . . , m*, where the user chooses *n* and *m*. For example, if the user picks 3 and 9, then the program should find the mean of 3, 4, 5, 6, 7, 8, and 9, which is 6.

## LAB 5.4   Nested Loops

Bring in program `nested.cpp` from the Lab 5 folder (this is Sample Program 5.6 from the Pre-lab Reading Assignment). The code is shown below:

```
// This program finds the average time spent programming by a student
// each day over a three day period.

// PLACE YOUR NAME HERE

#include <iostream>
using namespace std;

int main()
{
    int numStudents;
    float numHours, total, average;
    int student,day = 0;      // these are the counters for the loops

    cout << "This program will find the average number of hours a day"
         << " that a student spent programming over a long weekend\n\n";
    cout << "How many students are there ?" << endl << endl;
    cin >> numStudents;

    for(student = 1; student <= numStudents; student++)
    {
        total = 0;
        for(day = 1; day <= 3; day++)
        {
            cout << "Please enter the number of hours worked by student "
                 << student <<" on day " << day << "." << endl;
            cin >> numHours;
```

*continues*

```
        total = total + numHours;
    }


    average = total / 3;

    cout << endl;
    cout <<   "The average number of hours per day spent programming by "
         <<   "student " << student << " is " << average
         <<   endl << endl << endl;
    }

    return 0;
}
```

*Exercise 1:* Note that the inner loop of this program is always executed exactly three times—once for each day of the long weekend. Modify the code so that the inner loop iterates $n$ times, where $n$ is a positive integer input by the user. In other words, let the user decide how many days to consider just as they choose how many students to consider.

*Sample Run:*

**This program will find the average number of hours a day that a student spent programming over a long weekend**

**How many students are there?**
2
**Enter the number of days in the long weekend**
2

**Please enter the number of hours worked by student 1 on day 1**
4

**Please enter the number of hours worked by student 1 on day 2**
6

**The average number of hours per day spent programming by student 1 is 5**


**Please enter the number of hours worked by student 2 on day 1**
9

**Please enter the number of hours worked by student 2 on day 2**
13

**The average number of hours per day spent programming by student 2 is 11**

*Exercise 2:* Modify the program from Exercise 1 so that it also finds the average number of hours per day that a given student studies biology as well as programming. For each given student include two prompts, one for each subject. Have the program print out which subject the student, on average, spent the most time on.

## LAB 5.5    Student Generated Code Assignments

*Option 1:* Write a program that performs a survey tally on beverages. The program should prompt for the next person until a sentinel value of –1 is entered to terminate the program. Each person participating in the survey should choose their favorite beverage from the following list:

1. Coffee    2. Tea    3. Coke    4. Orange Juice

*Sample Run:*

```
Please input the favorite beverage of person #1: Choose 1, 2, 3, or 4 from the
above menu or -1 to exit the program
4


Please input the favorite beverage of person #2: Choose 1, 2, 3, or 4 from the
above menu or -1 to exit the program
1


Please input the favorite beverage of person #3: Choose 1, 2, 3, or 4 from the
above menu or -1 to exit the program
3


Please input the favorite beverage of person #4: Choose 1, 2, 3, or 4 from the
above menu or -1 to exit the program
1


Please input the favorite beverage of person #5: Choose 1, 2, 3, or 4 from the
above menu or -1 to exit the program
1


Please input the favorite beverage of person #6: Choose 1, 2, 3, or 4 from the
above menu or -1 to exit the program
-1


The total number of people surveyed is 5. The results are as follows:


Beverage        Number of Votes
*******************************
Coffee          3
Tea             0
Coke            1
Orange Juice    1
```

*Option 2:* Suppose Dave drops a watermelon off a high bridge and lets it fall until it hits the water. If we neglect air resistance, then the distance $d$ in meters fallen by the watermelon after $t$ seconds is $d = 0.5 * g * t^2$, where the acceleration of gravity $g$ = 9.8 meters/second². Write a program that asks the user to input the number of seconds that the watermelon falls and the height $h$ of the bridge above the water. The program should then calculate the distance fallen for each second from $t$ = 0 until the value of $t$ input by the user. If the total distance fallen is greater than the height of the bridge, then the program should tell the user that the distance fallen is not valid.

*Sample Run 1:*

**Please input the time of fall in seconds:**
2
**Please input the height of the bridge in meters:**
100


**Time Falling (seconds) Distance Fallen (meters)**
**********************************************
0                       0
1                       4.9
2                       19.6

*Sample Run 2:*

**Please input the time of fall in seconds:**
4
**Please input the height of the bridge in meters:**
50


**Time Falling (seconds) Distance Fallen (meters)**
**********************************************
0                       0
1                       4.9
2                       19.6
3                       44.1
4                       78.4


**Warning-Bad Data: The distance fallen exceeds the height of the bridge**

*Option 3:* Write a program that prompts the user for the number of tellers at Nation's Bank in Hyatesville that worked each of the last three years. For each worker the program should ask for the number of days out sick for each of the last three years. The output should provide the number of tellers and the total number of days missed by all the tellers over the last three years.

See the sample output below.

*Sample Run:*

**How many tellers worked at Nation's Bank during each of the last three years ?**
2
**How many days was teller 1 out sick during year 1 ?**
5
**How many days was teller 1 out sick during year 2 ?**
8
**How many days was teller 1 out sick during year 3 ?**
2

**How many days was teller 2 out sick during year 1 ?**
1
**How many days was teller 2 out sick during year 2 ?**
0
**How many days was teller 2 out sick during year 3 ?**
3


**The 2 tellers were out sick for a total of 19 days during the last three years**

# 6.1 Introduction to Void Functions (Procedures)

| | |
|---|---|
| **PURPOSE** | 1. To introduce the concept of void functions (procedures) |
| | 2. To work with void functions (procedures) that have no parameters |
| | 3. To introduce and work with void functions (procedures) that have pass by value and pass by reference parameters |

| | |
|---|---|
| **PROCEDURE** | 1. Students should read the Pre-lab Reading Assignment before coming to lab. |
| | 2. Students should complete the Pre-lab Writing Assignment before coming to lab. |
| | 3. In the lab, students should complete labs assigned to them by their instructor. |

# PRE-LAB READING ASSIGNMENT

## Modules

A key element of structured (well organized and documented) programs is their modularity: the breaking of code into small units. These units, or **modules**, that do not return a value are called **procedures** in most languages and are called **void functions** in C++. Although procedures is the authors' preferred term, this manual uses the word **function** to describe both void functions (discussed in this lesson set) and **value returning functions** (studied in the next lesson set), as this is the terminology used in C++.

The `int main()` section of our program is a function and, up until now, has been the only coded module used in our programs. We also have used pre-defined functions such as `pow` and `sqrt` which are defined in library routines and "imported" to our program with the `#include <cmath>` directive. We now explore the means of breaking our own code into modules. In fact, the `main` function should contain little more than "calls" to other functions. Think of the `main` function as a contractor who hires sub-contractors to perform certain duties: plumbers to do the plumbing, electricians to do the electrical work, etc. The contractor is in charge of the order in which these sub-contract jobs are issued.

The `int main()` function consists mostly of calls to functions just like a contractor issues commands to sub-contractors to come and do their jobs. A computer does many simple tasks (modules) that, when combined, produce a set of complex operations. How one determines what those separate tasks should be is one of the skills learned in software engineering, the science of developing quality software. A good computer program consists of several tasks, or units of code, called modules or functions.

In simple programs most functions are called, or invoked, by the `main` function. Calling a function basically means starting the execution of the instructions contained in that module. Sometimes a function may need information "passed" in order to perform designated tasks.

If a function is to find the square root of a number, then it needs that number passed to it by the calling function. Information is passed to or from a function through **parameters**. Parameters are the components of communication between functions. Some functions do very simple tasks such as printing basic output statements to the screen. These may be instructions to the user or just documentation on what the program will do. Such functions are often called parameter-less functions since they do not require anything passed by the calling procedure.

*Sample Program 6.1a:*

```
#include <iostream>
using namespace std;


void printDescription();   // Function prototype

int main()
{
    cout << "Welcome to the Payroll Program."  << endl;
    printDescription();    // Call to the function
```

```
        cout << "We hoped you enjoyed this program."  << endl;

        return 0;
}


//**************************************************************
//                            printDescription
//
// Task:     This function prints a program description
// Data in:  none
//
//**************************************************************

void printDescription()  // The function heading
{
        cout << "**************************************************"
                << endl << endl;
        cout << "This program takes two numbers (pay rate and hours)"
                << endl;
        cout << "and outputs gross pay. " << endl;
        cout << "**************************************************"
                << endl << endl;


}
```

In this example, three areas have been highlighted. Starting from the bottom we have the function itself which is often called the function definition.

The function **heading** void printDescription() consists of the name of the function preceded by the word void. The word void means that this function will not return a value to the module that called it.[1] The function name is followed by a set of parentheses. Just like the main function, all functions begin with a left brace and end with a right brace. In between these braces are the instructions of the function. In this case they consist solely of cout statements that tell what the program does.

Notice that this function comes after the main function. How is this function activated? It must be called by either the main function or another function in the program. This function is called by main with the simple instruction printDescription();.

A **call** to a function can be classified as the sixth fundamental instruction (see Lesson Set 2). Notice the call consists only of the name of the function (not the word void preceding it) followed by the set of parentheses and a semicolon. By invoking its name in this way, the function is called. The program executes the body of instructions found in that function and then returns to the calling function (main in this case) where it executes the remaining instructions following the call. Let us examine the order in which the instructions are executed.

---

[1] In the next lesson set we will see that the word preceding the name of a function can be the data type of the value that the function will return to the calling function.

The `main` function is invoked which then executes the following instruction:

```
cout << "Welcome to the Pay Roll Program" << endl;
```

Next the call to the function `printDescription` is encountered which executes the following instructions:

```
cout << "***************************************************" << endl << endl;
cout << "This program takes two numbers (pay rate & hours)" << endl;
cout << "and outputs gross pay " << endl;
cout << "***************************************************" << endl << endl;
```

After all the instructions in `printDescription` are executed, control returns to `main` and the next instruction after the call is executed:

```
cout << "We hoped you enjoyed this program" << endl;
```

The first highlighted section of the example is found before `main()` in what we call the global section of the program. It is called a **prototype** and looks just like the function heading except it has a semicolon at the end. Since our example has the "definition of the function" after the call to the function, the program will give us an error when we try to call it if we do not have some kind of signal to the computer that the definition will be forthcoming. That is the purpose of the prototype. It is a promise (contract if you will) to the compiler that a `void` function called `printDescription` will be defined after the `main` function. If the `printDescription` function is placed in the file before the `main` function which calls it, then the prototype is not necessary. However, most C++ programs are written with prototypes so that `main()` can be the first function.

## Pass by Value

The following program, Sample Program 6.1b, is an extension of the code above. This program will take a pay rate and hours worked and produce the gross pay based on those numbers. This can be done in another function called `calPaycheck`.

*Sample Program 6.1b:*

```
#include <iostream>
using namespace std;

// Function prototypes
void printDescription();
void calPaycheck(float, int);

int main()
{
    float payRate;
    int hours;

    cout << "Welcome to the Payroll Program." << endl;
```

```
    printDescription();                // Call to the printDescription function

    cout << endl << "Please input the pay per hour." << endl;
    cin >> payRate;

    cout << endl << "Please input the number of hours worked."  << endl;
    cin >> hours;
    cout << endl << endl;

    calPaycheck(payRate, hours);   // Call to the calPaycheck function

    cout << "We hope you enjoyed this program."  << endl;

    return 0;
}


//********************************************************************
//                        printDescription
//
//  Task:     This function prints a program description
//  Data in:  no parameters received from the function call
//
//********************************************************************

void printDescription()  // The function heading
{
    cout << "***************************************************" << endl << endl;
    cout << "This program takes two numbers (pay rate and hours) " << endl;
    cout << "and outputs gross pay. " << endl;
    cout << "***************************************************" << endl << endl;
}


//********************************************************************
//                          calPaycheck
//
//  Task:      This function computes and outputs gross pay
//  Data in:   rate and time
//
//********************************************************************

void calPaycheck(float rate, int time)
{
    float gross;

    gross = rate * time;
    cout << "The pay is " << gross << endl;
}
```

The bold sections of this program show the development of another function. This function is a bit different in that it has parameters inside the parentheses of the call, heading and prototype. Recall that parameters are the components of communication to and from a function and the call to that function. The function `calPaycheck` needs information from the calling routine. In order to find the gross pay it needs the rate per hour and the number of hours worked to be passed to it. The call provides this information by having parameters inside the parentheses of the call `calPaycheck(payRate,hours);`. Both `payRate` and `hours` are called **actual parameters**. They match in a one-to-one correspondence with the parameters in the function heading which are called `rate` and `time`:

```
void calPaycheck(float rate, int time)
```

The parameters in a function heading are called **formal parameters**.

It is important to compare the call with the function heading.

**Call**                          **Function heading**

`calPaycheck(payRate,hours);`     `void calPaycheck(float rate, int time)`

1. The call does not have any word preceding the name whereas the function heading has the word `void` preceding its name.

2. The call must NOT give the data type before its actual parameters whereas the heading MUST give the data type of its formal parameters.

3. Although the formal parameters may have the same name as their corresponding actual parameters, they do not have to be the same. The first actual parameter, `payRate`, is paired with `rate`, the first formal parameter. This means that the value of `payRate` is given to `rate`. The second actual parameter, `hours`, is paired with `time`, the second formal parameter, and gives `time` its value. Corresponding (paired) parameters must have the same data type. Notice that `payRate` is defined as `float` in the `main` function and thus it can legally match `rate` which is also defined as `float` in the function heading. `hours` is defined as `int` so it can be legally matched (paired) with `time` which is defined as `int` in the function heading.

4. The actual parameters (`payRate` and `hours`) pass their values to their corresponding formal parameters. Whatever value is read into `payRate` in the `main` function will be given to `rate` in the `calPaycheck` function. This is called **pass by value**. It means that `payRate` and `rate` are two distinct memory locations. Whatever value is in `payRate` at the time of the call will be placed in `rate`'s memory location as its initial value. It should be noted that if the function `calPaycheck` were to alter the value of `rate`, it would not affect the value of `payRate` back in the `main` function. In essence, pass by value is like making a copy of the value in `payRate` and placing it in `rate`. Whatever is done to that copy in `rate` has no effect on the value in `payRate`. Recall that a formal parameter can have the same name as its corresponding actual parameter; however, they are still two different locations in memory.

How does the computer know which location to go to if there are two variables with the same name? The answer is found in a concept called **scope**. Scope refers to the location in a program where an indentifier is accessible. All variables defined in the `main` function become inactive when another function is called and are reactivated when the control returns to `main`. By the same token, all formal parameters and variables defined inside a function are active only during the time the function is executing. What this means is that an actual parameter and its corresponding formal parameter are never active at the same time. Thus there is no confusion as to which memory location to access even if corresponding parameters have the same name. More on scope will be presented in the next lesson set.

It is also important to compare the prototype with the heading.

**Prototype**

`void calPaycheck(float, int);`

**Function heading**

`void calPaycheck(float rate, int time)`

1. The prototype has a semicolon at the end and the heading does not.
2. The prototype lists only the data type of the parameters and not their name. However, the prototype can list both and thus be exactly like the heading except for the semicolon. Some instructors tell students to copy the prototype without the semicolon and paste it to form the function heading.

Let us look at all three parts—prototype, call and heading:

1. The heading MUST have both data type and name for all its **formal parameters**.
2. The prototype must have the data type and can have the name for its **formal parameters**.
3. The call MUST have the name but MUST NOT have the data type for its **actual parameters**.

## Pass by Reference

Suppose we want the `calPaycheck` function to only compute the gross pay and then pass this value back to the calling function rather than printing it. We need another parameter, not to get information from the call but to give information back to the call. This particular parameter can not be **passed by value** since any change made in a function to a *pass by value formal parameter* has no effect on its corresponding actual parameter. Instead, this parameter is **passed by ref-**

ins that the calling function will give the called function the parameter instead of a copy of the value that is stored in that allows the called function to go in and change the value of

at I have a set of lockers each containing a sheet of paper Making a copy of a sheet from a particular locker and ou will ensure that you will not change my original copy. . On the other hand, if I give you a spare key to a particu-go to that locker and change the number on the sheet of This is pass by reference.

The S gram know whether a parameter is passed by value or by ters are passed by value unless they have the character & pe, which indicates a pass by reference.

```
#include <iomanip>
using namespace std;

// Function prototypes
```

*continues*

```cpp
void printDescription();                // prototype for a parameter-less function
void calPaycheck(float, int, float&);  // prototype for a function with 3
                                        // parameters. The first two are passed
                                        // by value. The third is passed by
                                        // reference

int main()
{
    float payRate;
    float grossPay;
    float netPay;
    int hours;

    cout << "Welcome to the Payroll Program."  << endl;

    printDescription();                // Call to the  description function

    cout << endl << "Please input the pay per hour." << endl;
    cin >> payRate;
    cout << endl << "Please input the number of hours worked."  << endl;
    cin >> hours;
    cout << endl << endl;

    calPaycheck(payRate, hours, grossPay);   // Call to the calPaycheck function
    etPay = grossPay - (grossPay * .20);

    cout << "The net pay is " << netPay << endl;
    cout << "We hoped you enjoyed this program."  << endl;

    return 0;
}

//****************************************************************
//                        printDescription
//
// Task:     This function prints a program description
// Data in:  none
// Data out: no actual parameters altered
//
//****************************************************************

void printDescription()  // The function heading
{
    cout << "*****************************************************"  <<   endl << endl;
    cout << "This program takes two numbers (pay rate and hours) " << endl;
    cout << "and outputs gross pay. " << endl;
    cout << "*****************************************************"  <<   endl << endl;
}
```

```
//*****************************************************************
//                            calPaycheck
//
//  Task:      This function computes gross pay
//  Data in:   rate and time
//  Data out:  gross (alters the corresponding actual parameter)
//
//*****************************************************************

void calPaycheck(float rate, int time, float& gross)
{
    gross = rate * time;
}
```

Notice that the function `calPaycheck` now has three parameters. The first two, `rate` and `time`, are passed by value while the third has an & after its data type indicating that it is pass by reference. The actual parameter `grossPay` is paired with `gross` since they both are the third parameter in their respective lists. But since this pairing is pass by reference, these two names refer to the SAME memory location. Thus what the function does to its formal parameter `gross` changes the value of `grossPay`. After the `calPaycheck` function finds `gross`, control goes back to the `main` function that has this value in `grossPay`. `main` proceeds to find the net pay, by taking 20% off the gross pay, and printing it. Study this latest revision of the program very carefully. One of the lab exercises asks you to alter it.

## PRE-LAB WRITING ASSIGNMENT

### Fill-in-the-Blank Questions

1. The word _____ precedes the name of every function prototype and heading that does not return a value back to the calling routine.

2. Pass by _____ indicates that a copy of the actual parameter is placed in the memory location of its corresponding formal parameter.

3. _____ parameters are found in the call to a function.

4. A prototype must give the _____ _____ of its formal parameters and may give their _____.

5. A _____ after a data type in the function heading and in the prototype indicates that the parameter will be passed by reference.

6. Functions that do not return a value are often called _____ in other programming languages.

7. Pass by _____ indicates that the location of an actual parameter, rather than just a copy of its value, is passed to the called function.

8. A call must have the _____ of its actual parameters and must NOT have the _____ _____ of those parameters.

9. _____ refers to the region of a program where a variable is "active."

10. _____ parameters are found in the function heading.

# LESSON 6.1A

### LAB 6.1   Functions with No Parameters

Retrieve program `proverb.cpp` from the Lab 6.1 folder. The code is as follows:

```
// This program prints the proverb
// "Now is the time for all good men to come to the aid of their party"
// in a function (procedure) called writeProverb that is called by the main function

//PLACE YOUR NAME HERE

#include <iostream>
using namespace std;


void writeProverb();   //This is the prototype for the writeProverb function

int main()
{

        // Fill in the code to call the writeProverb function

      return 0;


}

//    ***********************************************************************
//                              writeProverb
//
//    task:      This function prints a proverb
//    data in:   none
//    data out:  no actual parameter altered
//
//    ***********************************************************************


// Fill in the function heading and the body of the function that will print
// to the screen the proverb listed in the comments at the beginning of the
// program
```

*Exercise 1:* Fill in the code (places in bold) so that the program will print out the proverb listed in the comments at the beginning of the program. The proverb will be printed by the function which is called by the main function.

### LAB 6.2   Introduction to Pass by Value

Retrieve program `newproverb.cpp` from the Lab 6.1 folder. The code is as follows:

```
// This program will allow the user to input from the keyboard
// whether the last word to the following proverb should be party or country:
```

```
// "Now is the time for all good men to come to the aid of their _____"
// Inputting a 1 will use the word party. Any other number will use the word country.
```

```
// PLACE YOUR NAME HERE
```

```
#include <iostream>
#include <string>
using namespace std;
```

```
// Fill in the prototype of the function writeProverb.
```

```
int main ()
{

    int wordCode;

    cout << "Given the phrase:" << endl;
    cout << "Now is the time for all good men to come to the aid of their ___"
        << endl;
    cout << "Input a 1 if you want the sentence to be finished with party"
        << endl;
    cout << "Input any other number for the word country" << endl;
    cout << "Please input your choice now" << endl;
    cin  >> wordCode;
    cout << endl;
    writeProverb(wordCode);

    return 0;
}
```

```
//   ****************************************************************************
//                        writeProverb
//
//   task:       This function prints a proverb. The function takes a number
//               from the call. If that number is a 1 it prints "Now is the time
//               for all good men to come to the aid of their party."
//               Otherwise, it prints "Now is the time for all good men
//               to come to the aid of their country."
//   data in:    code for ending word of proverb (integer)
//   data out:   no actual parameter altered
//
//   ****************************************************************************
```

```
void writeProverb (int number)
```

```
{
    // Fill in the body of the function to accomplish what is described above
}
```

*Exercise 1:* Some people know this proverb as "Now is the time for all good men to come to the aid of their country" while others heard it as "Now is the time for all good men to come to the aid of their party." This program will allow the user to choose which way they want it printed. Fill in the blanks of the program to accomplish what is described in the program comments. What happens if you inadvertently enter a float such as -3.97?

*Exercise 2:* Change the program so that an input of 1 from the user will print "party" at the end, a 2 will print "country" and any other number will be invalid so that the user will need to enter a new choice.

*Sample Run:*

```
Given the phrase:
Now is the time for all good men to come to the aid of their __
Input a 1 if you want the sentence to be finished with party
Input a 2 if you want the sentence to be finished with country
Please input your choice now
4
I'm sorry but that is an incorrect choice; Please input a 1 or 2
2
Now is the time for all good men to come to the aid of their country
```

*Exercise 3:* Change the previous program so the user may input the word to end the phrase. The string holding the user's input word will be passed to the proverb function instead of passing a number to it. Notice that this change requires you to change the proverb function heading and the prototype as well as the call to the function.

*Sample Run:*

```
Given the phrase:
Now is the time for all good men to come to the aid of their _____
Please input the word you would like to have finish the proverb
family
Now is the time for all good men to come to the aid of their family
```

# LESSON 6.1B

## Lab 6.3    Introduction to Pass by Reference

Retrieve program `paycheck.cpp` from the Lab 6.1 folder. This program is similar to Sample Program 6.1C that was given in the Pre-lab Reading Assignment. The code is as follows:

```
// This program takes two numbers (payRate & hours)
// and multiplies them to get grosspay.
// It then calculates net pay by subtracting 15%

//PLACE YOUR NAME HERE
```

```cpp
#include <iostream>
#include <iomanip>
using namespace std;


//Function prototypes
void printDescription();
void computePaycheck(float, int, float&, float&);

int main()
{
    float payRate;
    float grossPay;
    float netPay;
    int hours;

    cout << setprecision(2) << fixed;

    cout << "Welcome to the Pay Roll Program" << endl;

    printDescription(); //Call to Description function

    cout << "Please input the pay per hour" << endl;
    cin >> payRate;

    cout << endl << "Please input the number of hours worked" << endl;
    cin >> hours;
    cout << endl << endl;

    computePaycheck(payRate,hours,grossPay,netPay);

    //  Fill in the code to output grossPay

    cout << "The net pay is $" << netPay << endl;

    cout << "We hope you enjoyed this program" << endl;

    return 0;
}




//  ********************************************************************
//                      printDescription
//
//  task:    This function prints a program description
//  data in:  none
//  data out: no actual parameter altered
//
//  ********************************************************************
```

*continues*

```
void printDescription() // The function heading
{
    cout << "**************************************************"  << endl << endl;
    cout << "This program takes two numbers (payRate & hours)" << endl;
    cout << "and  multiplies them to get gross pay "          << endl;
    cout << "it then calculates net pay by subtracting 15%"   << endl;
    cout << "**************************************************"  << endl << endl;
}



// **********************************************************************
//                     computePaycheck
//
//    task:      This function takes rate and time and multiples them to
//               get gross pay and then finds net pay by subtracting 15%.
//    data in:   pay rate and time in hours worked
//    data out:  the gross and net pay
//
// **********************************************************************



void computePaycheck(float rate, int time, float& gross, float& net)

{
        // Fill in the code to find gross pay and net pay


}
```

*Exercise 1:* Fill in the code (places in bold) and note that the function computePaycheck determines the net pay by subtracting 15% from the gross pay. Both gross and net are returned to the main() function where those values are printed.

*Exercise 2:* Compile and run your program with the following data and make sure you get the output shown.

**Please input the pay per hour**
9.50
**Please input the number of hours worked**
40


**The gross pay is $380**
**The net pay is $323**
**We hoped you enjoyed this program**

*Exercise 3:* Are the parameters `gross` and `net`, in the modified `calPaycheck` function you created in Exercise 1 above, pass by value or pass by reference?

*Exercise 4:* Alter the program so that `gross` and `net` are printed in the function compute `computePaycheck` instead of in `main()`. The `main()` function executes the statement

```
cout << "We hoped you enjoyed this program" << endl;
```

after the return from the function `calPaycheck`.

*Exercise 5:* Run the program again using the data from Exercise 2. You should get the same results. All parameters should now be passed by value.

## LAB 6.4    Student Generated Code Assignments

*Option 1:* Write a program that will read two floating point numbers (the first read into a variable called `first` and the second read into a variable called `second`) and then calls the function `swap` with the actual parameters `first` and `second`. The `swap` function having formal parameters `number1` and `number2` should swap the value of the two variables. Note: This is similar to a program you did in Lesson Set 1; however, now you are required to use a function. You may want to look at `logicprob.cpp` from Lesson Set 1.

*Sample Run:*

**Enter the first number**
**Then hit enter**
80
**Enter the second number**
**Then hit enter**
70

**You input the numbers as 80 and 70.**
**After swapping, the first number has the value of 70 which was the value of the**
**second number**
**The second number has the value of 80 which was the value of the first number**

*Exercise 1:* Compile the program and correct it if necessary until you get no syntax errors.

*Exercise 2:* Run the program with the sample data above and see if you get the same results.

*Exercise 3:* The `swap` parameters must be passed by _____. (Assume that main produces the output.) Why?

*Option 2:* Write a program that will input miles traveled and hours spent in travel. The program will determine miles per hour. This calculation must be done in a function other than `main`; however, `main` will print the calculation. The function will thus have 3 parameters: `miles`, `hours`, and `milesPerHour`. Which parameter(s) are pass by value and which are passed by reference? Output is fixed with 2 decimal point precision.

*Sample Run:*

**Please input the miles traveled**
475
**Please input the hours traveled**
8
**Your speed is 59.38 miles per hour**

*Option 3:* Write a program that will read in grades, the number of which is also input by the user. The program will find the sum of those grades and pass it, along with the number of grades, to a function which has a "pass by reference" parameter that will contain the numeric average of those grades as processed by the function. The `main` function will then determine the letter grade of that average based on a 10-point scale.

|        |   |
|--------|---|
| 90–100 | A |
| 80–89  | B |
| 70–79  | C |
| 60–69  | D |
| 0–59   | F |

*Sample Run:*

**Enter the number of grades**
3
**Enter a numeric grade between 0-100**
90
**Enter a numeric grade between 0-100**
80
**Enter a numeric grade between 0-100**
50
**The grade is C**

# 6.2 Functions that Return a Value

| PURPOSE | | |
|---|---|---|
| | 1. | To introduce the concept of scope |
| | 2. | To understand the difference between static, local and global variables |
| | 3. | To introduce the concept of functions that return a value |
| | 4. | To introduce the concept of overloading functions |

| PROCEDURE | | |
|---|---|---|
| | 1. | Students should read the Pre-lab Reading Assignment before coming to lab. |
| | 2. | Students should complete the Pre-lab Writing Assignment before coming to lab. |
| | 3. | In the lab, students should complete labs assigned to them by the instructor. |

| Contents | Pre-requisites | Approximate completion time | Page number | Check when done |
|---|---|---|---|---|
| Pre-lab Reading Assignment | | 20 min. | 92 | |
| Pre-lab Writing Assignment | Pre-lab reading | 10 min. | 101 | |
| **LESSON 6.2A** | | | | |
| Lab 6.5 Scope of Variables | Basic understanding of scope rules and parameter passing | 15 min. | 101 | |
| Lab 6.6 Parameters and Local Variables | Basic understanding of formal and actual parameters and local variables | 35 min. | 104 | |
| **LESSON 6.2B** | | | | |
| Lab 6.7 Value Returning and Overloading Functions | Understanding of value returning functions and overloaded functions | 30 min. | 106 | |
| Lab 6.8 Student Generated Code Assignments | Basic understanding of pass by reference and value. | 30 min. | 110 | |

## PRE-LAB READING ASSIGNMENT

### Scope

As mentioned in Lesson Set 6.1, the scope of an identifier (variable, constant, function, etc.) is an indication of where it can be accessed in a program. There can be certain portions of a program where a variable or other identifier can not be accessed for use. Such areas are considered out of the scope for that particular identifier. The header (the portion of the program before `main`) has often been referred to as the global section. Any identifier defined or declared in this area is said to have **global scope**, meaning it can be accessed at any time during the execution of the program. Any identifier defined outside the bounds of all the functions have global scope. Although most constants and all functions are defined globally, variables should almost **never** be defined in this manner.

**Local scope** refers to identifiers defined within a block. They are active only within the bounds of that particular block. In C++ a **block** begins with a left brace { and ends with a right brace }. Since all functions (including `main`) begin and end with a pair of braces, the body of a function is a block. Variables defined within functions are called **local variables** (as opposed to **global variables** which have global scope). Local variables can normally be accessed anywhere within the function from the point where they are defined. However, blocks can be defined within other blocks, and the scope of an identifier defined in such an inner block would be limited to that inner block. A function's formal parameters (Lesson Set 6.1) have the same scope as local variables defined in the outmost block of the function. This means that the scope of a formal parameter is the entire function. The following sample program illustrates some of these scope rules.

*Sample Program 6.2a:*

```
#include <iostream>
using namespace std;

const PI = 3.14;

void printHeading();

int main()
{
    float circle;
    cout << "circle has local scope that extends the entire main function"
        << endl;

    {
        float square;
        cout << "square has local scope active for only a portion of main."
            << endl;
        cout << "Both square and circle can be accessed here "
            << "as well as the global constant PI." << endl;
    }
```

```
        cout << "circle is active here, but square is not." << endl;

        printHeading();

        return 0;
}

void printHeading()
{
        int triangle;

        cout << "The global constant PI is active here "
             << "as well as the local variable triangle." << endl;

}
```

Notice that the nested braces within the outer braces of main() indicate another block in which square is defined. square is active only within the bounds of the inner braces while circle is active for the entire main function. Neither of these are active when the function printHeading is called. triangle is a local variable of the function printHeading and is active only when that function is active. PI, being a global identifier, is active everywhere.

Formal parameters (Lesson Set 6.1) have the same scope as local variables defined in the outmost block of the function. That means that the scope of formal parameters of a function is the entire function. The question may arise about variables with the same name. For example, could a local variable in the function printHeading of the above example have the name circle? The answer is yes, but it would be a different memory location than the one defined in the main function. There are rules of **name precedence** which determine which memory location is active among a group of two or more variables with the same name. The most recently defined variable has precedence over any other variable with the same name. In the above example, if circle had been defined in the printHeading function, then the memory location assigned with that definition would take precedence over the location defined in main() as long as the function printHeading was active.

**Lifetime** is similar but not exactly the same as scope. It refers to the time during a program that an identifier has storage assigned to it.

## Scope Rules

1. The scope of a global identifier, any identifier declared or defined outside all functions, is the entire program.
2. Functions are defined globally. That means any function can call any other function at any time.
3. The scope of a local identifier is from the point of its definition to the end of the block in which it is defined. This includes any nested blocks that may be contained within, unless the nested block has a variable defined in it with the same name.
4. The scope of formal parameters is the same as the scope of local variables defined at the beginning of the function.

Why are variables almost never defined globally? Good structured programming assures that all communication between functions will be explicit through the use of parameters. Global variables can be changed by any function. In large projects, where more than one programmer may be working on the same program, global variables are unreliable since their values can be changed by any function or any programmer. The inadvertent changing of global variables in a particular function can cause unwanted side effects.

## Static Local Variables

One of the biggest advantages of a function is the fact that it can be called multiple times to perform a job. This saves programming time and memory space. The values of local variables do not remain between multiple function calls. What this means is that the value assigned to a local variable of a function is lost once the function is finished executing. If the same function is called again that value will not necessarily be present for the local variable. Local variables start "fresh," in terms of their value, each time the function is called. There may be times when a function needs to retain the value of a variable between calls. This can be done by defining the variable to be **static**, which means it is initialized at most once and its memory space is retained even after the function in which it is defined has finished executing. Thus the lifetime of a static variable is different than a normal local variable. Static variables are defined by placing the word **static** before the data type and name of the variable as shown below.

```
static int totalPay = 0;
static float interestRate;
```

## Default Arguments

Actual parameters (parameters used in the call to a function) are often called **arguments**. Normally the number of actual parameters or arguments must equal the number of formal parameters, and it is good programming practice to use this one-to-one correspondence between actual and formal parameters. It is possible, however, to assign default values to all formal parameters so that the calling instruction does not have to pass values for all the arguments. Although these default values can be specified in the function heading, they are usually defined in the prototype. Certain actual parameters can be left out; however, if an actual parameter is left out, then all the following parameters must also be left out. For this reason, pass by reference arguments should be placed first (since by their very nature they must be included in the call).

*Sample Program 6.2b:*

```
#include <iostream>
#include <iomanip>
using namespace std;



void calNetPay(float& net, int hours=40, float rate=6.00);
// function prototype with default arguments specified



int main()
{
```

```
        int hoursWorked = 20;
        float payRate = 5.00;
        float pay;                     // net pay calculated by the calNetPay function

        cout << setprecision(2) << fixed << showpoint;

        calNetPay(pay);                // call to the function with only 1 parameter
        cout << "The net pay is $" << pay << endl;

        return 0;
}




//
//************************************************************************
//                       calNetPay
//
//   task:       This function takes rate and hours and multiples them to
//               get net pay (no deductions in this pay check!!!).  It has two
//               default parameters.  If the third argument is missing from the
//               call, 6.00 will be passed as the rate to this function.  If the
//               second and third arguments are missing from the call, 40 will be
//               passed as the hours and 6.00 will be passed as the rate.
//
//   data in:    pay rate and time in hours worked
//   data out:   net pay (alters the corresponding actual parameter)
//
//
//************************************************************************




void calNetPay(float& net, int hours, float rate)

{
        net = hours * rate;


}
```

What will happen if pay is not listed in the calling instruction? An error will occur stating that the function can not take 0 arguments. The reason for this is that the net formal parameter does not have a default value and so the call must have at least one argument. In general there must be as many actual arguments as formal parameters that do not have default values. Of course some or all default values can be overridden.

The following calls are all legal in the example program. Fill in the values that the calNetpay function receives for hours and rate in each case. Also fill in the value that you expect net pay to have for each call.

```
calNetPay(pay);                            The net pay is $_____
     calNetPay receives the value of _____ for hours and _____ for rate.
```

```
calNetPay(pay,hoursWorked);          The net pay is $_____
    calNetPay receives the value of _____ for hours and _____ for rate.

calNetPay(pay, hoursWorked, payRate);     The net pay is $_____
    calNetPay receives the value of _____ for hours and _____ for rate.
```

The following are not correct. List what you think causes the error in each case.

```
calNetPay(pay, payRate);
calNetPay(hoursWorked, payRate);
calNetPay(payRate);
calNetPay();
```

## Functions that Return a Value

The functions discussed in the previous lesson set are not "true functions" because they do not return a value to the calling function. They are often referred to as procedures in computer science jargon. True functions, or value returning functions, are modules that return exactly one value to the calling routine. In C++ they do this with a `return` statement. This is illustrated by the `cubeIt` function shown in sample program 6.2c.

*Sample Program 6.2c:*

```
#include <iostream>
using namespace std;

int cubeIt(int x);              // prototype for a user defined function
                                // that returns the cube of the value passed
                                // to it.

int main()

{
    int x = 2;
    int cube;

    cube = cubeIt(x);           // This is the call to the cubeIt function.
    cout << "The cube of " << x << " is " << cube << endl;

    return 0;
}

//*****************************************************************
//                        cubeIt
//
//   task:          This function takes a value and returns its cube
//   data in:       some value x
//   data returned: the cube of x
//
//*****************************************************************


int cubeIt(int x)               // Notice that the function type is int
                                // rather than void

    {
```

```
    int num;

    num = x * x * x;
    return num;
}
```

The function `cubeIt` receives the value of `x`, which in this case is 2, and finds its cube which is placed in the local variable `num`. The function then returns the value stored in `num` to the function call `cubeIt(x)`. The value 8 replaces the entire function call and is assigned to cube. That is, `cube = cubeIt(x)` is replaced with `cube = 8`. It is not actually necessary to place the value to be returned in a local variable before returning it. The entire `cubeIt` function could be written as follows:

```
int cubeIt(int x)
{
    return x * x * x;
}
```

For value returning functions we replace the word `void` with the data type of the value that is returned. Since these functions return one value, there should be no effect on any parameters that are passed from the call. This means that all parameters of value returning functions should be pass by value, NOT pass by reference. Nothing in C++ prevents the programmer from using pass by reference in value returning functions; however, they should not be used.

The `calNetPay` program (Sample Program 6.2b) has a module that calculates the net pay when given the hours worked and the hourly pay rate. Since it calculates only one value that is needed by the call, it can easily be implemented as a value returning function, instead of by having `pay` passed by reference.

Sample program 6.2d, which follows, modifies Program 6.2b in this manner.

*Sample Program 6.2d:*

```
#include <iostream>
#include <iomanip>
using namespace std;

float calNetPay(int hours, float rate);

int main()

{
    int hoursWorked = 20;
    float payRate = 5.00;
    float netPay;

    cout << setprecision(2) << fixed << showpoint;

    netPay = calNetPay(hoursWorked, payRate);
    cout << " The net pay is $" << netPay << endl;

    return 0;
}
```

*continues*

```
//*********************************************************************
//                      calNetPay
//
//   task:              This function takes hours worked and pay rate and multiplies
//                      them to get the net pay which is returned to the calling function.
//
//   data in:           hours worked and pay rate
//   data returned: net pay
//
//*********************************************************************


float calNetPay(int hours, float rate)
{

      return hours * rate;

}
```

Notice how this function is called.

```
paynet = calNetPay (hoursWorked, payRate);
```

This call to the function is not a stand-alone statement, but rather part of an assignment statement. The call is used in an expression. In fact, the function will return a floating value that replaces the entire right-hand side of the assignment statement. This is the first major difference between the two types of functions (void functions and value returning functions). A void function is called by just listing the name of the function along with its arguments. A value returning function is called within a portion of some fundamental instruction (the right-hand side of an assignment statement, condition of a selection or loop statement, or argument of a cout statement). As mentioned earlier, another difference is that in both the prototype and function heading the word void is replaced with the data type of the value that is returned. A third difference is the fact that a value returning function MUST have a return statement. It is usually the very last instruction of the function. The following is a comparison between the implementation as a procedure (void function) and as a value returning function.

| | Value Returning Function | Procedure |
|---|---|---|
| **PROTOTYPE** | float calNetPay (int hours, float rate); | void calNetPay (float& net, int hours, float rate); |
| **CALL** | netpay=calNetPay (hoursWorked, payRate); | calNetPay (pay, hoursWorked, payRate); |
| **HEADING** | float calNetPay (int hours, float rate) | void calNetPay (float& net, int hours, float rate) |
| **BODY** | {<br>    return hours * rate;<br>} | {<br>    net = hours * rate;<br>} |

Functions can also return a Boolean data type to test whether a certain condition exists (true) or not (false).

## Overloading Functions

Uniqueness of identifier names is a vital concept in programming languages. The convention in C++ is that every variable, function, constant, etc. name with the same scope needs to be unique. However, there is an exception. Two or more functions may have the same name as long as their parameters differ in quantity or data type. For example, a programmer could have two functions with the same name that do the exact same thing to variables of different data types.

*Example:* Look at the following prototypes of functions. All have the same name, yet all can be included in the same program because each one differs from the others either by the number of parameters or the data types of the parameters.

```
int   add(int a, int b, int c);
int   add(int a, int b);
float add(float a, float b, float c);
float add(float a, float b);
```

When the add function is called, the actual parameter list of the call is used to determine which add function to call.

## Stubs and Drivers

Many IDEs (Integrated Development Environments) have software debuggers which are used to help locate logic errors; however, programmers often use the concept of stubs and drivers to test and debug programs that use functions and procedures. A **stub** is nothing more than a dummy function that is called instead of the actual function. It usually does little more than write a message to the screen indicating that it was called with certain arguments. In structured design, the programmer often wants to delay the implementation of certain details until the overall design of the program is complete. The use of stubs makes this possible.

*Sample Program 6.2e:*

```
#include <iostream>
using namespace std;

int findSqrRoot(int x);   // prototype for a user defined function that
                          // returns the square root of the number passed to it

int main()
{
    int number;

    cout << "Input the number whose square root you want." << endl;
    cout << "Input a -99 when you would like to quit." << endl;
    cin >> number;

    while (number != -99)
    {
```

*continues*

```
                cout << "The square root of your number is "
                        << findSqrRoot(number) << endl;
                cout << "Input the number whose square root you want." << endl;
                cout << "Input a -99 when you would like to quit." << endl;
                cin >> number;
        }
        return 0;
}
```

```
int findSqrRoot(int x)
{
        cout << "findSqrRoot function was called with " << x
                << " as its argument\n";
        return 0;
}       // This bold section is the stub.
```

This example shows that the programmer can test the execution of main and the call to the function without having yet written the function to find the square root. This allows the programmer to concentrate on one component of the program at a time. Although a stub is not really needed in this simple program, stubs are very useful for larger programs.

A **driver** is a module that tests a function by simply calling it. While one programmer may be working on the main function, another programmer may be developing the code for a particular function. In this case the programmer is not so concerned with the calling of the function but rather with the body of the function itself. In such a case a driver (call to the function) can be used just to see if the function performs properly.

*Sample Program 6.2f:*

```
#include <iostream>
#include <cmath>
using namespace std;

int findSqrRoot(int x); // prototype for a user defined function that
                        // returns the square root of the number passed to it

int main()
{
        int number;

        cout << "Calling findSqrRoot function with a 4" << endl;
        cout << "The result is " << findSqrRoot(4) << endl;

        return 0;
}

int findSqrRoot(int x)
{
        return sqrt(x);
}
```

In this example, the main function is used solely as a tool (driver) to call the findSqrRoot function to see if it performs properly.

# PRE-LAB WRITING ASSIGNMENT

## Fill-in-the-Blank Questions

1. Variables of a function that retain their value over multiple calls to the function are called _____ variables.

2. In C++ all functions have _____ scope.

3. Default arguments are usually defined in the _____ of the function.

4. A function returning a value should never use pass by _____ parameters.

5. Every function that begins with a data type in the heading, rather than the word `void`, must have a(n) _____ statement somewhere, usually at the end, in its body of instructions.

6  A(n) _____ is a program that tests a function by simply calling it.

7. In C++ a block boundary is defined with a pair of _____.

8. A(n) _____ is a dummy function that just indicates that a function was called properly.

9. Default values are generally not given for pass by _____ parameters.

10. _____ functions are functions that have the same name but a different parameter list.

# LESSON 6.2A

## LAB 6.5   Scope of Variables

Retrieve program `scope.cpp` from the Lab 6.2 folder. The code is as follows:

```cpp
#include <iostream>
#include <iomanip>
using namespace std;


// This program will demonstrate the scope rules.

// PLACE YOUR NAME HERE


const double PI = 3.14;
const double RATE = 0.25;

void findArea(float, float&);
void findCircumference(float, float&);


int main()

{
```

*continues*

```cpp
            cout << fixed << showpoint << setprecision(2);
            float radius = 12;

            cout <<" Main function outer block" << endl;
            cout <<" LIST THE IDENTIFIERS THAT are active here" << endl << endl;
            {
                float area;
                cout << "Main function first inner block" << endl;
                cout << "LIST THE IDENTIFIERS THAT are active here" << endl << endl;

                // Fill in the code to call findArea here

                cout << "The radius = " << radius << endl;
                cout << "The area = " << area << endl << endl;
            }


            {
                float radius = 10;
                float circumference;

                cout << "Main function second inner block" << endl;
                cout << "LIST THE IDENTIFIERS THAT are active here" << endl << endl;

                // Fill in the code to call findCircumference here

                cout << "The radius = " << radius << endl;
                cout << "The circumference = " << circumference << endl << endl;

            }


            cout << "Main function after all the calls" << endl;
            cout << "LIST THE IDENTIFIERS THAT are active here" << endl << endl;

            return 0;
        }


//     ********************************************************************
//                         findArea
//
//     task:     This function finds the area of a circle given its radius
//     data in:  radius of a circle
//     data out: answer (which alters the corresponding actual parameter)
//
//     ********************************************************************


void findArea(float rad, float& answer)
{

        cout << "AREA FUNCTION" << endl << endl;
        cout << "LIST THE IDENTIFIERS THAT are active here"<< endl << endl;
```

```
    // FILL in the code, given that parameter rad contains the radius, that
    // will find the area to be stored in answer


}


//   ****************************************************************************
//                         findCircumference
//
//   task:     This function finds the circumference of a circle given its radius
//   data in:  radius of a circle
//   data out: distance (which alters the corresponding actual parameter)
//
//   ****************************************************************************



void findCircumference(float length, float& distance)


{
        cout << "CIRCUMFERENCE FUNCTION" << endl << endl;
        cout << "LIST THE IDENTIFIERS THAT are active here" << endl << endl;

        // FILL in the code, given that parameter length contains the radius,
        // that will find the circumference to be stored in distance


}
```

*Exercise 1:* Fill in the following chart by listing the identifiers (function names, variables, constants)

| GLOBAL | Main | Main (inner 1) | Main (inner 2) | Area | Circum-ference |
|--------|------|----------------|----------------|------|-----------------|
|        |      |                |                |      |                 |
|        |      |                |                |      |                 |
|        |      |                |                |      |                 |
|        |      |                |                |      |                 |
|        |      |                |                |      |                 |
|        |      |                |                |      |                 |
|        |      |                |                |      |                 |
|        |      |                |                |      |                 |

*Exercise 2:* For each cout instruction that reads:

```
cout << " LIST THE IDENTIFIERS THAT are active here" << endl;
```

Replace the words in all caps by a list of all identifiers active at that location. Change it to have the following form:

```
cout << "area, radius and PI are active here" << endl;
```

*Exercise 3:* For each comment in bold, place the proper code to do what it says.

NOTE:  area = $\pi\,r^2$

circumference = $2\pi r$

*Exercise 4:* Before compiling and running the program, write out what you expect the output to be.

What value for `radius` will be passed by `main` (first inner block) to the `findArea` function?

What value for `radius` will be passed by `main` function (second inner block) to the `findCircumference` function?

*Exercise 5:* Compile and run your program. Your instructor may ask to see the program run or obtain a hard copy.

### LAB 6.6   Parameters and Local Variables

Retrieve program `money.cpp` from the Lab 6.2 folder. The code is as follows:

```cpp
#include <iostream>
#include <iomanip>
using namespace std;

// PLACE YOUR NAME HERE

void normalizeMoney(float& dollars, int cents = 150);
// This function takes cents as an integer and converts it to dollars
// and cents.  The default value for cents is 150 which is converted
// to 1.50 and stored in dollars

int main()

{
  int cents;
  float dollars;


  cout << setprecision(2) << fixed << showpoint;

  cents = 95;
  cout << "\n We will now add 95 cents to our dollar total\n";

  //  Fill in the code to call normalizeMoney to add 95 cents

  cout << "Converting cents to dollars resulted in " << dollars << " dollars\n";

  cout << "\n We will now add 193 cents to our dollar total\n";

  // Fill in the code to call normalizeMoney to add 193 cents

  cout << "Converting cents to dollars resulted in " << dollars << " dollars\n";

  cout << "\n We will now add the default value to our dollar total\n";

  // Fill in the code to call normalizeMoney to add the default value of cents

  cout << "Converting cents to dollars resulted in " << dollars << " dollars\n";
```

```
      return 0;
}


//
*********************************************************************************
//                              normalizeMoney
//
//    task:      This function is given a value in cents.  It will convert cents
//               to dollars and cents which is stored in a local variable called
//               total which is sent back to the calling function through the
//               parameter dollars.  It will keep a running total of all the money
//               processed in a local static variable called sum.
//
//    data in:   cents which is an integer
//    data out:  dollars  (which alters the corresponding actual parameter)
//
//
*********************************************************************************



void normalizeMoney(float& dollars, int cents)

{

        float total=0;


        // Fill in the definition of sum as a static local variable
        _____ sum = 0.0;


        // Fill in the code to convert cents to dollars

        total = total + dollars;
        sum = sum + dollars;


        cout << "We have added another $" << dollars <<"  to our total" << endl;
        cout << "Our total so far is  $" << sum << endl;


        cout << "The value of our local variable total is $" << total << endl;

}
```

*Exercise 1:* You will notice that the function has to be completed. This function
will take `cents` and convert it to `dollars`. It also keeps a running total of
all the money it has processed. Assuming that the function is complete,
write out what you expect the program will print.

*Exercise 2:* Complete the function. Fill in the blank space to define `sum` and
then write the code to convert `cents` to `dollars`. Example: 789 cents
would convert to 7.89. Compile and run the program to get the expected
results. Think about how `sum` should be defined.

## LESSON 6.2B

### LAB 6.7    Value Returning and Overloading Functions

Retrieve program convertmoney.cpp from the Lab 6.2 folder. The code is as follows:

```cpp
#include <iostream>
#include <iomanip>
using namespace std;


// This program will input American money and convert it to foreign currency

// PLACE YOUR NAME HERE

// Prototypes of the functions
void  convertMulti(float dollars, float& euros, float& pesos);
void  convertMulti(float dollars, float& euros, float& pesos, float& yen);
float convertToYen(float dollars);
float convertToEuros(float dollars);
float convertToPesos(float dollars);


int main ()


{
    float dollars;
    float euros;
    float pesos;
    float yen;

    cout << fixed << showpoint << setprecision(2);

    cout << "Please input the amount of American Dollars you want converted "
        << endl;
    cout << "to euros and pesos" << endl;
    cin >> dollars;

    // Fill in the code to call convertMulti with parameters dollars, euros, and pesos
    // Fill in the code to output the value of those dollars converted to both euros
    // and pesos


    cout << "Please input the amount of American Dollars you want converted\n";
    cout << "to euros, pesos and yen" << endl;
    cin >> dollars;

    // Fill in the code to call convertMulti with parameters dollars, euros, pesos and yen
    // Fill in the code to output the value of those dollars converted to euros,
    // pesos and yen
```

```
    cout << "Please input the amount of American Dollars you want converted\n";
    cout << "to yen" <<endl;
    cin >> dollars;

    // Fill in the code to call convertToYen
    // Fill in the code to output the value of those dollars converted to yen

    cout << "Please input the amount of American Dollars you want converted\n";
    cout << " to euros" << endl;
    cin  >> dollars;

    // Fill in the code to call convert ToEuros
    // Fill in the code to output the value of those dollars converted to euros

    cout << "Please input the amount of American Dollars you want converted\n";
    cout << " to pesos " << endl;
    cin >> dollars;

    // Fill in the code to call convertToPesos
    // Fill in the code to output the value of those dollars converted to pesos

    return 0;
}



// All of the functions are stubs that just serve to test the functions
// Replace with code that will cause the functions to execute properly




//     **********************************************************************
//                       convertMulti
//
//    task:        This function takes a dollar value and converts it to euros
//                 and pesos
//    data in:   dollars
//    data out: euros and pesos
//
//     **********************************************************************

void  convertMulti(float dollars, float& euros, float& pesos)

{
      cout << "The function convertMulti with dollars, euros and pesos "
          << endl <<" was called with " << dollars <<" dollars" << endl << endl;


}
```

*continues*

```
//    ************************************************************************
//                         convertMulti
//
//    task:      This function takes a dollar value and converts it to euros
//               pesos and yen
//    data in:   dollars
//    data out:  euros pesos yen
//
//    ************************************************************************

void  convertMulti(float dollars, float& euros, float& pesos, float& yen)

{
        cout << "The function convertMulti with dollars, euros, pesos and yen"
            << endl << " was called with " << dollars << " dollars" << endl << endl;



}


//    ************************************************************************
//                         convertToYen
//
//    task:          This function takes a dollar value and converts it to yen
//    data in:       dollars
//    data returned: yen
//
//    ************************************************************************

float convertToYen(float dollars)

{

        cout << "The function convertToYen was called with " << dollars <<" dollars"
            << endl << endl;

        return 0;
}


//    ************************************************************************
//                         convertToEuros
//
//    task:          This function takes a dollar value and converts it to euros
//    data in:       dollars
//    data returned: euros
//
//    ************************************************************************
```

```
float convertToEuros(float dollars)
{
        cout << "The function convertToEuros was called with " << dollars
             << " dollars" << endl << endl;


        return 0;
}


//    ***********************************************************************
//                      convertToPesos
//
//    task:           This function takes a dollar value and converts it to pesos
//    data in:        dollars
//    data returned:  pesos
//
//    ***********************************************************************
float convertToPesos(float dollars)

{
        cout << "The function convertToPesos was called with " << dollars
             << " dollars" << endl;


        return 0;
}
```

*Exercise 1:* Run this program and observe the results. You can input anything that you like for the dollars to be converted. Notice that it has stubs as well as overloaded functions. Study the stubs carefully. Notice that in this case the value returning functions always return 0.

*Exercise 2:* Complete the program by turning all the stubs into workable functions. Be sure to call true functions differently than procedures. Make sure that functions return the converted dollars into the proper currency. Although the exchange rates vary from day to day, use the following conversion chart for the program. These values should be defined as constants in the global section so that any change in the exchange rate can be made there and nowhere else in the program.

One Dollar =   1.06 euros
               9.73 pesos
               124.35 yen

*Sample Run:*

**Please input the amount of American Dollars you want converted to euros and pesos**
**9.35**

**$9.35 is converted to 9.91 euros and 90.98 pesos**

**Please input the amount of American Dollars you want converted to euros and pesos and yen**
**10.67**

**$10.67 is converted to 11.31 euros, 103.82 pesos, and 1326.81 yen**

**Please input the amount of American Dollars you want converted to yen**
12.78
**$12.78 is converted to 1589.19 yen**

**Please input the amount of American Dollars you want converted to euros**
2.45
**$2.45 is converted to 2.60 euros**

**Please input the amount of American Dollars you want converted to pesos**
8.75
**$8.75 is converted to 85.14 pesos**

## LAB 6.8   Student Generated Code Assignments

*Option 1:* Write a program that will convert miles to kilometers and kilometers to miles. The user will indicate both a number (representing a distance) and a choice of whether that number is in miles to be converted to kilometers or kilometers to be converted to miles. Each conversion is done with a value returning function. You may use the following conversions.

> 1 kilometer = .621 miles
> 1 mile = 1.61 kilometers

*Sample Run:*

**Please input**
**1 Convert miles to kilometers**
**2 Convert kilometers to miles**
**3 Quit**

1
**Please input the miles to be converted**
120
**120 miles = 193.2 kilometers**

**Please input**
**1 Convert miles to kilometers**
**2 Convert kilometers to miles**
**3 Quit**
2
**Please input the kilometers to be converted**
235
**235 kilometers = 145.935 miles**

**Please input**
**1 Convert miles to kilometers**
**2 Convert kilometers to miles**
**3 Quit**
3

*Option 2:* Write a program that will input the number of wins and losses that a baseball team acquired during a complete season. The wins should be input in a parameter-less value returning function that returns the wins to the `main` function. A similar function should do the same thing for the losses. A third value returning function calculates the percentage of wins. It receives the wins and losses as parameters and returns the percentage (float) to the `main` program which then prints the result. The percentage should be printed as a percent to two decimal places.

*Sample Run:*

**Please input the number of wins**
80
**Please input the number of losses**
40
**The percentage of wins is 66.67%**

*Option 3:* Write a program that outputs a dentist bill. For members of a dental plan, the bill consists of the service charge (for the particular procedure performed) and test fees, input to the program by the user. To non-members the charges consist of the above services plus medicine (also input by the user). The program first asks if the patient is a member of the dental plan. The program uses two overloaded functions to calculate the total bill. Both are value returning functions that return the total charge.

*Sample Run 1:*

**Please input a one if you are a member of the dental plan**
**Input any other number if you are not**
1
**Please input the service charge**
7.89
**Please input the test charges**
89.56
**The total bill is $97.45**

*Sample Run 2:*

**Please input a one if you are a member of the dental plan**
**Input any other number if you are not**
2
**Please input the service charge**
75.84
**Please input the test charges**
49.78
**Please input the medicine charges**
40.22
**The total bill is $165.84**

# 7

# Arrays

**PURPOSE**

1. To introduce and allow students to work with arrays
2. To introduce the `typedef` statement
3. To work with and manipulate multidimensional arrays

**PROCEDURE**

1. Students should read the Pre-lab Reading Assignment before coming to lab.
2. Students should complete the Pre-lab Writing Assignment before coming to lab.
3. In the lab, students should complete labs assigned to them by the instructor.

| Contents | Pre-requisites | Approximate completion time | Page number | Check when done |
|---|---|---|---|---|
| Pre-lab Reading Assignment | | 20 min. | 114 | |
| Pre-lab Writing Assignment | Pre-lab reading | 10 min. | 122 | |
| **LESSON 7A** | | | | |
| Lab 7.1 Working with One-Dimensional Arrays | Basic understanding of one-dimensional arrays | 30 min. | 123 | |
| Lab 7.2 Strings as Arrays of Characters | Basic understanding of arrays of characters | 20 min. | 126 | |
| **LESSON 7B** | | | | |
| Lab 7.3 Working with Two-Dimensional Arrays | Understanding of multi-dimensional arrays | 30 min. | 129 | |
| Lab 7.4 Student Generated Code Assignments | Basic understanding of arrays | 30 min. | 134 | |

# PRE-LAB READING ASSIGNMENT

## One-Dimensional Arrays

So far we have talked about a variable as a single location in the computer's memory. It is possible to have a collection of memory locations, all of which have the same data type, grouped together under one name. Such a collection is called an **array**. Like every variable, an array must be defined so that the computer can "reserve" the appropriate amount of memory. This amount is based upon the type of data to be stored and the number of locations, i.e., size of the array, each of which is given in the definition.

*Example:* Given a list of ages (from a file or input from the keyboard), find and display the number of people for each age.

The programmer does not know the ages to be read but needs a space for the total number of occurrences of each "legitimate age." Assuming that ages 1, 2, . . . , 100 are possible, the following array definition can be used.

```
const int TOTALYEARS = 100;

int main()
{
    int ageFrequency[TOTALYEARS];     //reserves memory for 100 ints
    :
    return 0;

}
```

Following the rules of variable definition, the data type (integer in this case) is given first, followed by the name of the array (ageFrequency), and then the total number of memory locations enclosed in brackets. The number of memory locations must be an integer expression greater than zero and can be given either as a named constant (as shown in the above example) or as a literal constant (an actual number such as 100).

Each element of an array, consisting of a particular memory location within the group, is accessed by giving the name of the array and a position with the array (subscript). In C++ the subscript, sometimes referred to as index, is enclosed in square brackets. The numbering of the subscripts always begins at 0 and ends with one less than the total number of locations. Thus the elements in the ageFrequency array defined above are referenced as ageFrequency[0] through ageFrequency[99].

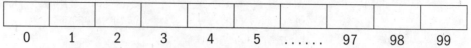

0    1    2    3    4    5   . . . . . .   97    98    99

If in our example we want ages from 1 to 100, the number of occurrences of age 4 will be placed in subscript 3 since it is the "fourth" location in the array. This odd way of numbering is often confusing to new programmers; however, it quickly becomes routine.[1]

---

[1] Some students actually add one more location and then ignore location 0, letting 1 be the first location. In the above example such a process would use the following definition: int agefrequency[101]; and use only the subscripts 1 through 100. Our examples will use location 0. Your instructor will tell you which method to use.

## Array Initialization

In our example, ageFrequency[0] keeps a count of how many 1s we read in, ageFrequency[1] keeps count of how many 2s we read in, etc. Thus, keeping track of how many people of a particular age exist in the data read in requires reading each age and then adding one to the location holding the count for that age. Of course it is important that all the counters start at 0. The following shows the initialization of all the elements of our sample array to 0.

```
for (int pos = 0;  pos < TOTALYEARS;  pos++)
        // pos acts as the array subscript
{
    ageFrequency[pos] = 0;
}
```

A simple for loop will process the entire array, adding one to the subscript each time through the loop. Notice that the subscript (pos) starts with 0. Why is the condition pos < TOTALYEARS used instead of pos <= TOTALYEARS? Remember that the last subscript is one less than the total number of elements in the array. Hence the subscripts of this array go from 0 to 99.

## Array Processing

Arrays are generally processed inside loops so that the input/output processing of each element of the array can be performed with minimal statements. Our age frequency program first needs to read in the ages from a file or from the keyboard. For each age read in, the "appropriate" element of the array (the one corresponding to that age) needs to be incremented by one. The following examples show how this can be accomplished:

**from a file using** infile **as a logical name**

```
infile >> currentAge;
while (infile)

{
  ageFrequency[currentAge-1] =
  ageFrequency[currentAge-1] + 1;
  infile >> currentAge;



}
```

**from a keyboard with –99 as sentinel data**

```
cout << "Please input an age from one"
        << "to 100. input -99 to stop"
        << endl;
cin >> currentAge;

while (currentAge != -99)
{
  ageFrequency[currentAge-1] =
  ageFrequency[currentAge-1] + 1;
  cout << "Please input an age from "
          << "one to 100. input -99 to stop"
          << endl;
cin >> currentAge;

}
```

The while(infile) statement means that while there is more data in the file infile, the loop will continue to process.

To read from a file or from the keyboard we **prime the read**,[2] which means the first value is read in before the test condition is checked to see if the loop

---

[2] Priming the read for a while loop means having an input just before the loop condition (just before the while) and having another one as the last statement in the loop.

should be executed. When we read an age, we increment the location in the array that keeps track of the amount of people in the corresponding age group. Since C++ array indices always start with 0, that location will be at the subscript one value less than the age we read in.

| 4 | 0 | 14 | 5 | 0 | 6 |  | 1 | 0 |
|---|---|----|---|---|---|---|---|---|
| 0 | 1 | 2 | 3 | 4 | 5 | ...... | 98 | 99 |
| 1 year | 2 years | 3 years | 4 years | 5 years | 6 years | | 99 years | 100 years |

Each element of the array contains the number of people of a given age. The data shown here is from a random sample run. In writing the information stored in the array, we want to make sure that only those array elements that have values greater than 0 are output. The following code will do this.

```
for (int ageCounter = 0; ageCounter < TOTALYEARS; ageCounter++)

    if (ageFrequency[ageCounter] > 0)
        cout << "The number of people " << ageCounter + 1 <<" years old is "
            << ageFrequency[ageCounter] << endl;
```

The `for` loop goes from 0 to one less than TOTALYEARS (0 to 99). This will test every element of the array. If a given element has a value greater than 0, it will be output. What does outputting `ageCounter + 1` do? It gives the age we are dealing with at any given time, while the value of `ageFrequency[ageCounter]` gives the number of people in that age group.

The complete age frequency program will be given as one of the lab assignments in Lab 7.4.

## Arrays as Arguments

Arrays can be passed as arguments (parameters) to functions. Although variables can be passed by value or reference, arrays are always **passed by pointer**, which is similar to pass by reference, since it is not efficient to make a "copy" of all elements of the array. Pass by pointer is discussed further in Lesson Set 9. This means that arrays, like pass by reference parameters, can be altered by the calling function. However, they NEVER have the & symbol between the data type and name, as pass by reference parameters do. Sample Program 7.1 illustrates how arrays are passed as arguments to functions.

*Sample Program 7.1:*

```
//  The grade average program
//  This program illustrates how one-dimensional arrays are used and how
//  they are passed as arguments to functions.  It contains two functions.
//  The first function is called to allow the user to input a set of grades and
//  store them in an array.  The second function is called to find the average
//  grade.

#include <iostream>
using namespace std;
```

```
const int TOTALGRADES = 50;        // TOTALGRADES is the maximum size of the array


// function prototypes

void getData(int array[], int& sizeOfArray);
  // the procedure that will read values into the array

float findAverage(const int array[], int sizeOfArray);
 // the procedure that will find the average of values
 // stored in an array.  The word const in front of the
 // data type of the array prevents the function from
 // altering the array

int main()
{
      int grades[TOTALGRADES];        // defines an array that holds up to 50 ints
      int numberOfGrades = 0;         // the number of grades read in
      float average;                  // the average of all grades read in

      getData(grades, numberOfGrades); // getData is called to read the grades into
                                       // the array and store how many grades there
                                       // are in numberOfGrades


      average = findAverage(grades, numberOfGrades);

      cout << endl << "The average of the  " << numberOfGrades
           << " grades read in is " << average << "." << endl << endl;


      return 0;

}




//*****************************************************************
//                    getData
//
// task:     This function inputs and stores data in the grades array.
// data in:  none (the parameters contain no information needed by the
//               getData function)
// data out: an array containing grades and the number of grades
//*****************************************************************

void getData(int array[], int& sizeOfArray)
{
      int pos = 0;               // array index which starts at 0
      int grade;                 // holds each individual grade read in

      cout << "Please input a grade or type -99 to stop: " << endl;
      cin >> grade;
```

*continues*

```
          while (grade != -99)
          {
                  array[pos] = grade;      // store grade read in to next array location
                  pos ++;                  // increment array index

                  cout << "Please input a grade or type -99 to stop: " << endl;
                  cin >> grade;
          }

          sizeOfArray = pos;             // upon exiting the loop, pos holds the
                                         // number of grades read in, which is sent
                                         // back to the calling function
    }


//****************************************************************************
//                              findAverage
//
// task:        This function finds and returns the average of the values
//
// data in:     the array containing grades and the array size
// data returned: the average of the grades contained in that array
//****************************************************************************

float findAverage (const int array[], int sizeOfArray)
{
        int sum = 0;                     // holds the sum of all grades in the array

        for (int pos = 0;  pos < sizeOfArray;  pos++)
        {
            sum = sum + array[pos];
          // add grade in array position pos to sum
        }

      return float(sum)/sizeOfArray;
}
```

Notice that a set of empty brackets [ ] follows the parameter of an array which indicates that the data type of this parameter is in fact an array. Notice also that no brackets appear in the call to the functions that receive the array.

Since arrays in C++ are passed by pointer, which is similar to pass by reference, it allows the original array to be altered, even though no & is used to designate this. The getData function is thus able to store new values into the array. There may be times when we do not want the function to alter the values of the array. Inserting the word **const** before the data type on the formal parameter list prevents the function from altering the array even though it is passed by pointer. This is why in the preceding sample program the findAverage function and header had the word const in front of the data type of the array.

```
        float findAverage (const int array[], int sizeOfArray);  // prototype
        float findAverage (const int array[], int sizeOfArray)   // function header
```

The variable `numberOfGrades` contains the number of elements in the array to be processed. In most cases not every element of the array is used, which means the size of the array given in its definition and the number of actual elements used are rarely the same. For that reason we often pass the actual number of elements used in the array as a parameter to a procedure that uses the array. The variable `numberOfGrades` is explicitly passed by reference (by using &) to the `getData` function where its corresponding formal parameter is called `sizeOfArray`.

Prototypes can be written without named parameters. Function headers must include named parameters.

```
float findAverage (const int [], int);  // prototype without named parameters
```

The use of brackets in function prototypes and headings can be avoided by declaring a programmer defined data type. This is done in the global section with a **typedef** statement.

*Example:* `typedef int GradeType[50];`

This declares a data type, called `GradeType`, that is an array containing 50 integer memory locations. Since `GradeType` is a data type, it can be used in defining variables. The following defines `grades` as an integer array with 50 elements.

```
GradeType grades;
```

It has become a standard practice (although not a requirement) to use an uppercase letter to begin the name of a data type. It is also helpful to include the word "type" in the name to indicate that it is a data type and not a variable.

Sample Program 7.2 shows the revised code (in bold) of Sample Program 7.1 using `typedef`.

*Sample Program 7.2:*

```
//  Grade average program
//  This program illustrates how one-dimensional arrays are used and how
//  they are passed as arguments to functions.  It contains two functions.
//  The first function is called to input a set of grades and store them
//  in an array.  The second function is called to find the average grade.

#include <iostream>
using namespace std;


const int TOTALGRADES = 50;          // maximum size of the array

// function prototypes

typedef int GradeType[TOTALGRADES];  // declaration of an integer array data type
                                     // called GradeType
```

*continues*

```
void getData(GradeType array, int& sizeOfArray);
 // the procedure that will read values into the array

float findAverage(const GradeType array, int sizeOfArray);
 // the procedure that will find the average of values
 // stored in an array.  The word const in front of the
 // data type of the array prevents the function from
 // altering the array

int main()
{
        GradeType grades;               // defines an array that holds up to 50 ints
        int numberOfGrades = 0;         // the number of grades read in
        float average;                  // the average of all grades read in

        getData(grades, numberOfGrades);// getData is called to read the grades into
                                        // the array and store how many grades there
                                        // are in numberOfGrades


        average = findAverage(grades, numberOfGrades);

        cout << endl << "The average of the  " << numberOfGrade
            << " grades read in is " << average << "." << endl << endl;

        return 0;
}


//**********************************************************************
//                      getData
//
// task:    This function inputs and stores data in the grades array.
// data in:  none
// data out: an array containing grades and the number of grades
//**********************************************************************

void getData(GradeType array, int& sizeOfArray)
{
        int pos = 0;                    // array index which starts at 0
        int grade;                      // holds each individual grade read in

        cout << "Please input a grade or type -99 to stop: " << endl;
        cin >> grade;

        while (grade != -99)
        {
                array[pos] = grade;     // store grade read in to next array location
                pos ++;                 // increment array index

                cout << "Please input a grade or type -99 to stop: " << endl;
                cin >> grade;
        }
```

```
        sizeOfArray = pos;        // upon exiting the loop, pos holds the
                                  // number of grades read in, which is sent
                                  // back to the calling function
}


//*************************************************************************
//                            findAverage
//
// task:          This function finds and returns the average of the values
//
// data in:       the array containing grades and the array size
// data returned: the average of the grades contained in that array
//*************************************************************************

float findAverage (const GradeType array, int sizeOfArray)
{
        int sum = 0;              // holds the sum of all grades in the array

        for (int pos = 0;  pos < sizeOfArray;  pos++)
        {
            sum = sum + array[pos];
            // add grade in array position pos to sum
        }

        return float(sum)/sizeOfArray;
}
```

This method of using `typedef` to eliminate brackets in function prototypes and headings is especially useful for multi-dimensional arrays such as those introduced in the next section.

## Two-Dimensional Arrays

Data is often contained in a table of rows and columns that can be implemented with a two-dimensional array. Suppose we want to read data representing profits (in thousands) for a particular year and quarter.

| Quarter 1 | Quarter 2 | Quarter 3 | Quarter 4 |
|-----------|-----------|-----------|-----------|
| 72        | 80        | 10        | 100       |
| 82        | 90        | 43        | 42        |
| 10        | 87        | 48        | 53        |

This can be done using a **two-dimensional array**.

*Example:*

```
const NO_OF_ROWS = 3;
const NO_OF_COLS = 4;

typedef float ProfitType[NO_OF_ROWS][NO_OF_COLS]; //declares a new data type
                                                  //which is a 2 dimensional
                                                  //array of floats
```

*continues*

```
int main()
{
    ProfitType profit;          // defines profit as a 2 dimensional array

    for (int row_pos = 0; row_pos < NO_OF_ROWS; row_pos++)
      for (int col_pos = 0; col_pos < NO_OF_COLS;  col_pos++)
      {
          cout << "Please input a profit" << endl;
          cin  >> profit[row_pos][col_pos];
      }
    return 0;
}
```

A two dimensional array normally uses two loops (one nested inside the other) to read, process, or output data.

How many times will the code above ask for a profit? It processes the inner loop NO_OF_ROWS * NO_OF_COLS times, which is 12 times in this case.

## Multi-Dimensional Arrays

C++ arrays can have any number of dimensions (although more than three is rarely used). To input, process or output every item in an *n*-dimensional array, you need *n* nested loops.

## Arrays of Strings

Any variable defined as **char** holds only one character. To hold more than one character in a single variable, that variable needs to be an array of characters. A string (a group of characters that usually form meaningful names or words) is really just an array of characters. A complete lesson on characters and strings is given in Lesson Set 10.

# PRE-LAB WRITING ASSIGNMENT

## Fill-in-the-Blank Questions

1. The first subscript of every array in C++ is _____ and the last is _____ less than the total number of locations in the array.

2. The amount of memory allocated to an array is based on the _____ and the _____ of locations or size of the array.

3. Array initialization and processing is usually done inside a _____.

4. The _____ statement can be used to declare an array type and is often used for multidimensional array declarations so that when passing arrays as parameters, brackets do not have to be used.

5. Multi-dimensional arrays are usually processed within _____ loops.

6. Arrays used as arguments are always passed by _____.

7. In passing an array as a parameter to a function that processes it, it is often necessary to pass a parameter that holds the _____ of _____ used in the array.

8. A string is an array of _____.

9. Upon exiting a loop that reads values into an array, the variable used as a(n) _____ to the array will contain the size of that array.

10. An *n*-dimensional array will be processed within _____ nested loops when accessing all members of the array.

## LESSON 7A

### LAB 7.1  Working with One-Dimensional Arrays

Retrieve program `testscore.cpp` from the Lab 7 folder. The code is as follows:

```cpp
// This program will read in a group of test scores (positive integers from 1 to 100)
// from the keyboard and then calculate and output the average score
// as well as the highest and lowest score. There will be a maximum of 100 scores.

// PLACE YOUR NAME HERE

#include <iostream>
using namespace std;

typedef int GradeType[100];         // declares a new data type:
                                    // an integer array of 100 elements



float findAverage (const GradeType, int);  // finds average of all grades
int   findHighest (const GradeType, int);  // finds highest of all grades
int   findLowest  (const GradeType, int);  // finds lowest of all grades


int main()

{
        GradeType grades;                // the array holding the grades.
        int numberOfGrades;              // the number of grades read.
        int pos;                         // index to the array.

        float avgOfGrades;               // contains the average of the grades.
        int highestGrade;                // contains the highest grade.
        int lowestGrade;                 // contains the lowest grade.

        // Read in the values into the array

        pos = 0;
        cout << "Please input a grade from 1 to 100, (or -99 to stop)" << endl;
```

*continues*

```
        cin  >> grades[pos];

        while (grades[pos] != -99)
        {

            // Fill in the code to read the grades

        }

        numberOfGrades = _____;   // Fill blank with appropriate identifier

        // call to the function to find average

        avgOfGrades = findAverage(grades, numberOfGrades);

        cout << endl << "The average of all the grades is " << avgOfGrades << endl;

        // Fill in the call to the function that calculates highest grade

        cout << endl << "The highest grade is " << highestGrade << endl;

        // Fill in the call to the function that calculates lowest grade
        // Fill in code to write the lowest to the screen

        return 0;
}


//****************************************************************************
//                              findAverage
//
// task:        This function receives an array of integers and its size.
//              It finds and returns the average of the numbers in the array
// data in:     array of floating point numbers
// data returned: average of the numbers in the array
//
//****************************************************************************

float findAverage (const GradeType  array, int size)

{

    float sum = 0;    // holds the sum of all the numbers

    for (int pos = 0; pos < size; pos++)

      sum = sum + array[pos];

    return (sum / size);   //returns the average

}
```

```
//**********************************************************************
//                        findHighest
//
// task:          This function receives an array of integers and its size.
//                It finds and returns the highest value of the numbers in the array
// data in:       array of floating point numbers
// data returned: highest value of the numbers in the array
//
//**********************************************************************

int   findHighest (const GradeType array, int size)

{

        / Fill in the code for this function

}




//**********************************************************************
//                        findLowest
//
// task:          This function receives an array of integers and its size.
//                It finds and returns the lowest value of the numbers in the array
// data in:       array of floating point numbers
// data returned: lowest value of the numbers in the array
//
//**********************************************************************

int   findLowest  (const GradeType array, int size)

{
        // Fill in the code for this function

}
```

*Exercise 1:* Complete this program as directed.

*Exercise 2:* Run the program with the following data:  90  45  73  62  -99
and record the output here:

_____

_____

_____

*Exercise 3:* Modify your program from Exercise 1 so that it reads the information from the gradfile.txt file, reading until the end of file is encountered. You will need to first retrieve this file from the Lab 7 folder and place it in the same folder as your C++ source code. Run the program.

## Lab 7.2    Strings as Arrays of Characters

Retrieve program `student.cpp` from the Lab 7 folder.

```
// This program will input an undetermined number of student names
// and a number of grades for each student. The number of grades is
// given by the user. The grades are stored in an array.
// Two functions are called for each student.
// One function will give the numeric average of their grades.
// The other function will give a letter grade to that average.
// Grades are assigned on a 10 point spread.
// 90-100 A    80-89 B  70-79 C    60-69 D    Below 60 F


// PLACE YOUR NAME HERE


#include <iostream>
#include <iomanip>
using namespace std;

const  int MAXGRADE = 25;              // maximum number of grades per student
const  int MAXCHAR = 30;               // maximum characters used in a name

typedef char StringType30[MAXCHAR + 1];// character array data type for names
                                       // having 30 characters or less.
typedef  float GradeType[MAXGRADE];    // one dimensional integer array data type

float findGradeAvg(GradeType, int);    // finds grade average by taking array of
                                       // grades and number of grades as parameters


char  findLetterGrade(float);          // finds letter grade from average given
                                       // to it as a parameter

int main()

{
     StringType30 firstname, lastname;// two arrays of characters defined
     int numOfGrades;                 // holds the number of grades
     GradeType  grades;               // grades defined as a one dimensional array
     float average;                   // holds the average of a student's grade
     char moreInput;                  // determines if there is more input

     cout << setprecision(2) << fixed << showpoint;

   // Input the number of grades for each student

     cout << "Please input the number of grades each student will receive." << endl
          << "This must be a number between 1 and " << MAXGRADE << " inclusive"
          << endl;

     cin >> numOfGrades;
```

```cpp
while (numOfGrades > MAXGRADE || numOfGrades < 1)
{
        cout << "Please input the number of grades for each student." << endl
            << "This must be a number between 1 and " << MAXGRADE
            << " inclusive\n";

        cin >> numOfGrades;

}

// Input names and grades for each student

  cout << "Please input a y if you want to input more students"
        << " any other character will stop the input" << endl;
  cin >> moreInput;

  while (moreInput == 'y' || moreInput == 'Y')

  {
        cout << "Please input the first name of the student" << endl;
        cin >> firstname;
        cout << endl << "Please input the last name of the student" << endl;
        cin >> lastname;

        for (int count = 0; count < numOfGrades; count++)

        {

                cout << endl << "Please input a grade" << endl;

                // Fill in the input statement to place grade in the array

        }

         cout << firstname << " " << lastname << " has an average of ";

           // Fill in code to get and print average of student to screen
           // Fill in call to get and print letter grade of student to screen

        cout << endl << endl << endl;
        cout << "Please input a y if you want to input more students"
            << " any other character will stop the input" << endl;
        cin >> moreInput;

  }

  return 0;
}
```

*continues*

```
//****************************************************************
//                          findGradeAvg
//
//   task:            This function finds the average of the
//                    numbers stored in an array.
//
//   data in:         an array of integer numbers
//   data returned:   the average of all numbers in the array
//
//****************************************************************

float findGradeAvg(GradeType array, int numGrades)


{
    // Fill in the code for this function
}


//****************************************************************
//                          findLetterGrade
//
//   task:            This function finds the letter grade for the number
//                    passed to it by the calling function
//
//   data in:         a floating point number
//   data returned:   the grade (based on a 10 point spread) based on the number
//                    passed to the function
//
//****************************************************************

char  findLetterGrade(float numGrade)


{
    // Fill in the code for this function


}
```

*Exercise 1:* Complete the program by filling in the code. (Areas in bold)

Run the program with 3 grades per student using the sample data below.

Mary Brown    100 90 90
George Smith   90 30 50
Dale Barnes    80 78 82
Sally Dolittle  70 65 80
Conrad Bailer  60 58 71

You should get the following results:

**Mary Brown has an average of 93.33 which gives the letter grade of A**
**George Smith has an average of 56.67 which gives the letter grade of F**
**Dale Barnes has an average of 80.00 which gives the letter grade of B**
**Sally Dolittle has an average of 71.67 which gives the letter grade of C**
**Conrad Bailer has an average of 63.00 which gives the letter grade of D**

# LESSON 7B

### LAB 7.3    Working with Two-Dimensional Arrays

Look at the following table containing prices of certain items:

| 12.78 | 23.78 | 45.67 | 12.67 |
|-------|-------|-------|-------|
| 7.83  | 4.89  | 5.99  | 56.84 |
| 13.67 | 34.84 | 16.71 | 50.89 |

These numbers can be read into a two-dimensional array.

Retrieve `price.cpp` from the Lab 7 folder. The code is as follows:

```cpp
// This program will read in prices and store them into a two-dimensional array.
// It will print those prices in a table form.

// PLACE YOUR NAME HERE

#include <iostream>
#include <iomanip>
using namespace std;


const  MAXROWS = 10;
const  MAXCOLS = 10;

typedef float PriceType[MAXROWS][MAXCOLS];      // creates a new data type
                                                // of a 2D array of floats

void    getPrices(PriceType, int&, int&);       // gets the prices into the array
void    printPrices(PriceType, int, int);       // prints data as a table


int main()

{
    int rowsUsed;                        // holds the number of rows used
    int colsUsed;                        // holds the number of columns used
    PriceType priceTable;                // a 2D array holding the prices

    getPrices(priceTable, rowsUsed, colsUsed);   // calls getPrices to fill the array
    printPrices(priceTable, rowsUsed, colsUsed);// calls printPrices to display array

    return 0;
}
```

*continues*

```
//****************************************************************************
//                      getPrices
//
// task:      This procedure asks the user to input the number of rows and
//            columns. It then asks the user to input (rows * columns) number of
//            prices.  The data is placed in the array.
// data in:  none
// data out: an array filled with numbers and the number of rows
//            and columns used.
//
//****************************************************************************

void   getPrices(PriceType table, int& numOfRows, int& numOfCols)
{

     cout << "Please input the number of rows from 1 to "<< MAXROWS << endl;
     cin >> numOfRows;

     cout << "Please input the number of columns from 1 to "<< MAXCOLS << endl;
     cin >> numOfCols;


     for (int row = 0;  row < numOfRows;  row++)
     {
        for (int col = 0; col < numOfCols;  col++)

        // Fill in the code to read and store the next value in the array
     }
}


//****************************************************************************
//                      printPrices
//
// task:      This procedure prints the table of prices
// data in:  an array of floating point numbers and the number of rows
//            and columns used.
// data out: none
//
//****************************************************************************

void   printPrices(PriceType table, int numOfRows, int numOfCols)
{

     cout << fixed << showpoint << setprecision(2);

     for (int row = 0;  row < numOfRows; row++)
     {
          for (int col = 0;  col < numOfCols; col++)

          // Fill in the code to print the table

     }
}
```

*Exercise 1:* Fill in the code to complete both functions `getPrices` and
`printPrices`, then run the program with the following data:

```
Please input the number of rows from 1 to 10
2

Please input the number of columns from 1 to 10
3

Please input the price of an item with 2 decimal places
1.45

Please input the price of an item with 2 decimal places
2.56

Please input the price of an item with 2 decimal places
12.98

Please input the price of an item with 2 decimal places
37.86

Please input the price of an item with 2 decimal places
102.34

Please input the price of an item with 2 decimal places
67.89

        1.45    2.56      12.98
        37.86   102.34    67.89
```

*Exercise 2:* Why does `getPrices` have the parameters `numOfRows` and
`numOfCols` passed by reference whereas `printPrices` has those parameters
passed by value?

*Exercise 3:* The following code is a function that returns the highest price in
the array. After studying it very carefully, place the function in the above
program and have the program print out the highest value.

```
float   findHighestPrice(PriceType table, int numOfRows, int numOfCols)
// This function returns the highest price in the array
{

    float highestPrice;

    highestPrice = table[0][0];   // make first element the highest price

    for (int row = 0;   row < numOfRows;  row++)
        for (int col = 0;   col < numOfCols; col++)
            if ( highestPrice < table[row][col] )

                highestPrice = table[row][col];

    return highestPrice;
}
```

*continues*

NOTE: This is a value returning function. Be sure to include its prototype in the global section.

*Exercise 4:* Create another value returning function that finds the lowest price in the array and have the program print that value.

*Exercise 5:* After completing all the exercises above, run the program again with the values from Exercise 1 and record your results.

*Exercise 6:* (Optional) Look at the following table that contains quarterly sales transactions for three years of a small company. Each of the quarterly transactions are integers (number of sales) and the year is also an integer.

| YEAR | Quarter 1 | Quarter 2 | Quarter 3 | Quarter 4 |
|------|-----------|-----------|-----------|-----------|
| 2000 | 72 | 80 | 60 | 100 |
| 2001 | 82 | 90 | 43 | 98 |
| 2002 | 64 | 78 | 58 | 84 |

We could use a two-dimensional array consisting of 3 rows and 5 columns. Even though there are only four quarters we need 5 columns (the first column holds the year).

Retrieve `quartsal.cpp` from the Lab 7 folder. The code is as follows:

```
// This program will read in the quarterly sales transactions for a given number
// of years. It will print the year and transactions in a table format.
// It will calculate year and quarter total transactions.

// PLACE YOUR NAME HERE

#include <iostream>
#include <iomanip>
using namespace std;

const  MAXYEAR = 10;
const  MAXCOL = 5;

typedef int SalesType[MAXYEAR][MAXCOL];     // creates a new 2D integer data type

void    getSales(SalesType, int&);      // places sales figures into the array
void    printSales(SalesType, int);     // prints data as a table
void    printTableHeading();            // prints table heading


int main()

{
        int yearsUsed;                  // holds the number of years used

        SalesType sales;                // 2D array holding
                                        // the sales transactions


        getSales(sales, yearsUsed);     // calls getSales to put data in array
```

```
        printTableHeading();                 // calls procedure to print the heading
        printSales(sales, yearsUsed);        // calls printSales to display table

        return 0;
}




//**************************************************************************
//                         printTableHeading
//  task:     This procedure prints the table heading
//  data in:  none
//  data out: none
//
//**************************************************************************


void printTableHeading()

{

        cout << setw(30) << "YEARLY QUARTERLY SALES" << endl << endl << endl;

        cout << setw(10) << "YEAR" << setw(10) << "Quarter 1"
             << setw(10) << "Quarter 2" << setw(10) << "Quarter 3"
             << setw(10) << "Quarter 4" << endl;
}




//**************************************************************************
//                         getSales
//
//  task:     This procedure asks the user to input the number of years.
//            For each of those years it asks the user to input the year
//            (e.g. 2004), followed by the sales figures for each of the
//            4 quarters of that year.  That data is placed in a 2D array
//  data in:  a 2D array of integers
//  data out: the total number of years
//
//**************************************************************************


void   getSales(SalesType  table, int&  numOfYears)
{

        cout << "Please input the number of years (1-" << MAXYEAR << ')' << endl;
        cin >> numOfYears;


        // Fill in the code to read and store the next value
```

*continues*

```
}


//*************************************************************************
//                      printSales
//
// task:      This procedure prints out the information in the array
// data in:   an array containing sales information
// data out:  none
//
//*************************************************************************




void   printSales(SalesType table, int numOfYears)
{
       // Fill in the code to print the table
}
```

---

Fill in the code for both getSales and printSales.

This is similar to the price.cpp program in Exercise 1; however, the code will be different. This is a table that contains something other than sales in column one.

*Exercise 7:* Run the program so that the chart from Exercise 6 is printed.

## LAB 7.4   Student Generated Code Assignments

*Option 1:* Write the complete age population program given in the Pre-lab Reading Assignment.

Statement of the problem:

Given a list of ages (1 to 100) from the keyboard, the program will tally how many people are in each age group.

*Sample Run:*

**Please input an age from one to 100, put -99 to stop**
5
**Please input an age from one to 100, put -99 to stop**
10
**Please input an age from one to 100, put -99 to stop**
100
**Please input an age from one to 100, put -99 to stop**
20
**Please input an age from one to 100, put -99 to stop**
5
**Please input an age from one to 100, put -99 to stop**
8
**Please input an age from one to 100, put -99 to stop**
20

```
Please input an age from one to 100, put -99 to stop
5
Please input an age from one to 100, put -99 to stop
9
Please input an age from one to 100, put -99 to stop
17
Please input an age from one to 100, put -99 to stop
-99


The number of people 5 years old is 3
The number of people 8 years old is 1
The number of people 9 years old is 1
The number of people 10 years old is 1
The number of people 17 years old is 1
The number of people 20 years old is 2
The number of people 100 years old is 1
```

*Option 2:* Write a program that will input temperatures for consecutive days. The program will store these values into an array and call a function that will return the average of the temperatures. It will also call a function that will return the highest temperature and a function that will return the lowest temperature. The user will input the number of temperatures to be read. There will be no more than 50 temperatures. Use typedef to declare the array type. The average should be displayed to two decimal places.

*Sample Run:*

```
Please input the number of temperatures to be read
5
Input temperature 1:
68
Input temperature 2:
75
Input temperature 3:
36
Input temperature 4:
91
Input temperature 5:
84


The average temperature is 70.80
The highest temperature is 91.00
The lowest temperature is 36.00
```

*Option 3:* Write a program that will input letter grades (A, B, C, D, F), the number of which is input by the user (a maximum of 50 grades). The grades will be read into an array. A function will be called five times (once for each letter grade) and will return the total number of grades in that category. The input to the function will include the array, number of elements in the array and the letter category (A, B, C, D or F). The program will print the number of grades that are A, B, etc.

*Sample Run:*

**Please input the number of grades to be read in. (1-50)**
**6**
**All grades must be upper case A B C D or F**
**Input a grade**
**A**
**Input a grade**
**C**
**Input a grade**
**A**
**Input a grade**
**B**
**Input a grade**
**B**
**Input a grade**
**D**

**Number of A=2**
**Number of B=2**
**Number of C=1**
**Number of D=1**
**Number of F=0**

# 8 Searching and Sorting Arrays

| | |
|---|---|
| **PURPOSE** | 1. To introduce the concept of a search routine |
| | 2. To introduce the linear and binary searches |
| | 3. To introduce the concept of a sorting algorithm |
| | 4. To introduce the bubble and selection sorts |
| **PROCEDURE** | 1. Students should read the Pre-lab Reading Assignment before coming to lab. |
| | 2. Students should complete the Pre-lab Writing Assignment before coming to lab. |
| | 3. In the lab, students should complete labs assigned to them by the instructor. |

| Contents | Pre-requisites | Approximate completion time | Page number | Check when done |
|---|---|---|---|---|
| Pre-lab Reading Assignment | | 20 min. | 138 | |
| Pre-lab Writing Assignment | Pre-lab reading | 10 min. | 148 | |
| **LESSON 8A** | | | | |
| Lab 8.1 Working with the Linear Search | Understanding of character arrays | 15 min. | 149 | |
| Lab 8.2 Working with the Binary Search | Understanding of integer arrays | 20 min. | 150 | |
| Lab 8.3 Working with Sorts | Understanding of arrays | 15 min. | 152 | |
| **LESSON 8B** | | | | |
| Lab 8.4 Student Generated Code Assignments | Understanding of arrays | 50 min. | 156 | |

# PRE-LAB READING ASSIGNMENT

## Search Algorithms

A search algorithm is a procedure for locating a specific datum from a collection of data.

For example, suppose you want to find the phone number for Wilson Electric in the phonebook. You open the phonebook to the business section under W and then look for all the entries that begin with the word Wilson. There are numerous such entries, so you look for the one(s) that end with Electric. This is an example of a **search algorithm**. Since each section in the phonebook is alphabetized, this is a particularly easy search. Of course, there are numerous types of "collections of data" that one could search. In this section we will focus on searching arrays. Two algorithms, the linear and binary searches, will be studied. We will see that each algorithm has its advantages and disadvantages.

## Linear Search

The easiest array search to understand is probably the **linear search**. This algorithm starts at the beginning of the array and then steps through the elements sequentially until either the desired value is found or the end of the array is reached. For example, suppose we want to find the first occurrence of the letter "o" in the word "Harpoon." We can visualize the corresponding character array as follows:

| 0 | 1 | 2 | 3 | 4 | 5 | 6 | 7 |
|---|---|---|---|---|---|---|---|
| H | a | r | p | o | o | n | \0 |

In C++ we can initialize the character array with the desired string:

```
char word[8] = "Harpoon";
```

So word[0]='H', word[3] = 'p', and word[7] = '\0 '. The '\0' marks the end of the string and is called the null character. It is discussed further in Lesson Set 10. If we perform a linear search looking for 'o', then we first check word[0] which is not equal to 'o'. So we then move to word[1] which is also not equal to 'o'. We continue until we get to word[4]='o'. At this point the subscript 4 is returned so we know the position in the array that contains the first occurrence of the letter 'o'. What would happen if we searched for 'z'? Certainly we would step through the array until we reached the end and not find any occurrence of 'z'. What should the search function return in this case? It is customary to return –1 since this is not a valid array subscript. Here is the complete program that performs the linear search:

*Sample Program 8.1:*

```
// This program performs a linear search on a character array

#include <iostream>
using namespace std;

int searchList(char[], int, char); // function prototype
const int SIZE = 8;
```

```cpp
int main()
{
    char word[SIZE] = "Harpoon";
    int found;
    char ch;

    cout << "Enter a letter to search for:" << endl;
    cin >> ch;

    found = searchList(word, SIZE, ch);
    if (found == -1)
        cout << "The letter " << ch
            << " was not found in the list" << endl;
    else
        cout << "The letter " << ch <<" is in the " << found + 1
            << " position of the list" << endl;

    return 0;

}


//**************************************************************
//                   searchList
//
// task:        This searches an array for a particular value
// data in:     List of values in an array, the number of
//              elements in the array, and the value searched for
//              in the array
// data returned: Position in the array of the value or -1 if value
//              not found
//
//**************************************************************

int searchList(char list[], int numElems, char value)
{
    for (int count = 0;count < numElems; count++)
    {
        if (list[count] == value)
                // each array entry is checked to see if it contains
                // the desired value.
        return count;
                // if the desired value is found, the array subscript
                // count is returned to indicate the location in the array
    }
    return -1;       // if the value is not found, -1 is returned
}
```

For example, suppose we wish to search the word "Harpoon" for the letter 'o'. The function SearchList does the linear search and returns the index 4 of the array where 'o' is found. However, the program outputs 5 for the position since we want to output the character's position within the string rather than its storage location in the word array. You have certainly noticed that there is a second occurrence of 'o' in the word "Harpoon." However, the linear search does not find it since it quits after finding the first occurrence.

One advantage of the linear search is its simplicity. It is easy to step sequentially through an array and check each element for a designated value. Another advantage is that the elements of the array do not need to be in any order to implement the algorithm. For example, to search the integer arrays

| First Array | 23 | 45 | 12 | 456 | 99 |
|---|---|---|---|---|---|

| Second Array | 12 | 29 | 45 | 23 | 456 |
|---|---|---|---|---|---|

for the integer 99, the linear search will work. It will return 4 for the first array and –1 for the second. The main disadvantage of the linear search is that it is time-consuming for large arrays. If the desired piece of data is not in the array, then the search has to check every element of the array before it returns –1. Even if the desired piece of data is in the array, there is a very good chance that a significant portion of the array will need to be checked to find it. So we need a more efficient search algorithm for large arrays.

## The Binary Search

A more efficient algorithm for searching an array is the **binary search** which eliminates half of the array every time it does a check. The drawback is that the data in the array must be ordered to use a binary search. If we are searching an array of integers, then the values stored in the array must be arranged in order from largest to smallest or smallest to largest.

*Examples:* Consider the following three integer arrays:

| 1) | 19 | 15 | 13 | 13 | 11 | 6 | -1 | -3 |
|---|---|---|---|---|---|---|---|---|

| 2) | 19 | 15 | 16 | 13 | 13 | 11 | -1 | -3 |
|---|---|---|---|---|---|---|---|---|

| 3) | -3 | 0 | 1 | 1 | 12 | 14 | 18 | 25 |
|---|---|---|---|---|---|---|---|---|

The arrays in 1) and 3) could be searched using a binary search. In 1) the values are arranged largest to smallest and in 3) the values are arranged smallest to largest. However, the array in 2) could not be searched using a binary search due to the first three elements of the array: the values of the elements decrease from 19 to 15 but then increase from 15 to 16.

Now that we know which types of arrays are allowed, let us next describe what the binary search actually does. For the sake of argument, let us assume the values of an integer array are arranged from smallest to largest and the integer we are searching for is stored in the variable wanted. We first pick an element in the middle of the array—let us call it middle. Think about how the number, whether it be even or odd, of elements in the array affects this choice. If `middle =` `wanted`, then we are done. Otherwise, `wanted` must be either greater than or less than `middle`. If `wanted < middle`, then since the array is in ascending order we know that `wanted` must be before `middle` in the array so we can ignore the second half of the array and search the first half. Likewise, if `wanted > middle`, we can ignore the first half of the array and search just the second half. In both cases we can immediately eliminate half of the array. Once we have done this, we will choose the middle element of the half that is left over and then repeat the same process until either `wanted` is found or it is determined that `wanted` is not in the array.

The following program performs a binary search on an array of integers that is ordered from largest to smallest. Students should think about the logic of this search and how it differs from the argument given above for data ordered smallest to largest.

*Sample Program 8.2:*

```
// This program demonstrates a Binary Search


#include <iostream>
using namespace std;

int binarySearch(int [], int, int);  // function prototype

const int SIZE = 16;

int main()
{
    int found, value;
    int array[] = {34,19,19,18,17,13,12,12,12,11,9,5,3,2,2,0};
                // array to be searched

    cout << "Enter an integer to search for:" << endl;
    cin >> value;

    found = binarySearch(array, SIZE, value);
                // function call to perform the binary search
                // on array looking for an occurrence of value
    if (found == -1)
        cout << "The value " << value << " is not in the list" << endl;
    else
    {
        cout << "The value " << value << " is in position number "
            << found + 1 << " of the list" << endl;
    }
    return 0;
}
```

*continues*

```
//*****************************************************************
//                  binarySearch
//
// task:        This searches an array for a particular value
// data in:     List of values in an orderd array, the number of
//              elements in the array, and the value searched for
//              in the array
// data returned: Position in the array of the value or -1 if value
//              not found
//
//*****************************************************************
int binarySearch(int array[],int numElems,int value) //function heading
{
        int first = 0;              // First element of list
        int last = numElems - 1;    // last element of the list
        int middle;                 // variable containing the current
                                    // middle value of the list

        while (first <= last)
        {
            middle = first + (last - first) / 2;

        if (array[middle] == value)
            return middle;          // if value is in the middle, we are done

        else if (array[middle]<value)
            last = middle - 1;      // toss out the second remaining half of
                                    // the array and search the first
        else
            first = middle + 1;     // toss out the first remaining half of
                                    // the array and search the second

        }

        return -1;                  // indicates that value is not in the array
}
```

If you run this program and search for 2, the output indicates that 2 is in the 14th position of the array. Since 2 is in the 14th and 15th position, we see that the binary search found the first occurrence of 2 in this particular data set; however, in Lab 8.2 you will search for values other than 2 and see that there are other possibilities for which occurrence of a sought value is found.

## Sorting Algorithms

We have just seen how to search an array for a specific piece of data; however, what if we do not like the order in which the data is stored in the array? For example, if a collection of numerical values is not in order, we might like them to be so we can use a binary search to find a particular value. Or, if we have a list of names, we may want them put in alphabetical order. To sort data stored in an array, one uses a **sorting algorithm**. In this section we will consider two such algorithms—the bubble sort and the selection sort.

## The Bubble Sort

The bubble sort is a simple algorithm used to arrange data in either **ascending** (lowest to highest) or **descending** (highest to lowest) order. To see how this sort works, let us arrange the array below in ascending order.

| 9 | 2 | 0 | 11 | 5 |
|---|---|---|----|---|
| Element 0 | Element 1 | Element 2 | Element 3 | Element 4 |

The bubble sort begins by comparing the first two array elements. If `Element 0 > Element 1`, which is true in this case, then these two pieces of data are exchanged. The array is now the following:

| 2 | 9 | 0 | 11 | 5 |
|---|---|---|----|---|
| Element 0 | Element 1 | Element 2 | Element 3 | Element 4 |

Next elements 1 and 2 are compared. Since `Element 1 > Element 2`, another exchange occurs:

| 2 | 0 | 9 | 11 | 5 |
|---|---|---|----|---|
| Element 0 | Element 1 | Element 2 | Element 3 | Element 4 |

Now elements 2 and 3 are compared. Since 9 < 11, there is no exchange at this step. Next elements 3 and 4 are compared and exchanged:

| 2 | 0 | 9 | 5 | 11 |
|---|---|---|---|----|
| Element 0 | Element 1 | Element 2 | Element 3 | Element 4 |

At this point we are at the end of the array. Note that the largest value is now in the last position of the array. Now we go back to the beginning of the array and repeat the entire process over again. Elements 0 and 1 are compared. Since 2 > 0, an exchange occurs:

| 0 | 2 | 9 | 5 | 11 |
|---|---|---|---|----|
| Element 0 | Element 1 | Element 2 | Element 3 | Element 4 |

Next elements 1 and 2 are compared. Since 2 < 9, no swap occurs. However, when we compare elements 2 and 3 we find that 9 > 5 and so they are exchanged. Since `Element 4` contains the largest value (from the previous pass), we do not need to make any more comparisons in this pass.

The final result is:

| 0 | 2 | 5 | 9 | 11 |
|---|---|---|---|----|
| Element 0 | Element 1 | Element 2 | Element 3 | Element 4 |

The data is now arranged in ascending order and the algorithm terminates. Note that the larger values seem to rise "like bubbles" to the larger positions of the array as the sort progresses.

We just saw in the previous example how the first pass through the array positioned the largest value at the end of the array. This is always the case. Likewise, the second pass will always position the second to largest value in the second position from the end of the array. The pattern continues for the third pass, fourth pass, and so on until the array is fully sorted. Subsequent passes have one less array element to check than their immediate predecessor.

*Sample Program 8.3:*

```cpp
// This program uses a bubble sort to arrange an array of integers in
// ascending order

#include <iostream>
using namespace std;

// function prototypes

void bubbleSortArray(int [], int);
void displayArray(int[], int);

const int SIZE = 5;

int main()
{
    int values[SIZE] = {9,2,0,11,5};

    cout << "The values before the bubble sort is performed are:" << endl;
    displayArray(values,SIZE);

    bubbleSortArray(values,SIZE);

    cout << "The values after the bubble sort is performed are:" << endl;
    displayArray(values,SIZE);

    return 0;
}
//*****************************************************************
//                      displayArray
//
// task:           to print the array
// data in:        the array to be printed, the array size
// data out:       none
//
//*****************************************************************

void displayArray(int array[], int elems)      // function heading
{                                              // displays the array
    for (int count = 0; count < elems; count++)
        cout << array[count] << "   " << endl;
}


//*****************************************************************
//                      bubbleSortArray
//
// task:           to sort values of an array in ascending order
// data in:        the array, the array size
// data out:       the sorted array
//
//*****************************************************************
```

```
void bubbleSortArray(int array[], int elems)
{
      bool swap;
      int temp;
      int bottom = elems - 1;      // bottom indicates the end part of the
                                   // array where the largest values have
                                   // settled in order
do
      {
      swap = false;
      for (int count = 0; count < bottom; count++)
      {
            if (array[count] > array[count+1])
            {                   // the next three lines do a swap
               temp = array[count];
               array[count] = array[count+1];
               array[count+1] = temp;
               swap = true; // indicates that a swap occurred
            }
      }
      bottom--;      // bottom is decremented by 1 since each pass through
                     // the array adds one more value that is set in order

} while(swap != false);
            // loop repeats until a pass through the array with
            // no swaps occurs
}
```

While the bubble sort algorithm is fairly simple, it is inefficient for large arrays since data values only move one at a time.

## The Selection Sort

A generally more efficient algorithm for large arrays is the **selection sort**. As before, let us assume that we want to arrange numerical data in ascending order. The idea of the selection sort algorithm is to first locate the smallest value in the array and move that value to the beginning of the array (i.e., position 0). Then the next smallest element is located and put in the second position (i.e., position 1). This process continues until all the data is ordered. An advantage of the selection sort is that for $n$ data elements at most $n$-1 moves are required. The disadvantage is that $n(n-1)/2$ comparisons are always required. To see how this sort works, let us consider the array we arranged using the bubble sort:

| 9 | 2 | 0 | 11 | 5 |
|---|---|---|----|---|
| Element 0 | Element 1 | Element 2 | Element 3 | Element 4 |

First the smallest value is located. It is 0, so the contents of Element 0 and Element 2 are swapped:

| 0 | 2 | 9 | 11 | 5 |
|---|---|---|----|---|
| Element 0 | Element 1 | Element 2 | Element 3 | Element 4 |

Next we look for the second smallest value. The important point to note here is that we do not need to check Element 0 again since we know it already contains the smallest data value. So the sort starts looking at Element 1. We see that the second smallest value is 2, which is already in Element 1. Starting at Element 2 we see that 5 is the smallest of the remaining values. Thus the contents of Element 2 and Element 4 are swapped:

| 0 | 2 | 5 | 11 | 9 |
|---|---|---|----|---|
| Element 0 | Element 1 | Element 2 | Element 3 | Element 4 |

Finally, the contents of Element 3 and Element 4 are compared. Since 11 > 9, the contents are swapped leaving the array ordered as desired:

| 0 | 2 | 5 | 9 | 11 |
|---|---|---|---|----|
| Element 0 | Element 1 | Element 2 | Element 3 | Element 4 |

*Sample Program 8.4:*

```cpp
// This program uses a selection sort to arrange an array of integers in
// ascending order

#include <iostream>
using namespace std;

// function prototypes

void selectionSortArray(int [], int);
void displayArray(int[], int);
const int SIZE = 5;

int main()
{
     int values[SIZE] = {9,2,0,11,5};

     cout << "The values before the selection sort is performed are:" << endl;
     displayArray(values,SIZE);

     selectionSortArray(values,SIZE);
     cout << "The values after the selection sort is performed are:" << endl;
     displayArray(values,SIZE);

     return 0;
}


//*************************************************************
//                    displayArray
//
// task:          to print the array
// data in:       the array to be printed, the array size
// data out:      none
//
//*************************************************************
```

```
void displayArray(int array[], int elems)    // function heading
{                                            // Displays array
     for (int count = 0; count < elems; count++)
          cout << array[count] << "  ";
     cout << endl;
}


//*****************************************************************
//                    selectionSortArray
//
// task:          to sort values of an array in ascending order
// data in:       the array, the array size
// data out:      the sorted array
//
//*****************************************************************


void selectionSortArray(int array[], int elems)
{
     int seek;        // array position currently being put in order
     int minCount;    // location of smallest value found
     int minValue;    // holds the smallest value found

     for (seek = 0; seek < (elems-1); seek++)  // outer loop performs the swap
                                               // and then increments seek
     {
        minCount = seek;
        minValue = array[seek];
        for(int index = seek + 1; index < elems; index++)
        {
                // inner loop searches through array
                // starting at array[seek] searching
                // for the smallest value. When the
                // value is found, the subscript is
                // stored in minCount. The value is
                // stored in minValue.

             if(array[index] < minValue)
             {
                 minValue = array[index];
                 minCount = index;
             }
        }


             // the following two statements exchange the value of the
             // element currently needing the smallest value found in the
             // pass(indicated by seek) with the smallest value found
             // (located in minValue)
```

*continues*

```
        array[minCount] = array[seek];
        array[seek] = minValue;


    }

}
```

## PRE-LAB WRITING ASSIGNMENT

### Fill-in-the-Blank Questions

1. The advantage of a linear search is that it is _____.

2. The disadvantage of a linear search is that it is _____.

3. The advantage of a binary search over a linear search is that a binary search is _____.

4. An advantage of a linear search over a binary search is that the data must be _____ for a binary search.

5. After 3 passes of a binary search, approximately what fraction of the original array still needs to be searched (assuming the desired data has not been found)? _____

6. While the _____ sort algorithm is conceptually simple, it can be inefficient for large arrays because data values only move one at a time.

7. An advantage of the _____ sort is that, for an array of size $n$, at most $n - 1$ moves are required.

8. Use the bubble sort on the array below and construct the first 3 steps that actually make changes. (Assume the sort is from smallest to largest).

| 19 | -4 | 91 | 0 | -17 |
|---|---|---|---|---|
| Element 0 | Element 1 | Element 2 | Element 3 | Element 4 |

|  |  |  |  |  |
|---|---|---|---|---|
| Element 0 | Element 1 | Element 2 | Element 3 | Element 4 |

|  |  |  |  |  |
|---|---|---|---|---|
| Element 0 | Element 1 | Element 2 | Element 3 | Element 4 |

|  |  |  |  |  |
|---|---|---|---|---|
| Element 0 | Element 1 | Element 2 | Element 3 | Element 4 |

9. Use the selection sort on the array below and construct the first 3 steps that actually make changes. (Assume the sort if from smallest to largest).

| 19 | -4 | 91 | 0 | -17 |
|---|---|---|---|---|
| Element 0 | Element 1 | Element 2 | Element 3 | Element 4 |

|  |  |  |  |  |
|---|---|---|---|---|
| Element 0 | Element 1 | Element 2 | Element 3 | Element 4 |

|  |  |  |  |  |
|---|---|---|---|---|
| Element 0 | Element 1 | Element 2 | Element 3 | Element 4 |

|  |  |  |  |  |
|---|---|---|---|---|
| Element 0 | Element 1 | Element 2 | Element 3 | Element 4 |

# LESSON 8

## LAB 8.1    Working with the Linear Search

Bring in program `linear_search.cpp` from the Lab 8 folder. This is Sample Program 8.1 from the Pre-lab Reading Assignment. The code is the following:

```cpp
// This program performs a linear search on a character array

// Place Your Name Here

#include <iostream>
using namespace std;

int searchList(char[], int, char); // function prototype
const int SIZE = 8;

int main()
{
    char word[SIZE] = "Harpoon";
    int found;
    char ch;

    cout << "Enter a letter to search for:" << endl;
    cin >> ch;

    found = searchList(word, SIZE, ch);
    if (found == -1)
        cout << "The letter " << ch
            << " was not found in the list" << endl;
    else
        cout << "The letter " << ch <<" is in the " << found + 1
            << " position of the list" << endl;

    return 0;

}


//******************************************************************
//                    searchList
//
// task:          This searches an array for a particular value
// data in:       List of values in an array, the number of
//                elements in the array, and the value searched for
//                in the array
// data returned: Position in the array of the value or -1 if value
//                not found
//
//******************************************************************
```

```
int searchList(char List[], int numElems, char value)
{
      for (int count = 0; count <= numElems; count++)
      {
            if (List[count] == value)
                        // each array entry is checked to see if it contains
                        // the desired value.
                  return count;
                        // if the desired value is found, the array subscript
                        // count is returned to indicate the location in the array
      }
      return -1;       // if the value is not found, -1 is returned
}
```

*Exercise 1:* Re-write this program so that it searches an array of integers rather than characters. Search the integer array nums[8] =

| 3 | 6 | -19 | 5 | 5 | 0 | -2 | 99 |
|---|---|-----|---|---|---|----|----|

for several different integers. Make sure you try integers that are in the array and others that are not. What happens if you search for 5?

*Exercise 2:* Re-write the program so that the user can continue to input values that will be searched for, until a sentinel value is entered to end the program. Should a pre or post test loop be used?

## LAB 8.2   Working with the Binary Search

Bring in program binary_search.cpp from the Lab 8 folder. This is Sample Program 8.2 from the Pre-lab Reading Assignment. The code is the following:

```
// This program demonstrates a Binary Search

// PLACE YOUR NAME HERE

#include <iostream>
using namespace std;

int binarySearch(int [], int, int);   // function prototype

const int SIZE = 16;

int main()
{
      int found, value;
      int array[] = {34,19,19,18,17,13,12,12,12,11,9,5,3,2,2,0};
                  // array to be searched

      cout << "Enter an integer to search for:" << endl;
      cin >> value;

      found = binarySearch(array, SIZE, value);
```

```
                    // function call to perform the binary search
                    // on array looking for an occurrence of value
        if (found == -1)
            cout << "The value " << value << " is not in the list" << endl;
        else
        {
            cout << "The value " << value << " is in position number "
                << found + 1 << " of the list" << endl;
        }
        return 0;
}



//*******************************************************************
//                    binarySearch
//
// task:           This searches an array for a particular value
// data in:        List of values in an orderd array, the number of
//                 elements in the array, and the value searched for
//                 in the array
// data returned: Position in the array of the value or -1 if value
//                 not found
//
//*******************************************************************
int binarySearch(int array[],int numElems,int value) //function heading
{
        int first = 0;                  // First element of list
        int last = numElems - 1;        // last element of the list
        int middle;                     // variable containing the current
                                        // middle value of the list

        while (first <= last)
        {
            middle = first + (last - first) / 2;

        if (array[middle] == value)
            return middle;              // if value is in the middle, we are done

        else if (array[middle] < value)
            last = middle - 1;          // toss out the second remaining half of
                                        // the array and search the first
        else
            first = middle + 1;         // toss out the first remaining half of
                                        // the array and search the second

        }

        return -1;                      // indicates that value is not in the array
}
```

*Exercise 1:* The variable `middle` is defined as an integer. The program contains the assignment statement `middle=first+(last-first)/2`. Is the right side of this statement necessarily an integer in computer memory? Explain how the `middle` value is determined by the computer. How does this line of code affect the logic of the program? Remember that `first`, `last`, and `middle` refer to the array positions, not the values stored in those array positions.

*Exercise 2:* Search the array in the program above for 19 and then 12. Record what the output is in each case.

_____

Note that both 19 and 12 are repeated in the array. Which occurrence of 19 did the search find?

_____

Which occurrence of 12 did the search find?

_____

Explain the difference.

*Exercise 3:* Modify the program to search an array that is in ascending order. Make sure to alter the array initialization.

## LAB 8.3  Working with Sorts

Bring in either the program `bubble_sort.cpp` or `selection_sort.cpp` from the Lab 8 folder. These are Sample Programs 8.3 and 8.4, respectively, from the Pre-lab Reading Assignment. The code for both are given below.

```cpp
// This program uses a bubble sort to arrange an array of integers in
// ascending order

// PLACE YOUR NAME HERE

#include <iostream>
using namespace std;

// function prototypes

void bubbleSortArray(int [], int);
void displayArray(int[], int);

const int SIZE = 5;

int main()
{
    int values[SIZE] = {9,2,0,11,5};

    cout << "The values before the bubble sort is performed are:" << endl;
    displayArray(values,SIZE);

    bubbleSortArray(values,SIZE);
```

```
        cout << "The values after the bubble sort is performed are:" << endl;
        displayArray(values,SIZE);

        return 0;
}
//*****************************************************************
//                      displayArray
//
// task:          to print the array
// data in:       the array to be printed, the array size
// data out:      none
//
//*****************************************************************

void displayArray(int array[], int elems)    //.function heading
{                                             // displays the array
        for (int count = 0; count < elems; count++)
            cout << array[count] << "   " << endl;
}


//*****************************************************************
//                      bubbleSortArray
//
// task:          to sort values of an array in ascending order
// data in:       the array, the array size
// data out:      the sorted array
//
//*****************************************************************


void bubbleSortArray(int array[], int elems)
{
        bool swap;
        int temp;
        int bottom = elems - 1;     // bottom indicates the end part of the
                                    // array where the largest values have
                                    // settled in order
do
        {
            swap = false;
            for (int count = 0; count < bottom; count++)
            {
                    if (array[count] > array[count+1])
                    {                   // the next three lines do a swap
                        temp = array[count];
                        array[count] = array[count+1];
                        array[count+1] = temp;
                        swap = true; // indicates that a swap occurred
                    }
            }
```

```
        bottom--;        // bottom is decremented by 1 since each pass through
                         // the array adds one more value that is set in order


    } while(swap != false);
                // loop repeats until a pass through the array with
                // no swaps occurs
}
```

---

**selection_sort.cpp**

---

```cpp
// This program uses a selection sort to arrange an array of integers in
// ascending order

//PLACE YOUR NAME HERE

#include <iostream>
using namespace std;

// function prototypes

void selectionSortArray(int [], int);
void displayArray(int[], int);
const int SIZE = 5;

int main()
{
    int values[SIZE] = {9,2,0,11,5};

    cout << "The values before the selection sort is performed are:" << endl;
    displayArray(values,SIZE);

    selectionSortArray(values,SIZE);
    cout << "The values after the selection sort is performed are:" << endl;
    displayArray(values,SIZE);

    return 0;
}


//****************************************************************
//                      displayArray
//
// task:          to print the array
// data in:       the array to be printed, the array size
// data out:      none
//
//****************************************************************

void displayArray(int array[], int elems)     // function heading
{                                              // Displays array
    for (int count = 0; count < elems; count++)
        cout << array[count] << "  ";
    cout << endl;
```

```
}

//******************************************************************
//                    selectionSortArray
//
// task:          to sort values of an array in ascending order
// data in:       the array, the array size
// data out:      the sorted array
//
//******************************************************************


void selectionSortArray(int array[], int elems)
{
      int seek;       // array position currently being put in order
      int minCount;   // location of smallest value found
      int minValue;   // holds the smallest value found

      for (seek = 0; seek < (elems-1);seek++)   // outer loop performs the swap
                                                // and then increments seek
      {
          minCount = seek;
          minValue = array[seek];
          for(int index = seek + 1; index < elems; index++)
          {
              // inner loop searches through array
              // starting at array[seek] searching
              // for the smallest value. When the
              // value is found, the subscript is
              // stored in minCount. The value is
              // stored in minValue.

              if(array[index] < minValue)
                {
                    minValue = array[index];
                    minCount = index;
                }
          }

          // the following two statements exchange the value of the
          // element currently needing the smallest value found in the
          // pass(indicated by seek) with the smallest value found
          // (located in minValue)

          array[minCount] = array[seek];
          array[seek] = minValue;

      }
}
```

*Exercise 1:* Re-write the sort program you chose so that it orders integers from largest to smallest rather than smallest to largest.

*Exercise 2:* Modify your program from Exercise 1 so that it prints the array at each step of the algorithm. Try sorting the array

| 23 | 0 | 45 | -3 | -78 | 1 | -1 | 9 |
|----|---|----|----|-----|---|----|---|

by hand using whichever algorithm you chose. Then have your program do the sort. Does the output match what you did by hand?

## LAB 8.4 Student Generated Code Assignments

Write a program that prompts the user to enter the number of elements and the numbers themselves to be placed in an integer array that holds a maximum of 50 elements. The program should then prompt the user for an integer which will be searched for in the array using a binary search. Make sure to include the following steps along the way:

*i)* A sort routine must be called before the binary search. You may use either the selection sort or the bubble sort. However, the sort must be implemented in its own function and not in `main`.

*ii)* Next include a function called by `main` to implement the binary search. The ordered array produced by the sort should be passed to the search routine which returns the location in the sorted array of the sought value, or -1 if the value is not in the array.

*iii)* Add a value returning function that computes the **mean** of your data set. Recall that the mean is the sum of the data values divided by the number of pieces of data. Your program should output the size of the array entered, the array as entered by the user, the sorted array, the integer being searched for, the location of that integer in the sorted array (or an appropriate message if it is not in the array), and the mean of the data set.

*iv)* (Optional) Modify your program so that the data is entered from a file rather than from the keyboard. The first line of the file should be the size of the integer array. The second line should contain the integer searched for in the data set. Finally, the array elements are to start on the third line. Make sure you separate each array element with a space. The output, as described in *iii)*, should be sent to a file.

# 9 Pointers

**PURPOSE**

1. To introduce pointer variables and their relationship with arrays
2. To introduce the dereferencing operator
3. To introduce the concept of dynamic memory allocation

**PROCEDURE**

1. Students should read the Pre-lab Reading Assignment before coming to lab.
2. Students should complete the Pre-lab Writing Assignment before coming to lab.
3. In the lab, students should complete labs assigned to them by the instructor.

| Contents | Pre-requisites | Approximate completion time | Page number | Check when done |
|---|---|---|---|---|
| Pre-lab Reading Assignment | | 20 min. | 158 | |
| Pre-lab Writing Assignment | Pre-lab reading | 10 min. | 167 | |
| **LESSON 9A** | | | | |
| Lab 9.1 Introduction to Pointer Variables | Basic understanding of pointer variables | 15 min. | 167 | |
| Lab 9.2 Dynamic Memory | Basic understanding of dynamic memory, new and delete operators | 35 min. | 168 | |
| **LESSON 9B** | | | | |
| Lab 9.3 Dynamic Arrays | Basic understanding of the relationship of pointer variables and arrays | 25 min. | 170 | |
| Lab 9.4 Student Generated Code Assignments | Basic understanding of pointers, the (*) and (&) symbols, sort and search routines | 30 min. | 171 | |

## PRE-LAB READING ASSIGNMENT

### Pointer Variables

A distinction must always be made between a memory location's address and the data stored at that location. A street address like 119 Main St. is a location that is different than a description of what is at that location: the little red house of the Smith family. So far we have been concerned only with the data stored in a variable, rather than with its address (where in main memory the variable is located). In this lesson we will look at addresses of variables and at special variables, called **pointers**, which hold these addresses. The address of a variable is given by preceding the variable name with the C++ address operator (&):

```
cout << &sum; // This outputs the address of the variable sum
```

The & operator in front of the variable sum indicates that the address itself, and not the data stored in that location, is the value used. On most systems the above address will print as a hexadecimal value representing the physical location of the variable. Before this lesson where have you used the address operator in C++ programming? You may recall that it was used in the prototype and the function heading of a function for parameters being passed by reference. This connection will be explored in the next section.

To define a variable to be a pointer, we precede it with an asterisk (*):

```
int *ptr;
```

The asterisk in front of the variable indicates that ptr holds the address of a memory location. The int indicates that the memory location that ptr points to holds integer values. ptr is NOT an integer data type, but rather a pointer that holds the address of a location where an integer value is stored. This distinction is most important!

The following example illustrates this difference.

```
int  sum;        // sum holds an integer value.
int *sumPtr;     // sumPtr holds an address where an
                 // integer can be found.
```

By now there may be confusion between the symbols * and &, so we next discuss their use.

### Using the & Symbol

The & symbol is basically used on two occasions.

1.  The most frequent use we have seen is between the data type and the variable name of a pass by reference parameter in a function heading/ prototype. This is called a **reference variable**. The memory address of the parameter is sent to the function instead of the value at that address. When the parameter is used in the function, the compiler automatically **dereferences** the variable. Dereference means that the location of that reference variable (parameter in this case) is accessed to retrieve or store a value.

We have looked at the swap function on several occasions. We revisit this routine to show that the & symbol is used in the parameters that need to be swapped. The reason is that these values need to be changed by the function and, thus, we give the address (location in memory) of those values so that the function can write their new values into them as they are swapped.

*Example:*

```
void swap(int &first, int &second)
{                      // The & indicates that the parameters
                       // first and second are being passed by
                       // reference.

int temp;

temp = first;     // Since first is a reference variable,
                  // the compiler retrieves the value
                  // stored there and places it in temp.

first = second    // New values are written directly into
second = temp;    // the memory locations of first and second.
}
```

2.   The & symbol is also used whenever we are interested in the *address* of a variable rather than its *contents*.

*Example:*

```
cout  << sum;     // This outputs the value stored in the
                  // variable sum.
cout  << &sum;    // This outputs the address where
                  // sum is stored in memory.
```

Using the & symbol to get the address of a variable comes in handy when we are assigning values to pointer variables.

## Using the * Symbol

The * symbol is also basically used on two occasions.

1.   It is used to define pointer variables:

```
int *ptr;
```

2.   It is also used whenever we are interested in the contents of the *memory location* pointed to by a *pointer variable*, rather than the address itself. When used this way * is called the **indirection operator**, or **dereferencing operator**.

*Example:*

```
cout << *ptr; // Since ptr is a pointer variable, *
              // dereferences ptr. The value stored at the
              // location ptr points to will be printed.
```

## Using * and & Together

In many ways * and & are the opposites of each other. The * symbol is used just before a pointer variable so that we may obtain the actual data rather than the address of the variable. The & symbol is used on a variable so that the variable's address, rather than the data stored in it, will be used. The following program demonstrates the use of pointers.

*Sample Program 9.1:*

```
#include <iostream>
using namespace std;

int main()
{
   int one = 10;
   int *ptr1;      // ptr1 is a pointer variable that points to an int

   ptr1 = &one;    // &one indicates that the address, not the
                   // contents, of one is being assigned to ptr1.
                   // Remember that ptr1 can only hold an address.
                   // Since ptr1 holds the address where the variable
                   // one is stored, we say that ptr1 "points to" one.

   cout << "The value of one is   " << one   << endl << endl;
   cout << "The value of &one is  " << &one  << endl << endl;
   cout << "The value of ptr1 is  " << ptr1  << endl << endl;
   cout << "The value of *ptr1 is " << *ptr1 << endl << endl;

   return 0;
}
```

What do you expect will be printed if the address of variable one is the hexadecimal value 006AF0F4? The following will be printed by the program.

| Output | Comments |
|---|---|
| **The value of one is 10** | one is an integer variable, holding a 10. |
| **The value of &one is 006AF0F4** | &one is the "address of" variable one. |
| **The value of  ptr1  is 006AF0F4** | ptr1 is assigned one's address |
| **The value of *ptr1 is 10** | * is the dereferencing operator which means *ptr1 gives us the value of the variable ptr1 is pointing at. |

## Arrays and Pointers

When arrays are passed to functions they are passed by pointer. An array name is a pointer to the beginning of the array. Variables can hold just one value and so we can reference that value by just naming the variable. Arrays, however, hold many values. All of these values cannot be referenced just by naming the array. This is where pointers enter the picture. Pointers allow us to access all the array elements. Recall that the array name is really a pointer that holds the address of the first element in the array. By using an array index, we dereference the pointer which gives us the contents of that array location. If grades is an array of 5 integers, as shown below, grades is actually a pointer to the first location in the array, and grades[0] allows us to access the contents of that first location.

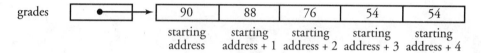

| grades | ● → | 90 | 88 | 76 | 54 | 54 |

starting address    starting address + 1    starting address + 2    starting address + 3    starting address + 4

From the last section we know it is also possible to dereference the pointer by using the * operator. What is the output of the following two statements?

```
cout << grades[0];    // Output the value stored in the 1st array element
cout << *grades;      // Output the value found at the address stored
                      // in grades (i.e., at the address of the 1st array
                      // element).
```

Both statements are actually equivalent. They both print out the contents of the first grades array location, a 90.

Access of an individual element of an array through an index is done by **pointer arithmetic**. We can access the second array location with grades[1], the third location with grades[2], and so on, because the indices allow us to move through memory to other addresses relative to the beginning address of the array. The phrase "address + 1" in the previous diagram means to move one array element forward from the staring address of the array. The third element is accessed by moving 2 elements forward and so forth. The amount of movement in bytes depends on how much memory is allocated for each element, and that depends on how the array is defined. Since grades is defined as an array of integers, if an integer is allocated 4 bytes, then +1 means to move forward 4 bytes from the starting address of the array, +2 means to move forward 8 bytes, etc. The compiler keeps track of how far forward to move to find a desired element based on the array index. Thus the following two statements are equivalent.

```
cout << grades[2];
cout << *(grades + 2);
```

Both statements refer to the value located two elements forward from the starting address of the array. Although the first may be the easiest, computer scientists need to understand how to access memory through pointers. The following program illustrates how to use pointer arithmetic rather than indexing to access the elements of an array.

*Sample Program 9.2:*

```
// This program illustrates how to use pointer arithmetic to
// access elements of an array.

#include <iostream>
using namespace std;

int main()
{
    int grades[] = {90, 88, 76, 54, 34};
        // This defines and initializes an int array.
        // Since grades is an array name, it is really a pointer
        // that holds the starting address of the array.

    cout << "The first grade is "        // The * before grades
         << *grades << endl;              // dereferences it so that the
                                          // contents of array location 0
                                          // is printed instead of its
                                          // address.

    cout << "The second grade is "       // The same is done for the other
         << *(grades + 1) << endl;        // elements of the array. In
    cout << "The third grade is "        // each case, pointer arithmetic
         << *(grades + 2) << endl;        // gives us the address of the
    cout << "The fourth grade is "       // next array element.  Then the
         << *(grades + 3) << endl;        // indirection operator * gives
    cout << "The fifth grade is "        // us the value of what is stored
         << *(grades + 4) << endl;        // at that address.

    return 0;
}
```

What is printed by the program?

```
The first grade is 90
The second grade is 88
The third grade is 76
The fourth grade is 54
The fifth grade is 34
```

## Dynamic Variables

In Lesson Set 7 on arrays, we saw how the size of an array is given at the time of its definition. The programmer must estimate the maximum number of elements that will be used by the array and this size is static, i.e., it cannot change during the execution of the program. Consequently, if the array is defined to be larger than is needed, memory is wasted. If it is defined to be smaller than is needed, there is not enough memory to hold all of the elements. The use of pointers (and the new and delete operators described below) allows us to dynamically allocate enough memory for an array so that memory is not wasted.

This leads us to **dynamic variables**. Pointers allow us to use dynamic variables, which can be created and destroyed as needed within a program. We have studied scope rules, which define where a variable is active. Related to this is the concept of **lifetime**, the time during which a variable exists. The lifetime of dynamic variables is controlled by the program through explicit commands to allocate (i.e., create) and deallocate (i.e., destroy) them. The operator **new** is used to allocate and the operator **delete** is used to deallocate dynamic variables. The compiler keeps track of where in memory non-dynamic variables (variables discussed thus far in this book) are located. Their contents can be accessed by just naming them. However, the compiler does not keep track of the address of a dynamic variable. When the new command is used to allocate memory for a dynamic variable, the system returns its address and the programmer stores it in a pointer variable. Through the pointer variable we can access the memory location.

*Example:*

```
int *one;        // one and two are defined to be pointer
int *two;        // variables that point to ints

int result;      // defines an int variable that will hold
                 // the sum of two values.

one = new int;   // These statements each dynamically
two = new int;   // allocate enough memory to hold an int
                 // and assign their addresses to pointer
                 // variables one and two, respectively.

*one = 10;       // These statements assign the value 10
*two = 20;       // to the memory location pointed to by one
                 // and 20 to the memory location pointed to
                 // by two.

result = *one + *two;
                 // This adds the contents of the memory
                 // locations pointed to by one and two.
cout << "result = " << result << endl;

delete one;      // These statements deallocate the dynamic
delete two;      // variables.  Their memory is freed and
                 // they cease to exist.
```

Now let us use dynamic variables to allocate an appropriate amount of memory to hold an array. By using the new operator to create the array, we can wait until we know how big the array needs to be before creating it. The following program demonstrates this idea. First the user is asked to input the number of grades to be processed. Then that number is used to allocate exactly enough memory to hold an array with the required number of elements for the grades.

*Sample Program 9.3:*

```cpp
// This program finds the average of a set of grades.
// It dynamically allocates space for the array holding the grades.

#include <iostream>
#include <iomanip>
using namespace std;

// function prototypes
void sortIt (float* grades, int numOfGrades);
void displayGrades(float* grades, int numOfGrades);

int main()
{
    float *grades;          // a pointer that will be used to point
                            // to the beginning of a float array
    float total = 0;        // total of all grades
    float average;          // average of all grades
    int numOfGrades;        // the number of grades to be processed
    int count;              // loop counter

    cout << fixed << showpoint << setprecision(2);

    cout << "How many grades will be processed " << endl;
    cin >> numOfGrades;

    while (numOfGrades <= 0)  // checks for a legal value
    {
        cout << "There must be at least one grade. Please reenter.\n";
        cout << "How many grades will be processed " << endl;
        cin >> numOfGrades;
    }

    grades = new float(numOfGrades);
                        // allocation memory for an array
                        // new is the operator that is allocating
                        // an array of floats with the number of
                        // elements specified by the user. grades
                        // is the pointer holding the starting
                        // address of the array.

    if (grades == NULL)    // NULL is a special identifier predefined
    {                      // to equal 0.  It indicates a non-valid
                           // address.  If grades is 0 it means the
                           // the operating system was unable to
                           // allocate enough memory for the array.

        cout << "Error allocating memory!\n";
                           // The program should output an appropriate
        return -1;         // error message and return with a value
    }                      // other than 0 to signal a problem.
    cout << "Enter the grades below\n";
```

```cpp
    for (count = 0; count < numOfGrades; count++)
    {
        cout << "Grade " << (count + 1) << ": " << endl;
        cin >> grades[count];
        total = total + grades[count];
    }

    average = total / numOfGrades;
    cout << "Average Grade is " << average << "%" << endl;

    sortIt(grades, numOfGrades);
    displayGrades(grades, numOfGrades);
    delete [] grades;            // deallocates all the array memory

    return 0;
}


//***************************************************
//              sortIt
//
// task:        to sort numbers in an array
// data in:     an array of floats and
//              the number of elements in the array
// data out:    sorted array
//
//***************************************************

void sortIt(float* grades, int numOfGrades)
{
  // Sort routine placed here
}


//***************************************************
//              displayGrades
//
// task:        to display numbers in an array
// data in:     an array of floats and
//              the number of elements in the array
// data out:    none
//
//***************************************************
void displayGrades(float* grades, int numOfGrades)
{
      // Code to display grades of the array
}
```

Notice how the dynamic array is passed as a parameter to the `sortIt` and `displayGrades` functions. In each case, the call to the function simply passes the name of the array, along with its size as an argument. The name of the array holds the array's starting address.

```cpp
    sortIt(grades, numOfGrades);
```

In the function header, the formal parameter that receives the array is defined to be a pointer data type.

```
void sortIt(float* grades, int numOfGrades)
```

Since the compiler treats an array name as a pointer, we could also have written the following function header.

```
void sortIt(float grades[], int numOfGrades)
```

In this program, dynamic allocation of memory was used to save memory. This is a minor consideration for the type of programs done in this course, but a major concern in professional programming environments where large fluctuating amounts of data are used.

## Review of * and &

The * symbol is used to define pointer variables. In this case it appears in the variable definition statement between the data type and the pointer variable name. It indicates that the variable holds an address, rather than the data stored at that address.

*Example 1:*   `int *ptr1;`

* is also used as a dereferencing operator. When placed in front of an already defined pointer variable, the data stored at the location the pointer points to will be used and not the address.

*Example 2:*   `cout << *ptr1;`

Since `ptr1` is defined as a pointer variable in Example 1, if we assume `ptr1` has now been assigned an address, the output of Example 2 will be the data stored at that address. * in this case dereferences the variable `ptr1`.

The & symbol is used in a procedure or function heading to indicate that a parameter is being passed by reference. It is placed between the data type and the parameter name of each parameter that is passed by reference.

The & symbol is also used before a variable to indicate that the address, not the contents, of the variable is to be used.

*Example 3:*

```
int *ptr1;
int one = 10;

ptr1 = &one;            // This assigns the address of variable
                        // one to ptr1

cout << "The value of &one is "
     << &one << endl;  // This prints an address

cout << "The value of *ptr1 is "
     << *ptr1 << endl;  // This prints 10, because ptr1 points to
                        // one and * is the dereferencing operator.
```

## PRE-LAB WRITING ASSIGNMENT

### Fill-in-the-Blank Questions

1. The _____ symbol is the dereferencing operator.

2. The _____ symbol means "address of."

3. The name of an array, without any brackets, acts as a(n) _____ to the starting address of the array.

4. An operator that allocates a dynamic variable is _____.

5. An operator that deallocates a dynamic variable is _____.

6. Parameters that are passed by _____ are similar to a pointer variable in that they can contain the address of another variable. They are used as parameters of a procedure (void function) whenever we want a procedure to change the value of the argument.

Given the following information, fill the blanks with either "an address" or "3.75".

```
float * pointer;
float pay = 3.75;
pointer = &pay;
```

7. cout << pointer; will print _____.

8. cout << *pointer; will print _____.

9. cout << &pay; will print _____.

10. cout << pay; will print _____.

## LESSON 9A

### LAB 9.1   Introduction to Pointer Variables

Retrieve program `pointers.cpp` from the Lab 9 folder.
The code is as follows:

```
// This program demonstrates the use of pointer variables
// It finds the area of a rectangle given length and width
// It prints the length and width in ascending order

// PLACE YOUR NAME HERE

#include <iostream>
using namespace std;

int main()
{

    int length;              // holds length
    int width;               // holds width
    int area;                // holds area

    int *lengthPtr;          // int pointer which will be set to point to length
    int *widthPtr;           // int pointer which will be set to point to width
```

*continues*

```
cout << "Please input the length of the rectangle" << endl;
cin >> length;
cout << "Please input the width of the rectangle" << endl;
cin >> width;


// Fill in code to make lengthPtr point to length (hold its address)
// Fill in code to make widthPtr point to width (hold its address)



area =  // Fill in code to find the area by using only the pointer variables
cout << "The area is " << area << endl;


if (// Fill in the condition length > width by using only the pointer variables)
    cout << "The length is greater than the width" << endl;

else if (// Fill in the condition of width > length by using only the pointer
        // variables)
    cout << "The width is greater than the length" << endl;

else
    cout << "The width and length are the same" << endl;



    return 0;
}


}
```

*Exercise 1:* Complete this program by filling in the code (places in bold). Note: use only pointer variables when instructed to by the comments in bold. This program is to test your knowledge of pointer variables and the & and * symbols.

*Exercise 2:* Run the program with the following data: 10 15. Record the output here _____.

## LAB 9.2   Dynamic Memory

Retrieve program `dynamic.cpp` from the Lab 9 folder.
The code is as follows:

```
// This program demonstrates the use of dynamic variables
// PLACE YOUR NAME HERE

#include <iostream>
using namespace std;

const int MAXNAME = 10;
```

```
int main()
{
    int pos;
    char * name;
    int * one;
    int * two;
    int * three;
    int result;

    //  Fill in code to allocate the integer variable one here
    //  Fill in code to allocate the integer variable two here
    //  Fill in code to allocate the integer variable three here
    //  Fill in code to allocate the character array pointed to by name

    cout << "Enter your last name with exactly 10 characters." << endl;
    cout << "If your name has < 10 characters, repeat last letter. " << endl
         << "Blanks at the end do not count." << endl;

    for (pos = 0;  pos < MAXNAME;   pos++)

        cin >>   // Fill in code to read a character into the name array
                 // WITHOUT USING a bracketed subscript

    cout << "Hi ";
    for (pos = 0;  pos < MAXNAME;  pos++)

        cout << // Fill in code to a print a character from the name array
                // WITHOUT USING a bracketed subscript

    cout << endl << "Enter three integer numbers separated by blanks" << endl;

    // Fill in code to input three numbers and store them in the
    // dynamic variables pointed to by pointers one, two, and three.
    // You are working only with pointer variables

    //echo print
    cout << "The three numbers are " << endl;

    // Fill in code to output those numbers

    result = // Fill in code to calculate the sum of the three numbers
    cout << "The sum of the three values is " << result << endl;

    // Fill in code to deallocate one, two, three and name

    return 0;
}
```

---

*Exercise 1:* Complete the program by filling in the code. (Areas in bold)
This problem requires that you study very carefully the code already
written to prepare you to complete the program.

*Sample Run:*

**Enter your last name with exactly 10 characters.**
**If your name < 10 characters, repeat last letter. Blanks do not count.**
DeFinooooo
**Hi DeFinooooo**
**Enter three integer numbers separated by blanks**
5 6 7
**The three numbers are 5 6 7**
**The sum of the three values is 18**

*Exercise 2:* In inputting and outputting the name, you were asked NOT to use a bracketed subscript. Why is a bracketed subscript unnecessary?

Would using name[pos] work for inputting the name? Why or why not?
Would using name[pos] work for outputting the name? Why or why not?

Try them both and see.

# LESSON 9B

### LAB 9.3   Dynamic Arrays

Retrieve program darray.cpp from the Lab 9 folder.
The code is as follows:

```
// This program demonstrates the use of dynamic arrays

// PLACE YOUR NAME HERE

#include <iostream>
#include <iomanip>
using namespace std;


int main()

{

    float   *monthSales;        // a pointer used to point to an array
                                // holding monthly sales
    float   total = 0;          // total of all sales
    float   average;            // average of monthly sales
    int     numOfSales;         // number of sales to be processed
    int     count;              // loop counter

    cout << fixed << showpoint << setprecision(2);

    cout << "How many monthly sales will be processed? ";
    cin >> numOfSales;

    // Fill in the code to allocate memory for the array pointed to by
    // monthSales.
```

```
if ( // Fill in the condition to determine if memory has been
      // allocated (or eliminate this if construct if your instructor
      // tells you it is not needed for your compiler)
   )


{
      cout << "Error allocating memory!\n";
      return 1;
}


cout << "Enter the sales below\n";

for (count = 0; count < numOfSales;  count++)
{
    cout << "Sales for Month number   "
         << // Fill in code to show the number of the month
         << ":";

    // Fill in code to bring sales into an element of the array
}


for (count = 0; count < numOfSales; count++)
{
    total = total + monthSales[count];
}


average = // Fill in code to find the average


cout << "Average Monthly sale is $" << average << endl;
// Fill in the code to deallocate memory assigned to the array.

return 0;
}
```

---

*Exercise 1:* Fill in the code as indicated by the comments in bold.

*Sample Run:*

```
How many monthly sales will be processed 3
Enter the sales below
Sales for Month number 1: 401.25
Sales for Month number 2: 352.89
Sales for Month number 3: 375.05
Average Monthly sale is $376.40
```

## LAB 9.4   Student Generated Code Assignments

In these assignments you are asked to develop functions that have dynamic arrays as parameters. Remember that dynamic arrays are accessed by a pointer variable and thus the parameters that serve as dynamic arrays are, in fact, pointer variables.

*Example:*

```
void sort(float* score, int num_scores);  // a prototype whose function has a
                                           // dynamic array as its first
                                           // parameter. It is a pointer variable
        .
        .
int main()
{
    float *score;                          // a pointer variable
         .
         .
    score  =  new float(num_scores);       // allocation of the array

    sort(score,scoreSize);                 // call to the function
```

*Option 1:* Write a program that will read scores into an array. The size of the array should be input by the user (dynamic array). The program will find and print out the average of the scores. It will also call a function that will sort (using a bubble sort) the scores in ascending order. The values are then printed in this sorted order.

*Sample Run:*

**Please input the number of scores**
5
**Please enter a score**
100
**Please enter a score**
90
**Please enter a score**
95
**Please enter a score**
100
**Please enter a score**
90
**The average of the scores is 95**

**Here are the scores in ascending order**
90
90
95
100
100

*Option 2:* This program will read in id numbers and place them in an array. The array is dynamically allocated large enough to hold the number of id numbers given by the user. The program will then input an id and call a function to search for that id in the array. It will print whether the id is in the array or not.

*Sample Run:*

**Please input the number of id numbers to be read**
4
**Please enter an id number**
96
**Please enter an id number**
97
**Please enter an id number**
98
**Please enter an id number**
99

**Please input an id number to be searched**
67
**67 is not in the array**

*Option 3:* Write a program that will read monthly sales into a dynamically allocated array. The program will input the size of the array from the user. It will call a function that will find the yearly sum (the sum of all the sales). It will also call another function that will find the average.

*Sample Run:*

**Please input the number of monthly sales to be input**
4
**Please input the sales for month 1**
1290.89
**Please input the sales for month 2**
905.95
**Please input the sales for month 3**
1567.98
**Please input the sales for month 4**
994.83
**The total sales for the year is $4759.65**
**The average monthly sale is $1189.91**

# 10 Characters and Strings

**PURPOSE**

1. To demonstrate the unique characteristics of character data
2. To view strings as an array of characters
3. To show how to input and output strings
4. To work with string functions

**PROCEDURE**

1. Students should read the Pre-lab Reading Assignment before coming to the lab.
2. Students should complete the Pre-lab Writing Assignment before coming to lab.
3. In the lab, students should complete labs assigned to them by the instructor.

| Contents | Pre-requisites | Approximate completion time | Page number | Check when done |
|---|---|---|---|---|
| Pre-lab Reading Assignment | | 20 min. | 176 | |
| Pre-lab Writing Assignment | Pre-lab reading | 10 min. | 186 | |
| **LESSON 10A** | | | | |
| Lab 10.1 Character Testing and String Validation | Pre-lab reading | 15 min. | 187 | |
| Lab 10.2 Case Conversion | Basic fundamental instructions | 5 min. | 190 | |
| Lab 10.3 Using `getline()` & `get()` | Basic knowledge of character arrays | 30 min. | 192 | |
| **LESSON 10B** | | | | |
| Lab 10.4 String Functions—`strcat` | Basic knowledge of character arrays | 15 min. | 193 | |
| Lab 10.5 Student Generated Code Assignments | Basic knowledge of character arrays | 35 min. | 193 | |

## PRE-LAB READING ASSIGNMENT

### Character Functions

C++ provides numerous *functions* for character testing. These functions will test a single character and return either a non-zero value (true) or zero (false). For example, `isdigit` tests a character to see if it is one of the digits between 0 and 9. So `isdigit(7)` returns a non-zero value whereas `isdigit(y)` and `isdigit($)` both return 0. We will not list all the character functions here. A complete list may be found in the text. The following program demonstrates some of the others. Note that the `cctype` header file must be included to use the character functions.

*Sample Program 10.1:*

```cpp
// This program utilizes several functions for character testing

#include <iostream>
#include <cctype>
using namespace std;

int main()
{
    char input;

    cout << "Please Enter Any Character:" << endl;
    cin >> input;
    cout << "The character entered is " << input << endl << endl;
    cout << "The ASCII code for " << input << " is " << int(input)
         << endl;

    if (isalpha(input))      // tests to see if character is a letter
    {
      cout << "The character is a letter" << endl;

      if (islower(input))    // tests to see if letter is lower case
            cout << "The letter is lower case" << endl;

      if (isupper(input))    // tests to see if letter is upper case
            cout << "The letter is upper case" << endl;
    }

    else if (isdigit(input)) // tests to see if character is a digit
            cout << "The character you entered is a digit" << endl;

    else
            cout << "The character entered is not a letter nor a digit"
                 << endl;

    return 0;
}
```

In Lab 10.1 you will see a more practical application of character testing functions.

## Character Case Conversion

The C++ library provides the `toupper` and `tolower` functions for converting the case of a character. `toupper` returns the uppercase equivalent for a letter and `tolower` returns the lower case equivalent. For example, `cout << tolower('F');` causes an `f` to be displayed on the screen. If the letter is already lowercase, then `tolower` will return the value unchanged. Likewise, any non-letter argument is returned unchanged by `tolower`. It should be clear to you now what `toupper` does to a given character.

While the `toupper` and `tolower` functions are conceptually quite simple, they may not appear to be very useful. However, the following program shows that they do have beneficial applications.

*Sample Program 10.2:*

```
// This program shows how the toupper and tolower functions can be
// applied in a C++ program

#include <iostream>
#include <cctype>
#include <iomanip>
using namespace std;

int main()
{
    int week, total, dollars;
    float average;
    char choice;

    cout << showpoint << fixed << setprecision(2);

    do
    {
      total = 0;
      for(week = 1; week <= 4; week++)
      {
            cout << "How much (to the nearest dollar) did you"
                 << " spend on food during week " << week
                 << " ?:" << endl;

            cin >> dollars;

            total = total + dollars;
      }
      average = total / 4.0;

      cout << "Your weekly food bill over the chosen month is $"
           << average << endl << endl;
      do
      {
            cout << "Would you like to find the average for "
                 << "another month?";
```

*continues*

```
              cout << endl << "Enter Y or N" << endl;
              cin >> choice;
       } while(toupper(choice) != 'Y' && toupper(choice) != 'N');

    } while (toupper(choice) == 'Y');

    return 0;
}
```

This program prompts the user to input weekly food costs, to the nearest dollar (an integer) for a four-week period. The average weekly total for that month is output. Then the user is asked whether they want to repeat the calculation for a different month. The flow of this program is controlled by a do-while loop. The condition toupper(choice) == 'Y' allows the user to enter 'Y' or 'y' for yes. This makes the program more user friendly than if we just allowed 'Y'. Note the second do-while loop near the end of the program. This loop also utilizes toupper. Can you determine the purpose of this second loop? How would the execution of the program be affected if we removed this loop (but left in the lines between the curly brackets)?

## String Constants

We have already talked about the character data type which includes letters, digits, and other special symbols such as $ and @. Often we need to put characters together to form strings. For example, the price "$1.99" and the phrase "one for the road!" are both strings of characters. The phrase contains blank space characters in addition to letters and an exclamation mark. In C++ a string is treated as a sequence of characters stored in consecutive memory locations. The end of the string in memory is marked by the null character \0. Do not confuse the null character with a sequence of two characters ( i.e., \ and 0 ). The null character is actually an escape sequence. Its ASCII code is 0. For example, the phrase above is stored in computer memory as

| o | n | e | | f | o | r | | t | h | e | | r | o | a | d | ! | \0 |
|---|---|---|---|---|---|---|---|---|---|---|---|---|---|---|---|---|----|

A **string constant** is a string enclosed in double quotation marks. For example,

"Learn C++"
"What time is it?"
"Code Word 7dF#c&Q"

are all string constants. When they are stored in the computer's memory, the null character is automatically appended. The string "Please enter a digit" is stored as

| P | l | e | a | s | e | | e | n | t | e | r | | a | | d | i | g | i | t | \0 |
|---|---|---|---|---|---|---|---|---|---|---|---|---|---|---|---|---|---|---|---|----|

When a string constant is used in C++, it is the memory address that is actually accessed. In the statement

```
cout << "Please enter a digit";
```

the memory address is passed to the cout object. cout then displays the consecutive characters until the null character is reached.

## Storing Strings in Arrays

Often we need to access parts of a string rather than the whole string. For instance, we may want to alter characters in a string or even compare two strings. If this is the case, then a string constant is not what we need. Rather, a character array is the appropriate choice. When using character arrays, enough space to hold the null character must be allocated. For example:

```
char last[10];
```

This code defines a 10-element character array called `last`. However, this array can hold no more than 9 non-null characters since a space is reserved for the null character. Consider the following:

```
char last[10];
cout << "Please enter your last name using no more than 9 letters";
cin >> last;
```

If the user enters `Symon`, then the following will be the contents of the `last` array:

| S | y | m | o | n | \0 |
|---|---|---|---|---|----|

Recall that the computer actually sees `last` as the beginning address of the array. There is a problem that can arise when using the `cin` object on a character array. `cin` does not "know" that `last` has only 10 elements. If the user enters `Newmanouskous` after the prompt, then `cin` will write past the end of the array. We can get around this problem by using the `getline` function. If we use

```
cin.getline(last,10)
```

then the computer knows that the maximum length of the string, including the null character, is 10. Consequently, `cin` will read until the user hits ENTER or until 9 characters have been read, whichever occurs first. Once the string is in the array, it can be processed character by character. In this next section we will see a program that uses `cin.getline()`.

## Library Functions for Strings

The C++ library provides many functions for testing and manipulating strings. For example, to determine the length of a given string one can use the `strlen` function. The syntax is shown in the following code:

```
char line[40] = "A New Day";
int length;
length = strlen(line);
```

Here `strlen(line)` returns the length of the string including white spaces but not the null character at the end. So the value of `length` is 9. Note this is smaller than the size of the actual array holding the string.

To see why we even need a function such as `strlen`, consider the problem of reading in a string and then writing it backwards. If we only allowed strings of a fixed size, say length 29 for example, then the task would be easy. We simply read the string into an array of size 30 or more. Then write the 28th entry followed by the 27th entry and so on, until we reach the 0th entry. However, what if we wish to allow the user to input strings of different lengths? Now it is unclear where the end of the string is. Of course, we could search the array until we find the null character and then figure out what position it is in. But this is precisely what the strlen function does for us. Sample Program 10.3 is a complete program that performs the desired task.

*Sample Program 10.3:*

```
#include <iostream>
#include <cstring>
using namespace std;

int main()
{
    char line[50];
    int length,count = 0;

    cout << "Enter a sentence of no more than 49 characters:\n";
    cin.getline(line,50);

    length = strlen(line);    // strlen returns the length of the
                              // string currently stored in line

    cout << "The sentence entered read backwards is:\n";

    for(count = length-1; count >= 0; count--)
    {
        cout << line[count];

    }

    cout << endl;
    return 0;
}
```

*Sample Run 1:*

**Enter a sentence of no more than 49 characters:**
luaP deiruB I
**The sentence you entered printed backwards is:**
I Buried Paul

*Sample Run 2:*

**Enter a sentence of no more than 49 characters:**
This sentence is too long to hold a mere 49 characters!
**The sentence you entered printed backwards is:**
arahc 94 erem a dloh ot gnol oot si ecnetnes sihT

Another useful function for strings is strcat, which concatenates two strings. strcat(string1,string2) attaches the contents of string2 to the end of string1. The programmer must make sure that the array containing string1 is large enough to hold the concatenation of the two strings plus the null character.

Consider the following code:

```
char string1[25] = "Total Eclipse ";    // note the space after the second
                                         // word - strcat does not insert a
                                         // space. The programmer must do this.

char string2[11] = "of the Sun";

cout << string1 << endl;
cout << string2 << endl;

strcat(string1,string2);

cout << string1 << endl;
```

These statements produce the following output:

**Total Eclipse**
**of the Sun**
**Total Eclipse of the Sun**

What would have happened if we had defined `string1` to be a character array of size 20?

There are several other string functions such as `strcpy` (copies the second string to the first string), `strcmp` (compares two strings to see if they are the same or, if not, which string is alphabetically greater than the other), and `strstr` (looks for the occurrence of a string inside of another string). Note that C-string functions require the `cstring` header file. For more details on these string functions and the others, see the text.

## The get and ignore functions

There are several ways of inputting strings. We could use the standard >> extraction operator for a character array or string class object. However, we know that using `cin` >> skips any leading whitespace (blanks, newlines). It will also stop at the first trailing whitespace character. So, for example, the name "John Wayne" cannot be read as a single string using `cin` >> because of a blank space between the first and last names. We have already seen the `getline` function which does allow blank spaces to be read and stored. In this section we will introduce the `get` and `ignore` functions, which are also useful for string processing.

The `get` function reads in the next character in the input stream, including whitespace. The syntax is

```
cin.get(ch);
```

Once this function call is made, the next character in the input stream is stored in the variable `ch`. So if we want to input

$ X

we can use the following:

```
cin.get(firstChar);
cin.get(ch);
cin.get(secondChar);
```

where `firstChar`, `ch`, and `secondChar` are all character variables. Note that after the second call to the `get` function, the blank character is stored in the variable `ch`.

The `get` function, like the `getline` function, can also be used to read strings. In this case we need two parameters:

```
cin.get(strName, numChar+1);
```

Here `strName` is a string variable and the integer expression `numChar+1` gives the number of characters that may be read into `strName`.

Both the `getline` and the `get` functions do not skip leading whitespace characters. The `get` statement above brings in the next input characters until it either has read `numChar+1` characters or it reaches the newline character `\n`. However, the newline character is not stored in `strName`. The null character is then appended to the end of the string. Since the newline character is not **consumed** (not read by the `get` function), it remains part of the input characters yet to be read.

*Example:*

```
char strName[21];
cin.get(strName,21);
```

Now suppose we input

**John Wayne**

Then "John Wayne" is stored in `strName`. Next input

**My favorite westerns star John Wayne**

In this case the string "My favorite westerns" is stored in `strName`.

We often work with records from a file that contain character data followed by numeric data. Look at the following data which has a name, hours worked, and pay rate for each record stored on a separate line.

*Pay Roll Data*

| | | |
|---|---|---|
| John Brown | 7 | 12.50 |
| Mary Lou Smith | 12 | 15.70 |
| Dominic DeFino | 8 | 15.50 |

Since names often have imbedded blank spaces, we can use the `get` function to read them. We then use an integer variable to store the number of hours and a floating point variable to store the pay rate. At the end of each line is the '\n' character. Note that the end of line character is not consumed by reading the pay rate and, in fact, is the next character to be read when reading the second name from the file. This creates problems. Whenever we need to read through characters in the input stream without storing them, we can use the `ignore` function. This function has two arguments, the first is an integer expression and the second is a character expression. For example, the call

```
cin.ignore(80,'\n');
```

says to skip over the next 80 input characters but stop if a newline character is read. The newline character is consumed by the `ignore` function. This use of `ignore` is often employed to find the end of the current input line.

The following program will read the sample pay roll data from a file called payRoll.dat and show the result to the screen. Note that the input file must have names that are no longer than 15 characters and the first 15 positions of each line are reserved for the name. The numeric data must be after the 15th position in each line.

*Sample Program 10.4:*

```cpp
#include <fstream>
#include <iostream>
using namespace std;

const int MAXNAME = 15;

int main()
{
    ifstream inData;

    inData.open("payRoll.dat");
    char name[MAXNAME+1];
    int hoursWorked;
    float payRate;

    inData.get(name,MAXNAME+1);   // prime the read
    while (inData)
    {
      inData >> hoursWorked;
      inData >> payRate;

      cout << name << endl;
      cout << "Hours Worked " << hoursWorked << endl;
      cout << "Pay Rate " << payRate << " per hour"
           << endl << endl;

      inData.ignore(80,'\n');
        // This will ignore up to 80 characters but will
        // stop (ignoring) when it reads the \n which is
        // consumed.

      inData.get(name,MAXNAME+1);

    }

    return 0;
}
```

*Summary of types of input for strings:*

```
cin >> strName;            // skips leading whitespace. Stops at the first
                           // trailing whitespace (which is not consumed)

cin.get(strName, 21);      // does not skip leading whitespace
                           // stops when either 20 characters are read or
                           // '\n' is encountered (which is not consumed)

cin.ignore(200,'\n');      // ignores at most 200 characters but stops if
                           // newline (which is consumed) is encountered
```

## Pointers and Strings

Pointers can be very useful for writing string processing functions. If one needs to process a certain string, the beginning address can be passed with a pointer variable. The length of the string does not even need to be known since the computer will start processing using the address and continue through the string until the null character is encountered.

Sample Program 10.5 below reads in a string of no more than 50 characters and then counts the number of letters, digits, and whitespace characters in the string. Notice the use of the pointer strPtr, which points to the string being processed. The three functions countLetters, countDigits, and countWhiteSpace all perform basically the same task—the while loop is executed until strPtr points to the null character marking the end of the string. In the countLetters function, characters are tested to see if they are letters. The if(isalpha(*strPtr)) statement determines if the character pointed at by strPtr is a letter. If so, then the counter occurs is incremented by one. After the character has been tested, strPtr is incremented by one to test the next character. The other two functions are analogous.

*Sample Program 10.5:*

```cpp
#include <iostream>
#include <cctype>

using namespace std;

//function prototypes
int countLetters(char*);
int countDigits(char*);
int countWhiteSpace(char*);

int main()
{
    int numLetters, numDigits, numWhiteSpace;
    char inputString[51];


    cout <<"Enter a string of no more than 50 characters: "
         << endl << endl;
```

```
        cin.getline(inputString,51);

        numLetters = countLetters(inputString);
        numDigits = countDigits(inputString);
        numWhiteSpace = countWhiteSpace(inputString);

        cout << "The number of letters in the entered string is "
             << numLetters << endl;
        cout << "The number of digits in the entered string is "
             << numDigits << endl;
        cout << "The number of white spaces in the entered string is "
             << numWhiteSpace << endl;

        return 0;
}
//*****************************************************************
//                    countLetters
//
// task:             This function counts the number of letters
//                   (both capital and lower case) in the string
// data in:          pointer that points to an array of characters
// data returned:    number of letters in the array of characters
//
//*****************************************************************

int countLetters(char *strPtr)
{
        int occurs = 0;
        while(*strPtr != '\0')        // loop is executed as long as
                                      // the pointer strPtr does not point
                                      // to the null character which
                                      // marks the end of the string

        {
            if (isalpha(*strPtr))     // isalpha determines if
                                      // the character is a letter
                  occurs++;
            strPtr++;
        }
        return occurs;
}
//*****************************************************************
//                    countDigits
//
// task:             This function counts the number of digits
//                   in the string
// data in:          pointer that points to an array of characters
// data returned:    number of digits in the array of characters
//
//*****************************************************************
```

*continues*

```
int countDigits(char *strPtr)
{
    int occurs = 0;
    while(*strPtr != '\0')
    {
        if (isdigit(*strPtr))    // isdigit determines if
                                 // the character is a digit.
            occurs++;
        strPtr++;
    }
    return occurs;
}


//********************************************************************
//                  countWhiteSpace
//
// task:            This function counts the number of whitespace
//                  characters in the string
// data in:         pointer that points to an array of characters
// data returned:   number of whitespaces in the array of
//                  characters
//
//********************************************************************

int countWhiteSpace(char *strPtr)    // this function counts the
                                     // number of whitespace characters.
                                     // These include, space, newline,
                                     // vertical tab, and tab
{
    int occurs = 0;
    while(*strPtr != '\0')
    {
        if (isspace(*strPtr))        // isspace determines if
                                     // the character is a
                                     // whitespace character
            occurs++;
        strPtr++;
    }
    return occurs;
}
```

## PRE-LAB WRITING ASSIGNMENT

### Fill-in-the-Blank Questions

1. The code `cout << toupper('b');` causes a _____ to be displayed on the screen.

2. The data type returned by `isalpha('g')` is _____.

3. After the assignment statement `result = isdigit('$')`, `result` has the value _____.

4. The code `cout << tolower('#');` causes a _____ to be displayed on the screen.

5. The end of a string is marked in computer memory by the _____.

6. In `cin.getline(name,25)`, the 25 indicates that the user can input at most _____ characters into `name`.

7. Consider the following:

```
char message[35] = "Like tears in the rain";
int length;
length = strlen(message);
```

Then the value of `length` is _____.

8. Consider the code

```
char string1[30] = "In the Garden";
char string2[15] = "of Eden";
strcat(string1,string2);
cout << string1;
```

The output for this is _____.

9. The _____ header file must be included to access the `islower` and `isspace` character functions.

10. In C++, a string constant must be enclosed in _____ whereas a character constant must be enclosed in _____.

## LESSON 10

### LAB 10.1 Character Testing and String Validation

The American Equities investment company offers a wide range of investment opportunities ranging from mutual funds to bonds. Investors can check the value of their portfolio from the American Equities' web page. Information about personal portfolios is protected via encryption and can only be accessed using a password. The American Equities company requires that a password consist of 8 characters, 5 of which must be letters and the other 3 digits. The letters and digits can be arranged in any order. For example,

> **rt56AA7q**
> **123actyN**
> **1Lo0Dwa9**
> **myNUM741**

are all valid passwords. However, the following are all invalid:

> **the476NEw**   // It contains more than 8 characters (also more than 5
>                 // letters)
>
> **be68moon**    // It contains less than 3 digits.
>
> **$retrn99**    // It contains only 2 digits and has an invalid character ('$')

American Equities needs a program for their web page that determines whether or not an entered password is valid. The program american_equities.cpp from the Lab 10 folder performs this task. The code is the following:

```cpp
// This program tests a password for the American Equities
// web page to see if the format is correct

// Place Your Name Here

#include <iostream>
#include <cctype>
#include <cstring>

using namespace std;

//function prototypes

bool testPassWord(char[]);
int countLetters(char*);
int countDigits(char*);

int main()
{
    char passWord[20];

    cout << "Enter a password consisting of exactly 5 "
        << "letters and 3 digits:" << endl;
    cin.getline(passWord,20);

    if (testPassWord(passWord))
        cout << "Please wait - your password is being verified" << endl;
    else
    {
        cout << "Invalid password. Please enter a password "
            << "with exactly 5 letters and 3 digits" << endl;
        cout << "For example, my37RuN9 is valid" << endl;
    }

    // Fill in the code that will call countLetters and
    // countDigits and will print to the screen both the number of
    // letters and digits contained in the password.

    return 0;
}
```

```
//*************************************************************
//                    testPassWord
//
// task:              determines if the word in the
//                    character array passed to it, contains
//                    exactly 5 letters and 3 digits.
// data in:           a word contained in a character array
// data returned:     true if the word contains 5 letters & 3
//                    digits, false otherwise
//
//*************************************************************
bool testPassWord(char custPass[])
{
    int numLetters, numDigits, length;

    length = strlen(custPass);
    numLetters = countLetters(custPass);
    numDigits = countDigits(custPass);
    if (numLetters == 5 && numDigits == 3 && length == 8 )
        return true;
    else
        return false;
}


// the next 2 functions are from Sample Program 10.5
//*************************************************************
//                     countLetters
//
// task:              counts the number of letters (both
//                    capital and lower case)in the string
// data in:           a string
// data returned:     the number of letters in the string
//
//*************************************************************
int countLetters(char *strPtr)
{
    int occurs = 0;

    while(*strPtr != '\0')

    {
        if (isalpha(*strPtr))
            occurs++;
        strPtr++;
    }

    return occurs;
}
```

*continues*

```
//***************************************************************
//                         countDigits
//
// task:               counts the number of digits in the string
// data in:            a string
// data returned:      the number of digits in the string
//
//***************************************************************
int countDigits(char *strPtr)
{
    int occurs = 0;

    while(*strPtr != '\0')
    {
        if (isdigit(*strPtr))    // isdigit determines if
                                 // the character is a digit
            occurs++;
        strPtr++;
    }

    return occurs;
}
```

*Exercise 1:* Fill in the code in bold and then run the program several times with both valid and invalid passwords. Read through the program and make sure you understand the logic of the code.

*Exercise 2:* Alter the program so that a valid password consists of 10 characters, 6 of which must be digits and the other 4 letters.

*Exercise 3:* Adjust your program from Exercise 2 so that only lower case letters are allowed for valid passwords.

## LAB 10.2  Case Conversion

Bring in `case_convert.cpp` from the Lab 10 folder. Note that this is Sample Program 10.2. The code is the following:

```
// This program shows how the toupper and tolower functions can be
// applied in a C++ program

// PLACE YOUR NAME HERE

#include <iostream>
#include <cctype>
#include <iomanip>
using namespace std;

int main()
{
    int week, total, dollars;
    float average;
    char choice;
```

```
        cout << showpoint << fixed << setprecision(2);

        do
        {
            total = 0;
            for(week = 1; week <= 4; week++)
            {
                cout << "How much (to the nearest dollar) did you"
                     << " spend on food during week " << week
                     << " ?:" << endl;
                cin  >> dollars;

                total = total + dollars;
            }
            average = total / 4.0;

            cout << "Your weekly food bill over the chosen month is $"
                 << average << endl << endl;
            do
            {
                cout << "Would you like to find the average for "
                     << "another month?";
                cout << endl << "Enter Y or N" << endl;
                cin >> choice;
            } while(toupper(choice) != 'Y' && toupper(choice) != 'N');

        } while (toupper(choice) == 'Y');


        return 0;
}
```

---

*Exercise 1:* Run the program several times with various inputs.

*Exercise 2:* Notice the following do-while loop which appears near the end of the program:

```
do
{
    cout << "Would you like to find the average for another month?";
    cout << endl << "Enter Y or N" << endl;
    cin >> choice;
} while(toupper(choice) != 'Y' && toupper(choice) != 'N');
```

How would the execution of the program be different if we removed this loop? Try removing the loop but leave the following lines in the program:

```
cout << "Would you like to find the average for another month?";
cout << endl << "Enter Y or N" << endl;
cin >> choice;
```

Record what happens when you run the new version of the program.

*Exercise 3:* Alter program case_convert.cpp so that it performs the same task but uses tolower rather than toupper.

## LAB 10.3 Using `getline()` & `get()`

*Exercise 1:* Write a short program called `readata.cpp` that defines a character array `last` which contains 10 characters. Prompt the user to enter their last name using no more than 9 characters. The program should then read the name into `last` and then output the name back to the screen with an appropriate message. Do not use the `getline()` or `get` functions!

*Exercise 2:* Once the program in Exercise 1 is complete, run the program and enter the name **Newmanouskous** at the prompt. What, if anything, happens? (Note that the results could vary depending on your system).

*Exercise 3:* Re-write the program above using the `getline()` function (and only allowing 9 characters to be input). As before, use the character array `last` consisting of 10 elements. Run your new program and enter **Newmanouskous** at the prompt. What is the output?

*Exercise 4:* Bring in program `grades.cpp` and `grades.txt` from the Lab 10 folder. Fill in the code in bold so that the data is properly read from `grades.txt`. and the desired output to the screen is as follows:

| OUTPUT TO SCREEN | | DATA FILE | |
|---|---|---|---|
| **Adara Starr** | **has a(n) 94 average** | **Adara Starr** | **94** |
| **David Starr** | **has a(n) 91 average** | **David Starr** | **91** |
| **Sophia Starr** | **has a(n) 94 average** | **Sophia Starr** | **94** |
| **Maria Starr** | **has a(n) 91 average** | **Maria Starr** | **91** |
| **Danielle DeFino** | **has a(n) 94 average** | **Danielle DeFino** | **94** |
| **Dominic DeFino** | **has a(n) 98 average** | **Dominic DeFino** | **98** |
| **McKenna DeFino** | **has a(n) 92 average** | **McKenna DeFino** | **92** |
| **Taylor McIntire** | **has a(n) 99 average** | **Taylor McIntire** | **99** |
| **Torrie McIntire** | **has a(n) 91 average** | **Torrie McIntire** | **91** |
| **Emily Garrett** | **has a(n) 97 average** | **Emily Garrett** | **97** |
| **Lauren Garrett** | **has a(n) 92 average** | **Lauren Garrett** | **92** |
| **Marlene Starr** | **has a(n) 83 average** | **Marlene Starr** | **83** |
| **Donald DeFino** | **has a(n) 73 average** | **Donald DeFino** | **73** |

The code of `grades.cpp` is as follows:

```cpp
#include <fstream>
#include <iostream>
using namespace std;

// PLACE YOUR NAME HERE

const int MAXNAME = 20;

int main()
{
    ifstream inData;
    inData.open("grades.txt");

    char name[MAXNAME + 1];  // holds student name
    float average;           // holds student average
```

```
inData.get(name,MAXNAME+1);
while (inData)
{
    inData >> average;
    // Fill in the code to print out name and
    // student average

    // Fill in the code to complete the while
    // loop so that the rest of the student
    // names and average are read in properly
}

return 0;
}
```

## LAB 10.4    String Functions—`strcat`

Consider the following code:

```
char string1[25] ="Total Eclipse ";
char string2[11] = "of the Sun";
cout << string1 << endl;
cout << string2 << endl;
strcat(string1,string2);
cout << string1 << endl;
```

*Exercise 1:* Write a complete program including the above code that outputs the concatenation of `string1` and `string2`. Run the program and record the result.

*Exercise 2:* Alter the program in Exercise 1 so that `string1` contains 20 characters rather than 25. Run the program. What happens?

## LAB 10.5    Student Generated Code Assignments

*Exercise 1:* A **palindrome** is a string of characters that reads the same forwards as backwards. For example, the following are both palindromes:

1457887541        madam

Write a program that prompts the user to input a string of a size 50 characters or less. Your program should then determine whether or not the entered string is a palindrome. A message should be displayed to the user informing them whether or not their string is a palindrome.

*Exercise 2:* The `strcmp(string1,string2)` function compares `string1` to `string2`. It is a value returning function that returns a negative integer if `string1 < string2`, 0 if `string1 == string2`, and a positive integer if `string1 > string2`. Write a program that reads two names (last name first followed by a comma followed by the first name) and then prints them in alphabetical order. The two names should be stored in separate character arrays holding a maximum of 25 characters each. Use the `strcmp()` function to make the comparison of the two names. Remember that `'a' < 'b'`, `'b' < 'c'`, etc. Be sure to include the proper header file to use `strcmp()`.

*Sample Run 1:*

**Please input the first name**

Brown, George

**Please input the second name**

Adams, Sally

**The names are as follows:**
**Adams, Sally**
**Brown, George**

*Sample Run 2:*

**Please input the first name**

Brown, George

**Please input the second name**

Brown, George

**The names are as follows:**
**Brown, George**
**Brown, George**
**The names are the same**

*Exercise 3:* (Optional) Write a program that determines how many consonants are in an entered string of 50 characters or less. Output the entered string and the number of consonants in the string.

# 11 Structures and Abstract Data Types

**PURPOSE**

1. To introduce the concept of an abstract data type
2. To introduce the concept of a structure
3. To develop and manipulate an array of structures
4. To use structures as parameters
5. To use hierarchical (nested) structures

**PROCEDURE**

1. Students should read the Pre-lab Reading Assignment before coming to lab.
2. Students should complete the Pre-lab Writing Assignment before coming to lab.
3. In the lab, students should complete labs assigned to them by the instructor.

| Contents | Pre-requisites | Approximate completion time | Page number | Check when done |
|---|---|---|---|---|
| Pre-lab Reading Assignment | | 20 min. | 196 | |
| Pre-lab Writing Assignment | Pre-lab reading | 10 min. | 205 | |
| **LESSON 11 A** | | | | |
| Lab 11.1 Working with Basic Structures | Knowledge of previous chapters | 15 min. | 205 | |
| Lab 11.2 Initializing Structures | Basic understanding of structures | 15 min. | 206 | |
| Lab 11.3 Arrays of Structures | Basic understanding of arrays and structures | 20 min. | 208 | |
| **LESSON 11 B** | | | | |
| Lab 11.4 Nested Structures | Basic understanding of functions and nested logic | 20 min. | 209 | |
| Lab 11.5 Student Generated Code Assignments | Completion of all the previous labs | 30 min. | 211 | |

# PRE-LAB READING ASSIGNMENT

So far we have learned of data types such as `float`, `int`, `char`, etc. In some applications the programmer needs to create their own data type. A user defined data type is often an **abstract data type (ADT)**. The programmer must decide which values are valid for the data type and which operations may be performed on the data type. It may even be necessary for the programmer to design new operations to be applied to the data. We will study this style of programming extensively when we introduce *object-oriented programming* in the lesson set from Chapter 13.

As an example, suppose you want to create a program to simulate a calendar. The program may contain the following ADTs: `year`, `month`, and `day`. Note that `month` could take on values January, February, . . . , December or even 1,2, . . . ,12 depending on the wishes of the programmer. Likewise, the range of values for `day` could be Monday, Tuesday, . . . , Sunday or even 1,2, . . . ,7. There is much more flexibility in the choice of allowable values for `year`. If the programmer is thinking short term they may wish to restrict `year` to the range 1990–2010. Of course there are many other possibilities.

In this lab we study the **structure**. Like arrays, structures allow the programmer to group data together. However, unlike an array, structures allow you to group together items of *different* data types. To see how this could be useful in practice, consider what a student must do to register for a college course. Typically, one obtains the current list of available courses and then selects the desired course or courses. The following is an example of a course you may choose:

```
CHEM 310          Physical Chemistry          4 Credits
```

Note that there are four items related to this course: the course discipline (CHEM), the course number (310), the course title (Physical Chemistry), and the number of credit hours (4). We could define variables as follows:

| Variable Definition | Information Held |
|---|---|
| char discipline[5] | 4-letter abbreviation for discipline |
| int courseNumber | Integer valued course number |
| char courseTitle[21] | First 20 characters of course title |
| short credits | Number of credit hours |

All of these variables are related because they can hold information about the same course. We can package these together by creating a structure. Here is the declaration:

```
struct course
{
    char   discipline[5];
    int    courseNumber;
    char   courseTitle[21];
    short  credits;
};   //note the semi-colon here
```

The **tag** is the name of the structure, `course` in this case. The tag is used like a data type name. Inside the braces we have the variable declarations that are the **members** of the structure. So the code above declares a structure named `course` which has four members: `discipline`, `courseNumber`, `courseTitle`, and `credits`.

The programmer needs to realize that the structure declaration does not define a variable. Rather it lets the compiler know what a `course` structure is composed of. That is, the declaration creates a new data type called `course`. We can now define variables of type `course` as follows:

```
course pChem;
course colonialHist;
```

Both `pChem` and `colonialHist` will contain the four members previously listed. We could have also defined these two structure variables on a single line:

```
course pChem, colonialHist;
```

Both `pChem` and `colonialHist` are called **instances** of the `course` structure. In other words, they are both user defined variables that exist in computer memory. Each structure variable contains the four structure members.

## Access to Structure Members

Certainly the programmer will need to assign the members values and also keep track of what values the members have. C++ allows you to access structure members using the **dot operator**. Consider the following syntax:

```
colonialHist.credits = 3;
```

In this statement the integer 3 is assigned to the `credits` member of `colonialHist`. The dot operator is used to connect the member name to the structure variable it belongs to.

Now let us put all of these ideas together into a program. Sample Program 11.1 below uses the `course` structure just described. This interactive program allows a student to add requested courses and keeps track of the number of credit hours for which they have enrolled. The execution is controlled by a `do-while` loop.

*Sample Program 11.1:*

```
#include <iostream>
#include <cctype>
using namespace std;

// This program demonstrates the use of structures

const int MAXDISCIPLINE = 4;
const int MAXCOURSE = 20;

// structure declaration

struct course
{
        char discipline[MAXDISCIPLINE + 1];
        int courseNumber;
        char courseTitle[MAXCOURSE + 1];
        short credits;
};
```

*continues*

```
int main()
{
        course nextClass;  // next class is a course structure
        int numCredits = 0;
        char addClass;
        do
        {
            cout << "Please enter course discipline area:  ";
            cin >> nextClass.discipline;
            cout << endl << "Pleae enter the course number: ";
            cin >> nextClass.courseNumber;
            cout << endl << "Please enter the course title: ";
            cin.ignore();  // necessary for the next line
            cin.getline(nextClass.courseTitle,MAXCOURSE + 1);
            // we add an extra space to read the end of line character
            // use getline because course title may have a blank space
            cout << "Please enter the number of credit hours: ";
            cin >> nextClass.credits;

            numCredits = numCredits + nextClass.credits;

            // output the selected course and pertinent information

            cout << "You have been registered for the following: " << endl;
            cout << nextClass.discipline << "      " << nextClass.courseNumber
                << "      " << nextClass.courseTitle
                << "      " << nextClass.credits << "credits" << endl;

            cout << "Would you like to add another class? (Y/N)" << endl;
            cin >> addClass;

        } while(toupper(addClass) == 'Y');

        cout << "The total number of credit hours registerd for is: "
            << numCredits << endl;

        return 0;
}
```

---

Make sure that you understand the logic of this program and, in particular, how structures are used. Notice the line at the end of the while loop that reads

```
while(toupper(addclass) == 'Y');
```

What do you think the purpose of toupper is?

As a second example, suppose we would like a simple program that computes the area and circumference of two circles input by the user. Although we can easily do this using previously developed techniques, let us see how this can be done using structures. We will also determine which circle's center is further from the origin.

*Sample Program 11.2:*

```cpp
#include <iostream>
#include <cmath>      // necessary for pow function
#include <iomanip>
using namespace std;


struct circle         // declares the structure circle
{                     // This structure has 6 members
     float centerX; // x coordinate of center
     float centerY; // y coordinate of center
     float radius;
     float area;
     float circumference;
     float distance_from_origin;
};

const float PI = 3.14159;

int main()
{
          circle circ1, circ2; // defines 2 circle structure variables

          cout << "Please enter the radius of the first circle: ";
          cin >> circ1.radius;
          cout << endl
              << "Please enter the x-coordinate of the center: ";
          cin >> circ1.centerX;
          cout << endl
              << "Please enter the y-coordinate of the center: ";
          cin >> circ1.centerY;

          circ1.area = PI * pow(circ1.radius, 2.0);
          circ1.circumference = 2 * PI * circ1.radius;
          circ1.distance_from_origin = sqrt(pow(circ1.centerX,2.0)
             + pow(circ1.centerY,2.0));
          cout << endl << endl;

          cout << "Please enter the radius of the second circle: ";
          cin >> circ2.radius;
          cout << endl
              << "Please enter the x-coordinate of the center: ";
          cin >> circ2.centerX;
          cout << endl
              << "Please enter the y-coordinate of the center: ";
          cin >> circ2.centerY;

          circ2.area = PI * pow(circ2.radius, 2.0);
          circ2.circumference = 2 * PI * circ2.radius;
          circ2.distance_from_origin = sqrt(pow(circ2.centerX,2.0)
             + pow(circ2.centerY,2.0));
```

*continues*

```
            cout << endl << endl;

            // This next section determines which circle's center is
            // closer to the origin

            if (circ1.distance_from_origin > circ2.distance_from_origin)
            {
                cout << "The first circle is further from the origin"
                    << endl << endl;
            }
            else if (circ1.distance_from_origin < circ2.distance_from_origin)
            {
                cout << "The first circle is closer to the origin"
                    << endl << endl;
            }
            else
                cout << "The two circles are equidistant from the origin";
            cout << endl << endl;

            cout << setprecision(2) << fixed << showpoint;

            cout << "The area of the first circle is : ";
            cout << circ1.area << endl;
            cout << "The circumference of the first circle is: ";
            cout << circ1.circumference << endl << endl;

            cout << "The area of the second circle is : ";
            cout << circ2.area << endl;
            cout << "The circumference of the second circle is: ";
            cout << circ2.circumference << endl << endl;

            return 0;
}
```

## Arrays of Structures

In the previous sample program we were interested in two instances of the circle structure. What if we need a much larger number, say 100, instances of this structure? Rather than define each one separately, we can use an **array of structures**. An array of structures is defined just like any other array. For example suppose we already have the following structure declaration in our program:

```
struct circle
{
    float centerX;    // x coordinate of center
    float centerY;    // y coordinate of center
    float radius;
    float area;
    float circumference;
    float distance_from_origin;   // distance of center from origin
};
```

Then the following statement defines an array, `circn`, which has 100 elements. Each of these elements is a `circle` structure variable:

```
circle circn[100];
```

Like the arrays encountered in previous lessons, you can access an array element using its subscript. So `circn[0]` is the first structure in the array, `circn[1]` is the second, and so on. The last structure in the array is `circn[99]`. To access a member of one of these array elements, we still use the dot operator. For instance, `circn[9].circumference` gives the `circumference` member of `circn[9]`. If we want to display the center and distance from the origin of the first 30 circles we can use the following:

```
for (int count = 0; count < 30; count++)
{
    cout << circn[count].centerX << endl;
    cout << circn[count].centerY << endl;
    cout << circn[count].distance_from_origin;
}
```

When studying arrays you may have seen two-dimensional arrays which allow one to have "a collection of collections" of data. An array of structures allows one to do the same thing. However, we have already noted that structures permit you to group together items of different data type, whereas arrays do not. So an array of structures can sometimes be used when a two-dimensional array cannot.

## Initializing Structures

We have already seen numerous examples of initializing variables and arrays at the time of their definition in the previous labs. Members of structures can also be initialized when they are defined. Suppose we have the following structure declaration in our program:

```
struct course
{
    char discipline[5];
    int courseNumber;
    char courseTitle[21];
    short credits;
};
```

A structure variable `colonialHist` can be defined and initialized:

```
course colonialHist = {"HIST",302,"Colonial History",3};
```

The values in this list are assigned to `course`'s members in the order they appear. Thus, the string `"HIST"` is assigned to `colonialHist.discipline`, the integer 302 is assigned to `colonialHist.courseNumber`, the string `"Colonial History"` is assigned to `colonialHist.courseTitle`, and the short value 3 is assigned to `colonialHist.credits`. It is not necessary to initialize all the members of a structure variable. For example, we could initialize just the first member:

```
course colonialHist = {"HIST"};
```

This statement leaves the last three members uninitialized. We could also initialize only the first two members:

```
course colonialHist = {"HIST",302};
```

There is one important rule, however, when initializing structure members. If one structure member is left uninitialized, then all structure members that follow it must be uninitialized. In other words, we cannot skip members of a structure during the initialization process.

It is also worth pointing out that you cannot initialize a structure member in the declaration of the structure. The following is an illegal declaration:

```
// illegal structure declaration
struct course
{
        char discipline[5] = "HIST";                  // illegal
        int courseNumber = 302;                       // illegal
        char courseTitle[20] = "Colonial History";    // illegal
        short credits = 3;                            // illegal
};
```

If we recall what a structure declaration does, it is clear why the above code is illegal. A structure declaration simply lets the compiler know what a structure is composed of. That is, the declaration creates a new data type (called course in this case). So the structure declaration does not define any variables. Hence there is nothing that can be initialized there.

## Hierarchical (Nested) Structures

Often it is useful to nest one structure inside of another structure. Consider the following:

*Sample Program 11.3:*

```
#include <iostream>
#include <iomanip>
#include <cmath>
using namespace std;

struct center_struct
{
        float x;       // x coordinate of center
        float y;       // y coordinate of center
};

struct circle
{
        float radius;
        float area;
        float circumference;
        center_struct coordinate;
};

const float PI = 3.14159;

int main()
{
        circle circ1, circ2; // defines 2 circle structure variables
```

```
cout << "Please enter the radius of the first circle: ";
cin >> circ1.radius;
cout << endl
     << "Please enter the x-coordinate of the center: ";
cin >> circ1.coordinate.x;
cout << endl
     << "Please enter the y-coordinate of the center: ";
cin >> circ1.coordinate.y;

circ1.area = PI * pow(circ1.radius, 2.0);
circ1.circumference = 2 * PI * circ1.radius;

cout << endl << endl;

cout << "Please enter the radius of the second circle: ";
cin >> circ2.radius;
cout << endl
     << "Please enter the x-coordinate of the center: ";
cin >> circ2.coordinate.x;
cout << endl
     << "Please enter the y-coordinate of the center: ";
cin >> circ2.coordinate.y;

circ2.area = PI * pow(circ2.radius, 2.0);
circ2.circumference = 2 * PI * circ2.radius;

cout << endl << endl;

cout << setprecision(2) << fixed << showpoint;

cout << "The area of the first circle is : ";
cout << circ1.area << endl;
cout << "The circumference of the first circle is: ";
cout << circ1.circumference << endl;
cout << "Circle 1 is centered at (" << circ1.coordinate.x
     << "," << circ1.coordinate.y << ")." << endl << endl;

cout << "The area of the second circle is : ";
cout << circ2.area << endl;
cout << "The circumference of the second circle is: ";
cout << circ2.circumference << endl ;
cout << "Circle 2 is centered at (" << circ2.coordinate.x
     << "," << circ2.coordinate.y << ")." << endl << endl;

    return 0;
}
```

Note that the programs in this lesson so far have not been modularized. Everything is done within the main function. In practice, this is not good structured programming. It can lead to unreadable and overly repetitious code. To solve this problem, we need to be able to pass structures and structure members to functions. In this next section, you will see how to do this.

## Structures and Functions

Just as we can use other variables as function arguments, structure members may be used as function arguments. Consider the following structure declaration:

```
struct circle
{
        float centerX;          // x coordinate of center
        float centerY;          // y coordinate of center
        float radius;
        float area;
};
```

Suppose we also have the following function definition in the same program:

```
float computeArea(float r)
{
        return PI * r * r;   // PI must previously be defined as a
                             // constant float
}
```

Let `firstCircle` be a variable of the `circle` structure type. The following function call passes `firstCircle.radius` into `r`. The return value is stored in `firstCircle.area`:

```
firstCircle.area = computeArea(firstCircle.radius);
```

It is also possible to pass an entire structure variable into a function rather than an individual member.

```
struct course
{
        char discipline[5];
        int courseNumber;
        char courseTitle[21];
        short credits;
};


course pChem;
```

Suppose the following function definition uses a `course` structure variable as its parameter:

```
void displayInfo(course c)
{
        cout << c.discipline << endl;
        cout << c.courseNumber << endl;
        cout << c.courseTitle << endl;
        cout << c.credits << endl;
}
```

Then the following call passes the `pChem` variable into `c`:

```
displayInfo(pChem);
```

There are many other topics relating to functions and structures such as returning a structure from a function and pointers to structures. Although we do not have time to develop these concepts in this lab, the text does contain detailed coverage of these topics for the interested programmer.

# PRE-LAB WRITING ASSIGNMENT

## Fill-in-the-Blank Questions

1. The name of a structure is called the _____.
2. An advantage of structures over arrays is that structures allow one to use items of _____ data types, whereas arrays do not.
3. One structure inside of another structure is an example of a _____.
4. The variables declared inside the structure declaration are called the _____ of the structure.
5. When initializing structure members, if one structure member is left uninitialized, then all the structure members that follow must be _____.
6. A user defined data type is often an _____.
7. Once an array of structures has been defined, you can access an array element using its _____.
8. The _____ allows the programmer to access structure members.
9. You may not initialize a structure member in the _____.
10. Like variables, structure members may be used as _____ arguments.

# LESSON 11 A

## LAB 11.1    Working with Basic Structures

Bring in program `rect_struct.cpp` from the Lab 11 folder. The code is shown below.

```cpp
#include <iostream>
#include <iomanip>
using namespace std;


// This program uses a structure to hold data about a rectangle
// PLACE YOUR NAME HERE

// Fill in code to declare a structure named rectangle which has
// members length, width, area, and perimeter all of which are floats

int main()
{
    // Fill in code to define a rectangle variable named box

    cout << "Enter the length of a rectangle: ";

    // Fill in code to read in the length member of box

    cout << "Enter the width of a rectangle: ";
```

*continues*

```
        // Fill in code to read in the width member of box

        cout << endl << endl;

        // Fill in code to compute the area member of box
        // Fill in code to compute the perimeter member of box

        cout << fixed << showpoint << setprecision(2);

        // Fill in code to output the area with an appropriate message
        // Fill in code to output the perimeter with an appropriate message

        return 0;
}
```

*Exercise 1:* Fill in the code as indicated by the comments in bold.

*Exercise 2:* Add code to the program above so that the modified program will determine whether or not the rectangle entered by the user is a square.

*Sample Run:*

Enter the length of a rectangle: 7
Enter the width of a rectangle: 7
The area of the rectangle is 49.00
The perimeter of the rectangle is 28.00
The rectangle is a square.

## LAB 11.2   Initializing Structures

Bring in program `init_struct.cpp` from the Lab 11 folder. The code is shown below.

```cpp
#include <iostream>
#include <iomanip>
using namespace std;


// This program demonstrates partially initialized structure variables

// PLACE YOUR NAME HERE

struct taxPayer
{
    char name[25];
    long  socialSecNum;
    float taxRate;
    float income;
    float taxes;
};


int main()
{
```

```
// Fill in code to initialize a structure variable named citizen1 so that
// the first three members are initialized.  Assume the name is Tim
// McGuiness, the social security number is 255871234, and the tax rate is .35

// Fill in code to initialize a structure variable named citizen2 so that
// the first three members are initialized.  Assume the name is John Kane,
// the social security number is 278990582, and the tax rate is .29

cout << fixed << showpoint << setprecision(2);

// calculate taxes due for citizen1

// Fill in code to prompt the user to enter this year's income for the citizen1
// Fill in code to read in this income to the appropriate structure member

// Fill in code to determine this year's taxes for citizen1

cout << "Name: " << citizen1.name << endl;
cout << "Social Security Number: " << citizen1.socialSecNum << endl;

cout << "Taxes due for this year: $" << citizen1.taxes << endl << endl;

// calculate taxes due for citizen2

// Fill in code to prompt the user to enter this year's income for citizen2
// Fill in code to read in this income to the appropriate structure member

// Fill in code to determine this year's taxes for citizen2

cout << "Name: " << citizen2.name << endl;
cout << "Social Security Number: " << citizen2.socialSecNum << endl;

cout << "Taxes due for this year: $" << citizen2.taxes << endl << endl;

    return 0;
}
```

*Exercise 1:* Fill in the code as indicated by the comments in bold.

*Sample Run:*

**Please input the yearly income for Tim McGuiness: 30000**
**Name: Tim McGuiness**
**Social Security Number: 255871234**
**Taxes due for this year: $10500.00**

**Please input the yearly income for John Kane: 60000**
**Name: John Kane**
**Social Security Number: 278990582**
**Taxes due for this year: $17400.00**

## LAB 11.3  Arrays of Structures

Bring in program `array_struct.cpp` from the Lab 11 folder. The code is shown below.

```cpp
#include <iostream>
#include <iomanip>

using namespace std;


// This program demonstrates how to use an array of structures
// PLACE YOUR NAME HERE

// Fill in code to declare a structure called taxPayer that has three
// members:  taxRate, income, and taxes — each of type float


int main()
{
    // Fill in code to define an array named citizen which holds
    // 5 taxPayers structures

    cout << fixed << showpoint << setprecision(2);

    cout << "Please enter the annual income and tax rate for 5 tax payers: ";
    cout << endl << endl << endl;

    for(int count = 0;count < 5;count++)
    {

        cout << "Enter this year's income for tax payer " << (count + 1);
        cout << ": ";

        // Fill in code to read in the income to the appropriate place

        cout << "Enter the tax rate for tax payer # " << (count + 1);
        cout << ": ";

        // Fill in code to read in the tax rate to the appropriate place

        // Fill in code to compute the taxes for the citizen and store it
        // in the appropriate place


        cout << endl;
    }
```

```
cout << "Taxes due for this year: " << endl << endl;


// Fill in code for the first line of a loop that will output the
// tax information
{
        cout << "Tax Payer # " << (index + 1) << ": " << "$ "
             << citizen[index].taxes << endl;
}


    return 0;
}
```

*Exercise 1:* Fill in the code as indicated by the comments in bold.

*Exercise 2:* In the previous code we have the following:

```
cout << "Tax Payer # " << (index+1) << ": " << "$ "
     << citizen[index].taxes << endl;
```

Why do you think we need (index+1) in the first line but index in the second?

*Sample Run:*

```
Enter this year's income for tax payer 1: 45000
Enter the tax rate for tax payer # 1: .19
Enter this year's income for tax payer 2: 60000
Enter the tax rate for tax payer # 2: .23
Enter this year's income for tax payer 3: 12000
Enter the tax rate for tax payer # 3: .01
Enter this year's income for tax payer 4: 104000
Enter the tax rate for tax payer # 4: .30
Enter this year's income for tax payer 5: 50000
Enter the tax rate for tax payer # 5: .22


Tax Payer # 1: $ 8550.00
Tax Payer # 2: $ 13800.00
Tax Payer # 3: $ 120.00
Tax Payer # 4: $ 31200.00
Tax Payer # 5: $ 11000.00
```

# LESSON 11 B

## LAB 11.4    Nested Structures

Bring in program `nestedRect_struct.cpp` from the Lab 11 folder. This code is very similar to the rectangle program from Lab 11.1. However, this time you will complete the code using nested structures. The code is shown below.

```
#include <iostream>
#include <iomanip>

using namespace std;
```

*continues*

```cpp
// This program uses a structure to hold data about a rectangle
// It calculates the area and perimeter of a box

// PLACE YOUR NAME HERE

// Fill in code to declare a structure named dimensions that
// contains 2 float members, length and width

// Fill in code to declare a structure named rectangle that contains
// 3 members, area, perimeter, and sizes. area and perimeter should be
// floats, whereas sizes should be a dimensions structure variable

int main()
{
    // Fill in code to define a rectangle structure variable named box.

    cout << "Enter the length of a rectangle: ";

    // Fill in code to read in the length to the appropriate location

    cout << "Enter the width of a rectangle: ";

    // Fill in code to read in the width to the appropriate location

    cout << endl << endl;

    // Fill in code to compute the area and store it in the appropriate
    // location
    // Fill in code to compute the perimeter and store it in the
    // appropriate location

    cout << fixed << showpoint << setprecision(2);
    cout << "The area of the rectangle is " << box.attributes.area << endl;
    cout << "The perimeter of the rectangle is " <<  box.attributes.perimeter
        << endl;

    return 0;
}
```

*Exercise 1:* Fill in the code as indicated by the comments in bold.

*Exercise 2:* Modify the program above by adding a third structure named results which has two members area and perimeter. Adjust the rectangle structure so that both of its members are structure variables.

*Exercise 3:* Modify the program above by adding functions that compute the area and perimeter. The structure variables should be passed as arguments to the functions.

*Sample Run:*

```
Enter the length of a rectangle: 9
Enter the width of a rectangle: 6
The area of the rectangle is 54.00
The perimeter of the rectangle is 30.00
```

## LAB 11.5   Student Generated Code Assignments

*Option 1:* Re-write Sample Program 11.2 so that it works for an array of structures. Write the program so that it compares 6 circles. You will need to come up with a new way of determining which circle's center is closest to the origin.

*Option 2:* Write a program that uses a structure to store the following information for a particular month at the local airport:

> Total number of planes that landed
> Total number of planes that departed
> Greatest number of planes that landed in a given day that month
> Least number of planes that landed in a given day that month

The program should have an array of twelve structures to hold travel information for the entire year. The program should prompt the user to enter data for each month. Once all data is entered, the program should calculate and output the average monthly number of landing planes, the average monthly number of departing planes, the total number of landing and departing planes for the year, and the greatest and least number of planes that landed on any one day (and which month it occurred in).

# 12 Advanced File Operations

**PURPOSE**

1. To review the basic concept of files
2. To understand the use of random access files
3. To understand and use various types of files (binary and text)

**PROCEDURE**

1. Students should read the Pre-lab Reading Assignment before coming to lab.
2. Students should complete the Pre-lab Writing Assignment before coming to lab.
3. In the lab, students should complete labs assigned to them by the instructor.

| Contents | Pre-requisites | Approximate completion time | Page number | Check when done |
|---|---|---|---|---|
| Pre-lab Reading Assignment | | 20 min. | 214 | |
| Pre-lab Writing Assignment | Pre-lab reading | 10 min. | 231 | |
| **LESSON 12A** | | | | |
| Lab 12.1 Introduction to Files (Optional) | General understanding of basic I/O | 15 min. | 231 | |
| Lab 12.2 Files as Parameters and Character Data | Understanding of get function and parameters | 20 min. | 233 | |
| Lab 12.3 Binary Files and the write Function | Completion of all previous labs | 30 min. | 235 | |
| **LESSON 12B** | | | | |
| Lab 12.4 Random Access Files | Completion of all previous labs | 20 min. | 238 | |
| Lab 12.5 Student Generated Code Assignments | Completion of all previous labs | 30 min. | 240 | |

# PRE-LAB READING ASSIGNMENT

## Review of Text Files

Chapter three introduced the basic use of files for input and output. We briefly review those concepts in this section.

A file is a collection of information stored (usually) on a disk. Files, just like variables, have to be defined in the program. The data type of a file depends on whether it is used as an input file, output file, or both. Output files have a data type called `ofstream`, input files have a data type of `ifstream`, and files used as both have the data type `fstream`. We must add the `#include <fstream>` directive when using files.

*Examples:*

```
ofstream outfile;      // defining outfile as an output file
ifstream infile;       // defining infile as an input file
fstream datafile;      // defining datafile to be both an input and
                       // output file
```

After their definition, files must still be opened, used (information stored to or data read from the file), and then closed.

## Opening Files

A file is opened with the `open` function. This ties the logical name of the file that is used in the definition to the physical name of the file used in the secondary storage device (disk). The statement `infile.open("payroll.dat");` opens the file `payroll.dat` and lets the program know that `infile` is the name by which this file will be referenced within the program. If the file is not located in the same directory as the C++ program, the full path (drive, etc.) MUST be indicated: `infile.open("a:\\payroll.dat");` This tying of the **logical name** `infile` with the **physical name** `payroll.dat` means that wherever `infile` is used in the program, data will be read from the physical file `payroll.dat`. A program should check to make sure that the physical file exists. This can be done by a conditional statement.

*Example:*
```
ifstream infile;
infile.open("payroll.dat");
if (!infile)
{
    cout << Error opening file.  It may not exist were indicated.\n;
    return 1;
}
```

In the previous example, `return 1` is used as an indicator of an abnormal occurrence. In this case the file in question can not be found.

## Reading from a File

Files have an "invisible" end of line marker at the end of each line of the file. Files also have an invisible end of file marker at the end of the file. When reading from an input file within a loop, the program must be able to detect that marker as the sentinel data (data that meets the condition to end the loop). There are several ways to do this.

*Sample Program 12.1:*

```
#include <fstream>
#include <iostream>
#include <iomanip>
using namespace std;

int main()
{
    ifstream infile;       // defining an input file
    ofstream outfile;      // defining an output file

    infile.open("payroll.dat");
    // This statement opens infile as an input file.
    // Whenever infile is used, data from the file payroll.dat
    // will be read.

    outfile.open("payment.out");
    // This statement opens outfile as an output file.
    // Whenever outfile is used, information will be sent
    // to the file payment.out

    int hours;             // The number of hours worked
    float payRate;         // The rate per hour paid
    float net;             // The net pay

    if (!infile)
    {
        cout << "Error opening file.\n";
        cout << "Perhaps the file is not where indicated.\n";
        return 1;

    }

    outfile << fixed << setprecision(2);
    outfile << "Hours    Pay Rate   Net Pay" << endl;

    infile >> hours;       // priming the read

    while (infile)
    {
        infile >> payRate;
        net = hours * payRate;
```

*continues*

```
            outfile    << hours << setw(10) << "$ " << setw(6)
                       << payRate << setw(5) << "$ " << setw(7)
                       << net << endl;

            infile >> hours;
        }

        infile.close();
        outfile.close();

        return 0;
    }
```

Notice the statement `outfile << fixed << setprecision(2);` in the above program. This shows that the format procedures learned for `cout` can be used for output files as well. Remember that `setw(x)` can be used as long as the `iomanip` header file is included.

This program assumes that a data file exists and contains an undetermined number of records with each record consisting of two data values, `hours` and `payRate`. Suppose the input data file (`payroll.dat`) contains the following:

```
40   10.00
30    6.70
50   20.00
```

The program will produce the following output file (`payment.out`).

| Hours | Pay Rate | Net Pay |
|-------|----------|---------|
| 40 | $ 10.00 | $ 400.00 |
| 30 | $  6.70 | $ 201.00 |
| 50 | $ 20.00 | $1000.00 |

The input file contains data for one employee on each line. Each time through the `while` loop, information is processed for one employee. The loop executes the same number of times as there are lines (employee records in this case) in the data file. Since there are two items of data for each line (`hours` and `payRate`), these items are read in each time through the loop. Notice that one of the input variables was input before the `while` loop. This is called "priming the read." Input can be thought of as a stream of values taken one at a time. Before the `while` loop condition can be tested, there has to be something in that stream. We **prime** the read by reading in at least one variable before the loop. Observe that the statement `infile >> hours;` is given twice in the program: once before the input loop and as the last statement in the loop. The other item, `payRate`, is read in at the very beginning of the loop. This way each variable is read every time through the loop. Also notice that the heading of the output file is printed outside the loop before it is executed.

There are other ways of determining when the end of the file is reached. The `eof( )` function reports when the end of a file is encountered. The loop in Sample Program 12.1 can be replaced with the following:

```
infile >> hours;
while (!infile.eof())
{
```

```
    infile >> payRate;
    net = hours * payRate;
    outfile << hours << setw(10) << "$ " << setw(6) << payRate << setw(5)
            << "$ " << setw(7) << net << endl;
    infile >> hours;
}
```

In addition to checking to see if a file exists, we can also check to see if it has any data in it. The following code checks first if the file exists and then if it is empty.

```
inData.open("sample2.dat");
```

**if(!inData)**
```
    cout << "file does not exist" << endl;
```
else **if((else if (inData.peek()) == EOF)**

```
    cout << "File is empty" << endl;
```
else
```
    //rest of program
```

The peek function actually looks ahead in the file for the next data item, in this case to determine if it is the end of file marker. ch must be defined as char data type.

Since the peek function looks "ahead" for the next data item, it can be used to test for end of file in reading values from a file within a loop without priming the read.

The following program accomplishes the same thing as Sample Program 12.1 without priming the read. The portions in bold differ from Sample Program 12.1.

*Sample Program 12.2:*

```
#include <fstream>
#include <iostream>
#include <iomanip>
using namespace std;

int main()
{
        ifstream infile;        // defining an input file
        ofstream outfile;       // defining an output file

        infile.open("payroll.dat");
        // This statement opens infile as an input file.
        // Whenever infile is used, data from the file payroll.dat
        // will be read.

        outfile.open("payment.out");
        // This statement opens outfile as an output file.
```

*continues*

```
// Whenever outfile is used, information will be sent
// to the file payment.out

int hours;              // The number of hours worked
float payRate;          // The rate per hour paid
float net;              // The net pay
char ch;                // ch is used to hold the next value
                        // (read as character) from the file

if (!infile)
{
    cout << "Error opening file.\n";
    cout << "Perhaps the file is not where indicated.\n";
    return 1;
}

outfile << fixed << setprecision(2);
outfile << "Hours     Pay Rate   Net Pay" << endl;


while ((ch = infile.peek()) != EOF)
{
    infile >> hours;
    infile >> payRate;
    net = hours * payRate;

    outfile  << hours << setw(10) << "$ " << setw(6)
             << payRate << setw(5) << "$ " << setw(7)
             << net << endl;



}

infile.close();
outfile.close();

return 0;
}
```

## Output Files

Output files are opened the same way: `outfile.open("payment.out")`. Whenever the program writes to `outfile`, the information will be placed in the physical file `payment.out`. Notice that the program generates a file stored in the same location as the source file. The user can indicate a different location for the file to be stored by indicating the full path (drive, etc.).

## Files Used for Both Input and Output

A file can be used for both input and output. The fstream data type, which is used for files that can handle both input and output, must have a **file access flag** as an argument to the open function so that the mode, input or output, can be determined. There are several access flags that are used to indicate the use of the file. The following chart lists frequently used access flags.

| Flag mode | Meaning |
| --- | --- |
| ios::in | Input mode. The file is used for "reading" information. If the file does not exist, it will not be created. |
| ios::out | Output mode. Information is written to the file. If the file already exists, its contents will be deleted. |
| ios::app | Append mode. If the file exists, its contents are preserved and all output is written to the end of the file. If it does not exist then the file will be created. Notice how this differs from ios::out. |
| ios::binary | Binary mode. Information is written to or read from in pure binary format (discussed later in this chapter). |

*Example:*

```
#include <fstream>
using namespace std;

int main()
{
    fstream test ("grade.dat", ios::out)
    // test is defined as an fstream file first used for output
    // ios::out is the file access flag

    // code of the program goes here
    // the code will put values in the test file

    test.close();              // close the file as an output file
    test.open("grade.dat", ios::in)
    // the same file is reopened now as an input file
    // ios::in is the file access flag

    //   other code goes here

    test.close();              // close the file

}
```

In the following example, we check for a file's existence before opening it. We first attempt to open the file for input. If the file does not exist, then the open operation fails and we open it as an output file.

*Example:*

```
fstream dataFile;
dataFile.open("grades.txt", ios::in);
if (dataFile.fail())
        // The fail directive indicates the file did not open
        // since it does not exist
{
        // The file does not exist, so create it.
dataFile.open("grades.txt", ios::out);
        // file is processed here:  data sent to the file
}
else  // the file already exists.

{
cout << "The file grades.txt already exists. \n";

     // process file here
 dataFile.close();

}
```

Just as `cin >>` is used to read from the keyboard and `cout <<` is used to write to the screen, `filename >>` is used to read from the file `filename` and `filename <<` is used to write to the file `filename`.

## Closing a File

Files should be closed before the program ends to avoid corrupting the file and/ or losing valuable data.

```
infile.close();
outfile.close();
dataFile.close();
```

## Passing Files as Parameters to Functions

Files can be passed as parameters just like variables. Files are always passed by reference. The & symbol must be included after the data type in the function heading and prototype.

*Example:*
```
void GetData(ifstream& infile, ofstream& outfile); // prototype of function
                                                    // with files as parameters

void GetData(ifstream& infile, ofstream& outfile)  // heading of function with
                                                    // files as parameters
```

## Review of Character Input

Chapter 10 introduced the basics of characters and strings. We briefly review those concepts since they apply to files as well.

Recall that each file has an end of line marker for each line as well as the end of file marker at the end of the file. Whenever whitespace (blanks, newlines, controls, etc.) is part of a file, a problem exists with the traditional >> operator in inputting character data. When reading input characters into a string object, the >> operator skips any leading whitespace. It then reads successive characters into the character array, stopping at the first trailing whitespace character (which is NOT consumed, but rather which remains as the next character to be read in the file). The >> operator also takes care of adding the null character to the end of the string. Stopping at the first trailing whitespace creates a problem for names containing spaces. A program reading first names into some string variable (array of characters) has a problem reading a name like Mary Lou since it has a blank space in it. The blank space between Mary and Lou causes the input to stop when using the >> operator. The get function can be used to input such strings.

```
infile.get(firstname, 20);
```

The get function does NOT skip leading whitespace characters but rather continues to read characters until it either has read, in the example above, 19 characters or it reaches the newline character \n (which it does NOT consume). Recall from Lesson Set 10 that the last space is reserved for the null character.

Since the get function does not consume the end of line character, there must be something done to consume it so that a new line can be read.

*Example:* Given the following data file

```
Mary Lou <eol>
Becky    <eol>
Debbie   <eol>
<eof>
```

Note: Both the <eol> and <eof> are NOT visible to the programmer or user. There are several options for reading and printing this data.

```
char dummy;                     // created to read the end of line character
char  firstname[80];            // array of characters for the first name
outfile << "Name  " << endl;
infile.get(firstname,80);       // priming the read   inputs the first name

while(infile)
{
    infile.get(dummy);          // reads the end of line character into dummy
    outfile << firstname << endl; // outputs the name
    infile.get(firstname,80);   // reads the next name
}
```

In the above example, dummy is used to consume the end of line character. input.get(firstname,80); reads the string Mary Lou and stops just before reading the <eol> end of line character. The infile.get(dummy) gets the end of line character into dummy.

Another way to do this is with the ignore function, which reads characters until it encounters the specific character it has been instructed to look for or until it has skipped the allotted number of characters, whichever comes first. The statement `infile.ignore(81,'\n')` skips up to 81 characters stopping if the new line `'\n'` character is encountered. This newline character IS consumed by the function, and thus there is no need for a dummy character variable.

*Example:*

```
char  firstname[80];

outfile << "Name  " << endl;
infile.get(firstname,80);

while(!infile.fail())
{
    infile.ignore(81,'\n');       // read and consume the end of line character
    outfile << firstname << endl;
    infile.get(firstname,80);
}
```

The following sample program shows how names with embedded whitespace along with numeric data can be processed. Parts in bold indicate the changes from Sample Program 12.2. Assume that the `payroll.dat` file has the following information:

| John Brown | 40 | 10.00 |
| Kelly Barr | 30 | 6.70 |
| Tom Seller | 50 | 20.00 |

The program will produce the following information in `payment.out`:

| Name | Hours | Pay Rate | Net Pay |
| --- | --- | --- | --- |
| John Brown | 40 | $10.00 | $  400.00 |
| Kelly Barr | 30 | $ 6.70 | $  201.00 |
| Tom Seller | 50 | $20.00 | $1000.00 |

*Sample Program 12.3:*

```
#include <fstream>
#include <iostream>
#include <iomanip>
using namespace std;

const int MAX_NAME = 11;

int main()
{
        ifstream infile;        // defining an input file
        ofstream outfile;       // defining an output file

        infile.open("payroll.dat");
        // This statement opens infile as an input file.
        // Whenever infile is used, data from the file payroll.dat
        // will be read.
```

```cpp
outfile.open("payment.out");
// This statement opens outfile as an output file.
// Whenever outfile is used, information will be sent
// to the file payment.out

int hours;                 // The number of hours worked
float payRate;             // The rate per hour paid
float net;                 // The net pay
char ch;                   // ch is used to hold the next value
                           // (read as character) from the file
char name[MAX_NAME];       // array of characters for the name of
                           // a student, with at most 10 characters

if (!infile)
{
    cout << "Error opening file.\n";
    cout << "Perhaps the file is not where indicated.\n";
    return 1;

}

outfile << fixed << setprecision(2);
outfile << "Name               Hours    Pay Rate    Net Pay" << endl;


while ((ch = infile.peek()) != EOF)    // no need to prime the read
{
        infile.get(name,MAX_NAME);       // gets names with blanks
        infile >> hours;
        infile >> payRate;
        infile.ignore(81,'\n');          // ignores the rest of the line
                                         // and consumes end of line marker
        net = hours * payRate;

        outfile << name << setw(10) << hours << setw(10) << "$ "
                << setw(6) << payRate << setw(5) << "$ " << setw(7)
                << net << endl;


}

infile.close();
outfile.close();

return 0;

}
```

Another way to read in lines containing whitespace characters is with the getline member function.

*Example:*

```
char firstName[80];
outfile << "Name " << endl;
infile.getline(firstName,81);

while (infile)
{
  outfile << firstName << endl;
  intfile.getline(firstName,81);
}
```

## Binary Files

So far all the files we have talked about have been text files, files formatted as ASCII text.[1] Even the numbers written to a file with the << operator are changed to ASCII text. ASCII is a code that stores every datum (letter of the alphabet, digit, punctuation mark, etc.) as a character with a unique number. Although ASCII text is the default method for storing information in files, we can specify that we want to store data in pure binary format by "opening" a file in binary mode with the ios::binary flag. The write member function is then used to write binary data to the file. This method is particularly useful for transferring an entire array of data to a file. Binary files are efficient since they store everything as 1s or 0s rather than as text.

*Example:*

```
fstream test("grade.dat", ios::out | ios::binary); // This defines and opens
                                                    // the file test as an
                                                    // output binary file

int grade[arraysize] = {98, 88, 78, 77, 67, 66, 56, 78, 98, 56}; // creates and
                                                                 // initializes
                                                                 // an integer
                                                                 // array

test.write((char*)grade, sizeof(grade));  // write all values of array to file

test.close();                             // close the file
```

`test.write((char*)grade, sizeof(grade));` in the above example calls the write function. The name of the file to be written to is test. The first argument is a character pointer pointing to the starting address of memory, in this case to the beginning of the grade array. The second argument is the size in bytes of the item written to the file. sizeof is a function that determines the size.

---

[1] Or some other alphanumberic code.

The following sample program initializes an array and then places those values into a file as binary numbers. The program then adds 10 to each element of the array and prints those values to the screen. Finally the program reads the values from the same file and prints them. These values are the original numbers. Study the program and its comments very carefully.

*Sample Program 12.4:*

```cpp
#include <fstream>
#include <iostream>
using namespace std;

const int ARRAYSIZE = 10;

int main()
{
        fstream test("grade.dat", ios::out | ios::binary);
        // note the use of | to separate file access flags
        int grade[ARRAYSIZE] = {98,88,78,77,67,66,56,78,98,56};
        int count;      // loop counter

        test.write((char*)grade, sizeof(grade));
                        // write values of array to file
        test.close();  // close file

        // now add 10 to each grade

        cout << "The values of grades with 10 points added\n";

        for (count =0; count < ARRAYSIZE; count++)
        {
            grade[count] = grade[count] + 10;
                    // this adds 10 to each elemnt of the array
            cout << grade[count] << endl;
                    // write the new values to the screen
        }

        test.open("grade.dat", ios::in);
                // reopen the file but now as an input file

        test.read((char*) grade, sizeof(grade));

        /*  The above statement reads from the file test and places
            the values found into the grade array.  As with the write
            function, the first argument is a character pointer even
            though the array itself is an integer.  It points to the
            starting address in memory where the file information is to
            be transferred
        */
```

*continues*

```
        cout << "The grades as they were read into the file"  << endl;

        for (count =0; count < ARRAYSIZE; count++)
        {
            cout << grade[count] << endl;
                // write the original values to the screen
        }

        test.close();
        return 0;

}
```

The output to the screen from this program is as follows:

**The values of grades with 10 points added**
**108**
**98**
**88**
**87**
**77**
**76**
**66**
**88**
**108**
**66**
**The grades as they were read into the file**
**98**
**88**
**78**
**77**
**67**
**66**
**56**
**78**
**98**
**56**

## Files and Records

Files are often used to store records. A "field" is one piece of information and a "record" is a group of fields that logically belong together in a unit.

| *Example:* | **Name** | **Test1** | **Test2** | **Final** |
|---|---|---|---|---|
| | Brown | 89 | 97 | 88 |
| | Smith | 99 | 89 | 97 |

Each record has four fields: Name, Test1, Test2, and Final. When records are stored in memory, rather than in files, C++ structures provide a good way to organize and store them.

```
struct Grades
{
    char name[10];
    int test1;
```

```
        int test2;
        int final;
};
```

An identifier defined to be a Grades structure can hold one record.

The write function, mentioned in the previous section, can be used to write records to a file.

```
fstream test("score.dat", ios::out|ios::binary);
Grades student;                              // defines a structure variable


// code that gets information into the student record
test.write((char *) &student, sizeof(student));
```

The test.write function used to write a record stored as a struct is similar to the write function used for an array with one big difference. Notice the inclusion of (&). Why is this necessary here and not when writing an array? In this example we need to pass by reference which requires the (&) symbol. Arrays are passed by pointer. The following sample program takes records from the user and stores them into a binary file.

*Sample Program 12.5:*

```
#include <fstream>
#include <iostream>
#include <cctype>              // for toupper function
using namespace std;

const int NAMESIZE = 31;

struct Grades                  // declaring a structure
{
        char name[NAMESIZE];
        int test1;
        int test2;
        int final;
};

int main()
{
        fstream tests("score.dat", ios::out | ios::binary);
        // defines tests as an output binary file

        Grades student; // defines student as a record (struct)
        char more;      // used to determine if there is more input

        do
        {
            cout << "Enter the following information" << endl;
            cout << "Student's name: ";
            cin.getline(student.name,NAMESIZE);
```

*continues*

```
            cout << "First test score :";
            cin >> student.test1;
            cin.ignore();      // ignore rest of line

            cout << "Second test score: ";
            cin >> student.test2;
            cin.ignore();

            cout << "Final test score: ";
            cin >> student.final;
            cin.ignore();

            // write this record to the file
            tests.write((char *) &student, sizeof(student));

            cout << "Enter a y if you would like to input more data\n ";
            cin >> more;
            cin.ignore();

      }   while (toupper(more) == 'Y');

      tests.close();
      return 0;
}
```

## Random Access Files

All the files studied thus far have performed **sequential file access**, which means that all data is read or written in a sequential order. If the file is opened for input, data is read starting at the first byte and continues sequentially through the file's contents. If the file is opened for output, bytes of data are written sequentially. The writing usually begins at the beginning of the file unless the ios::app mode is used, in which case data is written to the end of the file. C++ allows a program to perform **random file access**, which means that any piece of data can be accessed at any time. A cassette tape is an example of a sequential access medium. To listen to the songs on a tape, one has to listen to them in the order they were recorded or fast forward (reverse) through the tape to get to a particular song. A CD has properties of a random access medium. One simply jumps to the track where a song is located. It is not truly random access, however, since one can not jump to the middle of a song.

There are two file stream member functions that are used to move the read/write position to any byte in the file. The seekp function is used for output files and seekg is used for input files.

Example:

```
dataOut.seekp(30L, ios::beg);
```

This instruction moves the marker position of the file called dataOut to 30 positions from the beginning of the file. The first argument, 30L (L indicates a long integer), represents an offset (distance) from some point in the file that will be used to move the read/write position. That point in the file is indicated by the second argument (`ios::beg`). This access flag indicates that the offset is calculated from the beginning of the file. The offset can be calculated from the end (`ios::end`) or from the current (`ios::cur`) position in the file.

If the `eof` marker has been set (which means that the position has reached the end of the file), then the member function `clear` must be used before `seekp` or `seekg` is used.

Two other member functions may be used for random file access: `tellp` and `tellg`. They return a long integer that indicates the current byte of the file's read/write position. As expected, `tellp` is used to return the write position of an output file and `tellg` is used to return the read position of an input file.

Assume that a data file `letterGrades.txt` has the following single line of information:

ABCDEF

Marker positions always begin with 0. The mapping of the characters to their position is as follows:

A B C D E F
0 1 2 3 4 5

The following sample program demonstrates the use of `seekg` and `tellg`.

*Sample Program 12.6:*

```
#include <iostream>
#include <fstream>
#include <cctype>
using namespace std;


int main()
{
        fstream inFile("letterGrades.txt", ios::in);
        long offset;      // used to hold the offset
                          // of the read position from
                          // some point
        char ch;          // holds character read at some
                          // position in the file
        char more;        // used to indicate if more information
                          // is to be given

        do
        {
            cout << "The read position is currently at byte "
                << inFile.tellg() << endl;
```

*continues*

```
                    // This prints the current read position (found by the tellg
                    // function)

                    cout << "Enter an offset from the beginning of the file: ";
                    cin >> offset;

                    inFile.seekg(offset, ios::beg);

                    // This moves the position from the beginning of the file.
                    // offset contains the number of bytes that the read position
                    // will be moved from the beginning of the file

                    inFile.get(ch);
                    // This gets one byte of information from the file

                    cout << "The character read is " << ch << endl;

                    cout << "If you would like to input another offset enter a Y"
                         << endl;
                    cin >> more;

                    inFile.clear();
                    // This clears the file in case the eof flag was set

        }   while (toupper(more) == 'Y');
        inFile.close();
        return 0;

}
```

*Sample Run:*

**The read position is currently at byte 0**
**Enter an offset from the beginning of the file:** 2
**The character read is C**
**If you would like to input another offset enter a Y:** y
**The read position is currently at byte 3**
**Enter an offset from the beginning of the file:** 0
**The character read is A**
**If you would like to input another offset enter a Y:** y
**The read position is currently at byte 1**
**Enter an offset from the beginning of the file:** 5
**The character read is F**
**If you would like to input another offset enter a Y:** n

**CAUTION:** If you enter an offset that goes beyond the data stored, it prints the previous
character offset.

# PRE-LAB WRITING ASSIGNMENT

## Fill-in-the-Blank Questions

1. The _____ member function moves the read position of a file.
2. Files that will be used for both input and output should be defined as _____ data type.
3. The _____ member function returns the write position of a file.
4. The ios::_____ file access flag indicates that output to the file will be written to the end of the file.
5. _____ files are files that do not store data as ASCII characters.
6. The _____ member function moves the write position of a file.
7. The _____ function can be used to send an entire record or array to a binary file with one statement.
8. The >> operator _____ any leading whitespace.
9. The _____ function "looks ahead" to determine the next data value in an input file.
10. The _____ and _____ functions do not skip leading whitespace characters.

# LESSON 12A

## LAB 12.1   Introduction to Files (Optional)

(This is a good exercise for those needing a review of basic file operations)

Retrieve program `files.cpp` from the Lab 12 folder. The code is as follows:

```cpp
// This program uses hours, pay rate, state tax and fed tax to determine gross
// and net pay.

#include <fstream>
#include <iostream>
#include <iomanip>
using namespace std;

int main()
{
    // Fill in the code to define payfile as an input file
    float gross;
    float net;
    float hours;
    float payRate;
    float stateTax;
    float fedTax;
```

*continues*

```
cout << fixed << setprecision(2) << showpoint;
// Fill in the code to open payfile and attach it to the physical file
// named payroll.dat

// Fill in code to write a conditional statement to check if payfile
// does not exist.
{
        cout << "Error opening file. \n";
        cout << "It may not exist where indicated" << endl;
        return 1;
}


cout << "Payrate       Hours    Gross Pay        Net Pay"
        << endl   << endl;
// Fill in code to prime the read for the payfile file.
// Fill in code to write a loop condition to run while payfile has more
// data to process.
{
    payfile >> payRate >> stateTax >> fedTax;
    gross = payRate * hours;
    net = gross - (gross * stateTax) - (gross * fedTax);
    cout << payRate << setw(15) << hours << setw(12) << gross
        << setw(12)  << net << endl;
    payfile >> // Fill in the code to finish this with the appropriate
               // variable to be input
}
payfile.close();
return 0;
}
```

*Exercise 1:* Assume that the data file has `hours`, `payRate`, `stateTax`, and `fedTax` on one line for each employee. `stateTax` and `fedTax` are given as decimals (5% would be .05). Complete this program by filling in the code (places in bold).

*Exercise 2:* Run the program. Note: the data file does not exist so you should get the error message:

```
Error opening file.
It may not exist where indicated.
```

*Exercise 3:* Create a data file with the following information:

```
40   15.00   .05  .12
50   10      .05  .11
60   12.50   .05  .13
```

Save it in the same folder as the `.cpp` file. What should the data file name be?

*Exercise 4:* Run the program. Record the output here:

_____

_____

_____

_____

_____

*Exercise 5:* Change the program so that the output goes to an output file called pay.out and run the program. You can use any logical internal name you wish for the output file.

## Lab 12.2    Files as Parameters and Character Data

Retrieve program Grades.cpp and the data file graderoll.dat from the Lab 12 folder. The code is as follows:

```cpp
#include // FILL IN DIRECTIVE FOR FILES
#include <iostream>
#include <iomanip>
using namespace std;


// This program reads records from a file.  The file contains the
// following: student's name, two test grades and final exam grade.
// It then prints this information to the screen.


const int NAMESIZE = 15;
const int MAXRECORDS = 50;
struct Grades                           // declares a structure
{
      char name[NAMESIZE + 1];
      int test1;
      int test2;
      int final;

};


typedef Grades gradeType[MAXRECORDS];
 // This makes gradeType a data type
 // that holds MAXRECORDS
 // Grades structures.



// FIll IN THE CODE FOR THE PROTOTYPE OF THE FUNCTION ReadIt
// WHERE THE FIRST ARGUMENT IS AN INPUT FILE, THE SECOND IS THE
// ARRAY OF RECORDS, AND THE THIRD WILL HOLD THE NUMBER OF RECORDS
// CURRENTLY IN THE ARRAY.
```

*continues*

```cpp
int main()

{

    ifstream indata;
    indata.open("graderoll.dat");
    int numRecord;                        // number of records read in
    gradeType studentRecord;

    if(!indata)
    {
        cout << "Error opening file. \n";
        cout << "It may not exist where indicated" << endl;
        return 1;
    }


        // FILL IN THE CODE TO CALL THE FUNCTION ReadIt.

        // output the information
        for (int count = 0; count < numRecord; count++)
        {
            cout << studentRecord[count].name << setw(10)
                << studentRecord[count].test1
                << setw(10) << studentRecord[count].test2;
            cout << setw(10) << studentRecord[count].final << endl;
        }


        return 0;
}


//*************************************************************
//                         readIt
//
//  task:     This procedure reads records into an array of
//            records from an input file and keeps track of the
//            total number of records
//  data in:  data file containing information to be placed in
//            the array
//  data out: an array of records and the number of records
//
//*************************************************************


void readIt(// FILL IN THE CODE FOR THE FORMAL PARAMETERS AND THEIR
            // DATA  TYPES.
            // inData, gradeRec and total are the formal parameters
            // total is passed by reference)


{
    total = 0;

    inData.get(gradeRec[total].name, NAMESIZE);
    while (inData)
    {
```

```
// FILL IN THE CODE TO READ test1
// FILL IN THE CODE TO READ test2
// FILL IN THE CODE TO READ final

   total++;      // add one to total

// FILL IN THE CODE TO CONSUME THE END OF LINE
// FILL IN THE CODE TO READ name


   }


}
```

*Exercise 1:* Complete the program by filling in the code (areas in bold). This problem requires that you study very carefully the code and the data file already written to prepare you to complete the program. Notice that in the data file the names occupy no more than 15 characters. Why?

*Exercise 2:* Add another field called `letter` to the record which is a character that holds the letter grade of the student. This is based on the average of the grades as follows: `test1` and `test2` are each worth 30% of the grade while `final` is worth 40% of the grade. The letter grade is based on a 10 point spread. The code will have to be expanded to find the average.

| | |
|---|---|
| 90–100 | A |
| 80–89 | B |
| 70–79 | C |
| 60–69 | D |
| 0–59 | F |

# LESSON 12B

## LAB 12.3   Binary Files and the `write` Function

Retrieve program `budget.cpp` from the Lab 12 folder. The code is as follows:

```
// This program reads in from the keyboard a record of financial information
// consisting of a person's name, income, rent, food costs, utilities and
// miscellaneous expenses.  It then determines the net money
// (income minus all expenses)and places that information in a record
// which is then written to an output file.

#include <fstream>
#include <iostream>
#include <iomanip>
using namespace std;
```

*continues*

```cpp
const int NAMESIZE = 15;
struct budget  //declare a structure to hold name and financial information
{
        char name[NAMESIZE+1];
        float income;          // person's monthly income
        float rent;            // person's monthly rent
        float food;            // person's monthly food bill
        float utilities;       // person's monthly utility bill
        float miscell;         // person's other bills
        float net;             // person's net money after bills are paid


};


int main()

{
    fstream indata;
    ofstream outdata;                                       // output file of
                                                            // student.

    indata.open("income.dat", ios::out | ios::binary);      // open file as binary
                                                            // output.
    outdata.open("student.out");                            // output file that we
                                                            // will write student
                                                            // information to.

    outdata << left << fixed << setprecision(2);            // left indicates left
                                                            // justified for fields


    budget person;    //defines person to be a record

    cout << "Enter the following information" << endl;
    cout << "Person's name: ";
    cin.getline(person.name, NAMESIZE);
    cout << "Income :";
    cin >> person.income;


    // FILL IN CODE TO READ IN THE REST OF THE FIELDS:
    // rent, food, utilities AND miscell TO THE person RECORD

    // find the net field
    person.net = // FILL IN CODE TO DETERMINE NET INCOME (income - expenses)

    // write this record to the file
    // Fill IN CODE TO WRITE THE RECORD TO THE FILE indata (one instruction)

    indata.close();

    // FILL IN THE CODE TO REOPEN THE indata FILE, NOW AS AN INPUT FILE.
    // FILL IN THE CODE TO READ THE RECORD FROM indata AND PLACE IT IN THE
    // person RECORD (one instruction)
```

```
// write information to output file
outdata << setw(20) << "Name" << setw(10) << "Income" << setw(10) << "Rent"
                 << setw(10) << "Food" << setw(15) << "Utilities" << setw(15)
                 << "Miscellaneous" << setw(10) << "Net Money" << endl << endl;


// FILL IN CODE TO WRITE INDIVIDUAL FIELD INFORMATION OF THE RECORD TO
// THE outdata FILE.(several instructions)


    return 0;
}
```

*Exercise 1:* This program reads in a record with fields name, income, rent, food, utilities, and miscell from the keyboard. The program computes the net (income minus the other fields) and stores this in the net field. The entire record is then written to a binary file (indata). This file is then closed and reopened as an input file. Fill in the code as indicated by the comments in bold.

*Sample Run:*

**Enter the following information**
**Person's Name:** Billy Berry
**Income:** 2500
**Rent:** 700
**Food:** 600
**Utilities:** 400
**Miscellaneous:** 500

The program should write the following text lines to the output file student.out.

| Name | Income | Rent | Food | Utilities | Miscellaneous | Net Money |
|---|---|---|---|---|---|---|
| Billy Berry | 2500.00 | 700.00 | 600.00 | 400.00 | 500.00 | 300.00 |

*Exercise 2:* Alter the program to include more than one record as input. Use an array of records.

*Sample Run:*

**Enter the following information**
**Person's Name:** Billy Berry
**Income:** 2500
**Rent:** 700
**Food:** 600
**Utilities:** 400
**Miscellaneous:** 500

**Enter a Y if you would like to input more data**
Y

**Enter the following information**
**Person's Name:** Terry Bounds

> **Income:** 3000
> **Rent:** 750
> **Food:** 650
> **Utilities:** 300
> **Miscellaneous:** 400
>
> **Enter a Y if you would like to input more data**
> n
> **That's all the information**

The output file `student.out` should then have the following lines of text written to it.

| Name | Income | Rent | Food | Utilities | Miscellaneous | Net Money |
|------|--------|------|------|-----------|---------------|-----------|
| Billy Berry | 2500.00 | 700.00 | 600.00 | 400.00 | 500.00 | 300.00 |
| Terry Bounds | 3000.00 | 750.00 | 650.00 | 300.00 | 400.00 | 900.00 |

## Lab 12.4  Random Access Files

Retrieve program `randomAccess.cpp` and the data file `proverb.txt` from the Lab 12 folder. The code is as follows:

```cpp
#include <iostream>
#include <fstream>
#include <cctype>
using namespace std;

int main()
{
    fstream inFile("proverb.txt", ios::in);
    long offset;
    char ch;
    char more;

    do
    {
        //  Fill in the code to write to the screen
        //   the current read position (with label)

        cout << "Enter an offset from the current read position: ";
        cin >> offset;

        //  Fill in the code to move the read position "offset" bytes
        //   from the CURRENT read position.

        //  Fill in the code to get one byte of information from the file
        //   and place it in the variable "ch".

        cout << "The character read is " << ch << endl;
        cout << "If you would like to input another offset enter a Y"
             << endl;
```

```
    cin >> more;

    // Fill in the code to clear the eof flag.

} while (toupper(more) == 'Y');

inFile.close();
return 0;
}
```

*Exercise 1:* Fill in the code as indicated by the comments in bold.
The file `proverb.txt` contains the following information:

```
Now Is The Time fOr All GoOd Men to come to the aid of their Family
```

*Sample Run:*

**The read position is currently at byte 0**

**Enter an offset from the current position:  4**

**The character read is I**

**If you would like to input another offset enter a Y**  y


**The read position is currently at byte 5**

**Enter an offset from the current position:  2**

**The character read is T**

**If you would like to input another offset enter a Y**  y


**The read position is currently at byte 8**

**Enter an offset from the current position:  6**

**The character read is e**

**If you would like to input another offset enter a Y**  y


**The read position is currently at byte 15**

**Enter an offset from the current position:  44**

**The character read is r**

**If you would like to input another offset enter a Y**  y


**The read position is currently at byte 60**

**Enter an offset from the current position:  8**

**The character read is r**

**If you would like to input another offset enter a Y**  n


*Exercise 2:* Why do you think that the character printed at the last run was
another r? What would you have to do to get a different letter after the
position is beyond the `eof` marker?

*Exercise 3:* Change the program so that the read position is calculated from the end of the file. What type of offsets would you need to enter to get characters from the proverb? Do several sample runs with different numbers to test your program.

## LAB 12.5   Student Generated Code Assignments

*Option 1:* Write a program that will: 1) read an array of records from the keyboard, 2) store this information to a binary file, 3) read from the binary file back to the array of records, 4) store this information to a textfile. Left justify the information for each field. Each record will consist of the following fields:

| | |
|---|---|
| first name | 15 characters |
| last name | 15 characters |
| street address | 30 characters |
| city | 20 characters |
| state | 5 characters |
| zip | long integer |

You may assume a maximum of 20 records.

This assignment is very similar to the program found in Lab 12.3.

*Sample Run:*

```
Enter the following information
Person's First Name: Billy
Person's Last Name: Berry
Street: 205 Main Street
City: Cleveland
State: TX
Zip: 45679


Enter a Y if you would like to input more data
Y


Enter the following information
Person's First Name: Sally
Person's Last Name: Connely
Street: 348 Wiley Lane
City: San Francisco
State: Md
Zip: 54789


Enter a Y if you would like to input more data
n
That's all the information
```

The output file contains the following:

| First Name | Last Name | Street | City | State | Zip Code |
|---|---|---|---|---|---|
| Billy | Berry | 205 Main Street | Cleveland | Tx | 45679 |
| Sally | Connely | 348 Wiley Lane | San Francisco | Md | 54789 |

*Option 2:* Write a program that will read the radii of circles. Use an array of records where each record will have the radius of the circle read from the keyboard and the diameter and area of the circle will be calculated by the program. This information (radius, diameter and area) is stored in a binary file. The information in the binary file is then read back into the records and stored in a text output file. Left justify the information for each field. Each record will consist of the following fields:

| | |
|---|---|
| radius | float |
| diameter | float |
| area | float |

You may assume a maximum of 20 records. You may want to include the `cmath` library.

You need to know the formulas for finding the area and circumference of a circle.

This assignment is very similar to the program in Lab 12.3.

*Sample Run:*

```
Enter the following information:
Radius of circle: 5
Enter a Y if you would like to input more data
y


Enter the following information:
Radius of circle: 4
Enter a Y if you would like to input more data
y


Enter the following information:
Radius of circle: 7
Enter a Y if you would like to input more data
n


That's all the information.
```

The output file contains the following:

```
Radius   Area    Circumference

5.00     78.54    31.42
4.00     50.27    25.13
7.00    153.94    43.98
```

*Option 3:* Bring in the file `employee.in` from Lab 12 folder. Write a program that will read records from this file and store them in a binary file. That file will then be used as input to create an output file of the information. The data file contains employee information consisting of name, social security, department ID, years employed, and salary. In addition to displaying the information of each record, the program will also calculate the average salary and years employed of all the records. This additional information is stored in the same output file.

*Sample Data File:*

| Bill Tarpon | 182460678 | 789 | 8 | 30600 |
|---|---|---|---|---|
| Fred Caldron | 456905434 | 789 | 10 | 40700 |
| Sally Bender | 203932239 | 790 | 8 | 50000 |
| David Kemp | 568903493 | 790 | 9 | 60000 |

The output file should look like this:

| Name | Social Security | Department ID | Years Employed | Salary |
|---|---|---|---|---|
| Bill Tarpon | 182460678 | 789 | 8 | 30600.00 |
| Fred Caldron | 456905434 | 789 | 10 | 40700.00 |
| Sally Bender | 203932239 | 790 | 8 | 50000.00 |
| David Kemp | 568903493 | 790 | 9 | 60000.00 |

The average number of years employed is 8

The average salary is $45325.00

# 13 Introduction to Classes

**PURPOSE**

1.  To introduce object-oriented programming
2.  To introduce the concept of classes
3.  To introduce the concept of constructors and destructors
4.  To introduce arrays of objects

**PROCEDURE**

1.  Students should read Chapter 13 of the text.
2.  Students should read the Pre-lab Reading Assignment before coming to lab.
3.  Students should complete the Pre-lab Writing Assignment before coming to lab.
4.  In the lab, students should complete labs assigned to them by the instructor.

| Contents | Pre-requisites | Approximate completion time | Page number | Check when done |
|---|---|---|---|---|
| Pre-lab Reading Assignment | Chapter 13 of text | 20 min. | 244 | |
| Pre-lab Writing Assignment | Pre-lab reading | 10 min. | 260 | |
| **LESSON 13A** | | | | |
| Lab 13.1 Square as a Class | Basic understanding of structures and classes | 10 min. | 261 | |
| Lab 13.2 Circles as a Class | Completion of Pre-lab Reading Assignment | 40 min. | 263 | |
| **LESSON 13B** | | | | |
| Lab 13.3 Arrays as Data Members of Classes | Understanding of private data members of classes and files | 20 min. | 265 | |
| Lab 13.4 Arrays of Objects | Understanding of classes | 20 min. | 267 | |
| Lab 13.5 Student Generated Code Assignments | Completion of all the previous labs | 30 min. | 269 | |

# PRE-LAB READING ASSIGNMENT

## Introduction to Object-Oriented Programming

Up until now, we have been using the procedural programming method for writing all our programs. A procedural program has data stored in a collection of variables (or structures) and has a set of functions that perform certain operations. The functions and data are treated as separate entities. Although operational, this method has some serious drawbacks when applied to very large real-world situations. Even though procedural programs can be modularized (broken into several functions), in a large complex program the number of functions can become overwhelming and difficult to modify or extend. This can create a level of complexity that is difficult to understand.

**Object-Oriented Programming (OOP)** mimics real world applications by introducing **classes** which act as prototypes for **objects**. Objects are similar to nouns which can simulate persons, places, or things that exist in the real world. OOP enhances code reuse ability (use of existing code or classes) so time is not used on "reinventing the wheel."

Classes and objects are often confused with one another; however, there is a subtle but important difference explained by the following example. A plaster of Paris mold consists of the design of a particular figurine. When the plaster is poured into the mold and hardened, we have the creation of the figurine itself. A class is analogous to the mold, for it holds the definition of an object. The object is analogous to the figurine, for it is an **instance** of the class. Classes and structures are very similar in their construction. Object-oriented programming is not learned in one lesson. This lab gives a brief introduction into this most important concept of programming.

A **class** is a prototype (template) for a set of objects. An object can be described as a single instance of a class in much the same way that a variable is a single instance of a particular data type. Just as several figurines can be made from one mold, many objects can be created from the same class. A class consists of a name (its identity), its member data which describes what it is and its member functions which describe what it does.[1] Member data are analogous to nouns since they act as entities. Member functions are analogous to verbs in that they describe actions. A class is an **abstract data type (ADT)** which is a user defined data type that combines a collection of variables and operations. For example, a rectangle, in order to be defined, must have a length and width. In practical terms we describe these as its member data (`length`, `width`). We also describe a set of member functions that gives and returns values to and from the member data as well as perform certain actions such as finding the rectangle's perimeter and area. Since many objects can be created from the same class, each object must have its own set of member data.

As noted earlier, a class is similar to a structure except that classes encapsulate (contain) functions as well as data.[2] Functions and data items are usually designated

---

[1] In other object-oriented languages member functions are called methods and member data are called attributes.

[2] Although structures can contain functions, they usually do not, whereas classes always contain them

as either **private** or **public** which indicates what can access them. Data and functions that are defined as `public` can be directly accessed by code outside the class, while functions and data defined as `private` can be accessed only by functions belonging to the class. Usually, classes make data members `private` and require outside access to them through member functions that are defined as `public`. Member functions are thus usually defined as `public` and member data as `private`.

The following example shows how a rectangle class can be defined in C++:

```cpp
#include <iostream>
using namespace std;


// Class declaration (header file)

class Rectangle  // Rectangle is the name of the class (its identity).
{

public:

    //  The following are labeled as public.
    //  Usually member functions are defined public
    //  and are used to describe what the class can do.

    void setLength(float side_l);
    //  This member function receives the length of the
    //  Rectangle object that calls it and places that value in
    //  the member data called length.

    void setWidth(float side_w);
    //  This member function receives the width of the Rectangle
    //  object that calls it and places the value in the member
    //  data called width.

    float getLength();
    //  This member function returns the length of the Rectangle
    //  object that calls it.

    float getWidth();
    //  This member function returns the width of the Rectangle
    //  object that calls it.

    double findArea();
    //  This member function finds the area of the Rectangle object
    //  that calls it.

    double findPerimeter();
    //  This member function finds the perimeter of the Rectangle
    //  object that calls it.
```

*continues*

```
private:

    // The following are labeled as private.
    // Member data are usually declared private so they can
    // ONLY be accessed by functions that belong to the class.
    // Member data describe the attributes of the class

    float length;
    float width;

};
```

This example has six member functions. It has two member functions for each private member data: `setLength` and `getLength` for the member data `length` and `setWidth` and `getWidth` for the member data `width`. It is often the case that a class will have both a **set** and a **get** member function for each of its private data members. A set member function receives a value from the calling object and places that value into the corresponding private member data. A get member function returns the value of the corresponding private member data to the object that calls it. In addition to set and get member functions, classes usually have other member functions that perform certain actions such as finding area and perimeter in the `Rectangle` class.

## Client and Implementation Files

It is not necessary for someone to understand how a television remote control works in order to use the remote to change the stations or the volume. The user of the remote could be called a **client** that only knows how to use the remote to accomplish a certain task. The details of how the remote control performs the task are not necessary for the user to operate the remote. Likewise, an automobile is a complex mechanical machine with a simple interface that allows users without any (or very little) mechanical knowledge to start, drive, and use it for a variety of functions. Drivers do not need to know what goes on under the hood. In the same way, a program that uses `Rectangle` does not need to know the details of how its member functions perform their operations. The use of an object (an instance of a class) is thus separated into two parts: the **interface** (client file) which calls the functions and the **implementation** which contains the details of how the functions accomplish their task.

An object not only combines data and functions, but also restricts other parts of the program from accessing member data and the inner workings of member functions. Having programs or users access only certain parts of an object is called **data hiding**. The fact that the internal data and inner workings can be hidden from users makes the object more accessible to a greater number of programs.

Just like an automobile or a remote control, a piece of commercial software is usually a complex entity developed by many individuals. OOP (Object-Oriented Programming) allows programmers to create objects with hidden complex logic that have simple **interfaces** which are easily understood and used. This allows more sophisticated programs to be developed. Interfacing is a major concern for software developers.

User of an object ——▶Public
                         Interface ——▶ Private Internal Data
                                        (length, width)
                                        Implementation of the member functions

## Types of Objects

Objects are either general purpose or application-specific. General purpose objects are designed to create a specific data type such as currency or date. They are also designed to perform common tasks such as input verification and graphical output. Application-specific objects are created as a specific limited operation for some organization or task. A student class, for example, may be created for an educational institution.

## Implementations of Classes in C++

The class declaration is usually placed in the global section of a program or in a special file (called a **header** file). As noted earlier, the class declaration acts very much like a prototype or data type for an object. An object is defined much like a variable except that it uses the class name as the data type. This definition creates an **instance** (actual occurrence) of the class. Implementation of the member functions of a class are given either after the `main` function of the program or in a separate file called the **implementation** file. Use of the object is usually in the `main` function, other specialized functions, or in a separate program file called the **client** file.[3]

## Creation and Use of Objects

`Rectangle`, previously described, is a class (prototype) and not an object (an actual instance of the class). Objects are defined in the client file, `main`, or other functions just as variables are defined:

`Rectangle box1,box2;`

`box1` and `box2` are objects of class `Rectangle`.

`box1` has its own `length` and `width` that are possibly different from the `length` and `width` of `box2`.

To access a member function (method) of an object, we use the dot operator, just as we do to access data members of structures. The name of the object is given first, followed by the dot operator and then the name of the member function.

The following example shows a complete `main` function (or client file) that defines and uses objects which call member functions.

```
int main()

{
        Rectangle box1;      // box1 is defined as an object of Rectangle class
        Rectangle box2;      // box2 is defined as another Rectangle class object
```

[3] More will be given on header, implementation, and client files later in the lesson.

```
        box1.setLength(20); // This instruction has the object box1 calling the
                            // setLength member function which sets the member data
                            // length associated with box1 to the value of 20
        box1.setWidth(5);

        box2.setLength(9.5);// This instruction has the object box2 calling the
                            // setLength member function which sets the member data
                            // length associated with box2 to the value of 9.5
        box2.setWidth(8.5);

        cout << "The length of box1 is "  << box1.getLength() << endl;
        cout << "The width of box1 is " << box1.getWidth() << endl;
        cout << "The area of box1 is "  << box1.findArea() << endl;
        cout << "The perimeter of box1 is " << box1.findPerimeter() << endl;

        cout << "The length of box2 is "  << box2.getLength() << endl;
        cout << "The width of box2 is " << box2.getWidth() << endl;
        cout << "The area of box2 is "  << box2.findArea() << endl;
        cout << "The perimeter of box2 is " << box2.findPerimeter() << endl;

        return 0;

}
```

Since findArea and findPerimeter must have length and width before they can do the calculation, an object must call setLength and setWidth first. The user must remember to initialize both length and width by calling both set functions. It is not good programming practice to assume that a user will do the necessary initialization. Constructors (discussed later) solve this problem.

## Implementation of Member Functions

As previously noted, the implementation of the member function can be hidden from the users (clients) of the objects. However, they must be implemented by someone, somewhere. The following shows the implementation of the Rectangle member functions.

```
//*****************************************************************
//                              setLength
//
// task:     This member function of the class Rectangle receives
//           the length of the Rectangle object that calls it and
//           places that value in the member data called length.
// data in:  the length of the rectangle
// data out: none
//
//*****************************************************************
```

```
void Rectangle::setLength(float side_l)
{

    length = side_l;
}


//******************************************************************
//                              setWidth
//
//   task:     This member function of the class Rectangle receives the
//             the width of the Rectangle object that calls it and
//             places that value in the member data called width.
//   data in:  the width of the rectangle
//   data out: none
//
//******************************************************************


void Rectangle::setWidth(float side_w)
{

    width = side_w;
}




//******************************************************************
//                              getLength
//
//   task:     This member function of the class Rectangle returns
//             the length of the Rectangle object that calls it.
//   data in:  none
//   data returned: length
//
//******************************************************************


float Rectangle::getLength()

{
    return length;


}

//******************************************************************
//                              getWidth
//
//   task:     This member function of the class Rectangle returns
//             the width of the Rectangle object that calls it.
//   data in:          none
//   data returned:    width
//
//******************************************************************
```

*continues*

```
float Rectangle:: getWidth()
{
    return width;
}


//*******************************************************************
//                                  findArea
//
// task:            This member function of the class Rectangle
//                  calculates the area of the object that calls it.
// data in:         none (uses the values of member data length &
//                  width)
// data returned:   area
//
//*******************************************************************


double Rectangle::findArea()

{
    return length * width;
}



//*******************************************************************
//                                  findPerimeter
//
// task:            This member function of the class Rectangle
//                  calculates the perimeter of the object that calls it
// data in:         none  (uses the values of member data length &
//                          width)
// data returned:   perimeter
//
//*******************************************************************

double Rectangle::findPerimeter()
{

    return ((2 * length) + (2 * width));
}
```

Notice that in the heading of each member function the name of the function is preceded by the name of the class to which it is a member followed by a double colon. In the above example each name is preceded by **Rectangle::**. This is necessary to indicate in which class the function is a member. There can be more than one function with the same name associated with different classes. The :: symbol is called the **scope operator**. It acts as an indicator of the class association.

Usually classes are declared in a header file, while member functions are stored in an implementation file and objects are defined and used in a client file. These files are often bound together in a project. Various development environments have different means of creating and storing related files in a project. All could be located in three different sections of the same file.

## Complete Program

The following code shows the class declaration, member functions (methods), implementations and use (client) of the `Rectangle` class:

```cpp
#include <iostream>
using namespace std;


//_____
// Class declaration (header file)

class Rectangle  // Rectangle is the name of the class
{
public:

    //  The member functions are labeled as public.

    void setLength(float side_l);
    //  This member function receives the length of the
    //  Rectangle object that calls it and places that value in
    //  the member data called length.

    void setWidth(float side_w);
    //  This member function receives the width of the Rectangle
    //  object that calls it and places the value in the member
    //  data called width.

    float getLength();
    //  This member function returns the length of the Rectangle
    //  object that calls it.

    float getWidth();
    //  This member function returns the width of the Rectangle
    //  object that calls it.

    double findArea();
    //  This member function finds the area of the rectangle object
    //  that calls it.

    double findPerimeter();
    //  This member function finds the perimeter of the rectangle
    //  object that calls it.


private:

    //  The following are labeled as private.
    //  Member data are usually declared private so they can
    //  ONLY be accessed by functions that belong to the class.
    //  Member data describe the attributes of the class
```

*continues*

```
        float length;
        float width;

};

// _____
// Client file
int main()

{
    Rectangle box1;          // box1 is defined as an object of Rectangle class
    Rectangle box2;          // box2 is defined as another Rectangle class object

    box1.setLength(20);      // This instruction has the object box1 calling the
                             // setLength member function which sets the member
                             // data length associated with box1 to the value
                             // of 20
    box1.setWidth(5);

    box2.setLength(30.5);    // This instruction has the object box2 calling the
                             // setLength member function which sets the member
                             // data length associated with box2 to the value
                             // of 30.5

    box2.setWidth(8.5);

    cout << "The length of box1 is "  << box1.getLength() << endl;
    cout << "The width of box1 is " << box1.getWidth() << endl;
    cout << "The area of box1 is "  << box1.findArea() << endl;
    cout << "The perimeter of box1 is " << box1.findPerimeter() << endl;

    cout << "The length of box2 is "  << box2.getLength() << endl;
    cout << "The width of box2 is " << box2.getWidth() << endl;
    cout << "The area of box2 is "  << box2.findArea() << endl;
    cout << "The perimeter of box2 is " << box2.findPerimeter() << endl;

    return 0;

}
// _____
// Implementation file

//******************************************************************
//                              setLength
//
//  task:     This member function of the class Rectangle receives the
//            the length of the Rectangle object that calls it and
//            places that value in the member data called length.
//  data in:  the length of the rectangle
//  data out: none
//
//******************************************************************
```

```
void Rectangle::setLength(float side_l)
{

    length = side_l;
}


//******************************************************************
//                              setWidth
//
//  task:     This member function of the class Rectangle receives the
//            the width of the Rectangle object that calls it and
//            places that value in the member data called width.
//  data in:  the width of the rectangle
//  data out: none
//
//******************************************************************


void Rectangle::setWidth(float side_w)
{

    width = side_w;
}


//******************************************************************
//                              getLength
//
//  task:            This member function of the class Rectangle returns
//                   the length of the Rectangle object that calls it.
//  data in:         none
//  data returned:   length
//
//******************************************************************


float Rectangle::getLength()

{
    return length;

}


//******************************************************************
//                              getWidth
//
//  task:            This member function of the class Rectangle returns
//                   the width of the Rectangle object that calls it.
//  data in:         none
//  data returned:   width
//
//******************************************************************
```

*continues*

```
float Rectangle::getWidth()
{
    return width;
}


//*******************************************************************
//                              findArea
//
//  task:           This member function of the class Rectangle
//                  calculates the area of the object that calls it.
//  data in:        none  (uses the values of member data length &
//                  width)
//  data returned:  area
//
//*******************************************************************


double Rectangle::findArea()

{
    return length * width;
}



//*******************************************************************
//                              findPerimeter
//
//  task:           This member function of the class Rectangle
//                  calculates the perimeter of the object that calls it.
//  data in:        none  (uses the values of member data length & width)
//  data returned:  perimeter
//
//*******************************************************************


double Rectangle::findPerimeter()
{

    return ((2 * length) + (2 * width));
}
```

## Inline Member Functions

Sometimes the implementation of member functions is so simple that they can be defined inside a class declaration. Such functions are called inline member functions. In the `Rectangle` class, `findArea` and `findPerimeter` are so simple that they can be defined in the class declaration as follows:

```
double findArea(){ return length * width; }
double findPerimeter()  { return 2 * length + 2 * width; }
```

## Introduction to Constructors

As noted earlier, the methods (member functions) findArea and findPerimeter must have the length and width before they can do any calculation.  The user must remember to initialize both length and width by calling both of these functions. What happens if the user forgets? Suppose we call findArea without first calling both setLength and setWidth. The function will try to find the area of a rectangle that has no length or width. Thus, the creator of a class should never rely on the user to initialize essential data.

C++ provides a mechanism, called a **constructor**, to guarantee the initialization of an object. A constructor is a member function that is *implicitly* invoked whenever a class instance is created (whenever an object is defined).  A constructor is unique from other member functions in two ways:

1. It has the same name as the class itself.
2. It does not have a data type (or the word void) in front of it.  The only purpose of the constructor is to initialize an object's member data.

The following shows the Rectangle class using two constructors that set the values of length and width.

```
class Rectangle
{
public:
    Rectangle(float side_l, float side_w);
    // Constructor allowing a user to input the length and width
    Rectangle();
    // Constructor using default values for both length and width

    void setLength(float side_l);
    void setWidth(float side_w);
    float getLength();
    float getWidth();
    double findArea();
    double findPerimeter() ;
private:
    float length;
    float width;

};
```

This class includes two constructors, differentiated by their parameter lists. Recall from Lesson Set 6.2 that two or more functions can have the same name as long as their parameters differ in quantity or data type. The parameter-less constructor (the second constructor in the above example) is the **default constructor**. Like all member functions, constructors are defined in the implementation file (or function definition section of a program). The reason for a default constructor is explained in the next section.

## Constructor Definitions

The function definitions of the two constructors for the Rectangle class are as follows:

```
Rectangle::Rectangle(float side_l, float side_w)
{
    length = side_l;
    width = side_w;
}

Rectangle::Rectangle()
{
    length = 1;
    width = 1;
}
```

The first constructor allows the user to input a value for both length and width at the same time that the object is defined (shown later in the lab). The second constructor (the default constructor) sets both length and width to 1 whenever the object is defined. Actually they could be set to anything that the creator of the class wants to use as a default for an object of the class that is not initialized by the user. With the use of these constructors, every object of class Rectangle will have a value for both length and width. We still keep the two member functions setLength and setWidth to allow the user to change the values of length and width. We could create a third constructor that has just one parameter which gives the value of length and uses the default value for width. If we create this third constructor, however, we can not create a fourth constructor that gives the value of width and use the default value for length. Why? We would have two member functions with the same name and an identical parameter list in both data type and number.

## Invoking a Constructor

Although a constructor is a member function, it is never invoked (called) using the dot notation. It is invoked when an object is defined.

*Example:* `Rectangle box1(12,6);`
         `Rectangle box2;`

In this example, box1 is an object of Rectangle class that has length set to 12 and width set to 6. Since it has two parameters, box1 activates the constructor that has two parameters. The object box2 is defined with both length and width set to 1. Since box2 has no parameters, it activates the default constructor.

## Destructors

A **destructor** is a member function that is automatically called to destroy an object. Just like constructors, a destructor has the same name as the class; however, it is preceded by a tilde (~). Destructors are used to free up memory when the object is no longer needed. The destructor is automatically called when an object of the class goes out of scope. This occurs when the function (such as main), where the object is defined, ends. The following example shows how constructors and destructors operate.

*Example*:

```
#include <iostream>
using namespace std;

class Demo
{
public:
    Demo();  // Default constructor
    ~Demo(); // Destructor

};

int main()
{
    Demo demoObj;  // demoObj is defined and invokes
                   // the default constructor that
                   // prints the message "The constructor has
                   // been invoked"

    cout << "The program is now running" << endl;
    return 0;
}


// Now that the main program is over, the object demoObj is no
// longer active.  The destructor is invoked and the message
// "The destructor has been invoked" is printed.

//*********************************************************
//                    The Default Constructor Demo
// Notice that constructors do not have to set member data
// This constructor prints a message that the constructor
// has been invoked.
//*********************************************************

Demo::Demo()
{
    cout << "The constructor has been invoked"  << endl;
}


//*********************************************************
//                    The Destructor Demo
// Notice that destructors do not have to print anything but
// this destructor prints the message "The destructor has been
// invoked."  The primary purpose of destructors is to free
// memory space once an object is no longer needed.
//*********************************************************

Demo::~Demo()
{
    cout << "The destructor has been invoked"  << endl;
}
```

What order do you think the three `cout` statements will be executed? Note that a class can have only one default constructor and one destructor.

## Arrays of Objects

Arrays can also contain objects of a class. For example, we could have an array of `Rectangle` objects.

*Example*:

```
Rectangle box[4]; // box is defined as an array of Rectangle objects
```

This statement makes an array of 4 elements, each consisting of an object of the `Rectangle` class.

Since this class has a default constructor, the default values are assigned to each element (object) of the array. The length and width for each of the objects in the box array are equal to 1 since these are the default values assigned by the default constructor.

The following program demonstrates the use of an array of objects:

```cpp
#include <iostream>
using namespace std;


class Rectangle
{
public:

    // Constructor allowing a user to input the length and width
    Rectangle(float side_l, float side_w);
    Rectangle();        // Default constructor
    ~Rectangle();       // Destructor

    void setLength(float side_l);
    void setWidth(float side_w);
    float getLength();
    float getWidth();
    double findArea();
    double findPerimeter() ;

private:

    float length;
    float width;

};


const int NUMBEROFOBJECTS = 4;

int main()

{
```

```
Rectangle box[NUMBEROFOBJECTS];   // Box is defined as an array of
                                  // Rectangle objects

      for (int pos = 0; pos < NUMBEROFOBJECTS; pos++)

      {
          cout << "Information for box number  " << pos + 1 << endl << endl;

          cout << "The length of the box is "  << box[pos].getLength()
               << endl;
          cout << "The width of the box is " << box[pos].getWidth() << endl;
          cout << "The area of the box is "  << box[pos].findArea() << endl;
          cout << "The perimeter of the box is " << box[pos].findPerimeter()
               << endl << endl;

      }

      return 0;

}

void Rectangle::setLength(float side_l)
{
    length = side_l;
}

void Rectangle::setWidth(float side_w)
{
    width = side_w;
}


float Rectangle::getLength()
{
    return length;
}

float Rectangle:: getWidth()
{
    return width;
}

double Rectangle::findArea()
{
    return length * width;
}

double Rectangle::findPerimeter()
{
```

*continues*

```
        return ((2 * length) + (2 * width));
}


Rectangle::Rectangle(float side_l, float side_w)
{
    length = side_l;
    width = side_w;
}


Rectangle::Rectangle()
{
    length = 1;
    width = 1;
}


Rectangle::~Rectangle()
{
}
```

The output will be the same for each box because each has been initialized to the default values for length and width.

## PRE-LAB WRITING ASSIGNMENT

### Fill–in–the–Blank Questions

1. A(n)_____is used in C++ to guarantee the initialization of a class instance.

2. A constructor has the_____name as the class itself.

3. Member functions are sometimes called _____ in other object-oriented languages.

4. A(n) _____is a member function that is automatically called to destroy an object.

5. To access a particular member function, the code must list the object name and the name of the function separated from each other by a

   _____.

6. A _____ constructor has no parameters.

7. A _____ precedes the destructor name in the declaration.

8. A(n) _____ member function has its implementation given in the class declaration.

9. In an array of objects, if the default constructor is invoked, then it is applied to _____ object in the array.

10. A constructor is a member function that is _____ invoked whenever a class instance is created.

## LESSON 13A

### Lab 13.1    Squares as a Class

Retrieve program `square.cpp` from the Lab 13 folder. The code is as follows:

```
// This program declares the Square class and uses member functions to find
// the perimeter and area of the square

#include <iostream>
using namespace std;

// FILL IN THE CODE TO DECLARE A CLASS CALLED Square. TO DO THIS SEE
// THE IMPLEMENTATION SECTION.

int main()
{
    Square   box;   // box is defined as an object of the Square class
    float    size;  // size contains the length of a side of the square

    // FILL IN THE CLIENT CODE THAT WILL ASK THE USER FOR THE LENGTH OF THE
    // SIDE OF THE SQUARE. (This is stored in size)

    // FILL IN THE CODE THAT CALLS SetSide.

    // FILL IN THE CODE THAT WILL RETURN THE AREA FROM A CALL TO A FUNCTION
    // AND PRINT OUT THE AREA TO THE SCREEN.

    // FILL IN THE CODE THAT WILL RETURN THE PERIMETER FROM A CALL TO A
    // FUNCTION AND PRINT OUT THAT VALUE TO THE SCREEN.

    return 0;
}

//_____
//Implementation section    Member function implementation

//**************************************************
//              setSide
//
// task:    This procedure takes the length of a side and
//          places it in the appropriate member data
// data in: length of a side
//**************************************************

void Square::setSide(float length)

{
    side = length;
}
```

*continues*

```
//***************************************************
//                findArea
//
// task:    This finds the area of a square
// data in: none (uses value of data member side)
// data returned:  area of square
//***************************************************

float Square::findArea()
{
   return side * side;
}
//***************************************************
//                findPerimeter
//
// task:    This finds the perimeter of a square
// data in: none (uses value of data member side)
// data returned:  perimeter of square
//***************************************************
float Square::findPerimeter()
{
   return 4 * side;
}
```

*Exercise 1:* This program asks you to fill in the class declaration and client code based on the implementation of the member functions. Fill in the code so that the following input and output will be generated:

**Please input the length of the side of the square**
8
**The area of the square is 64**
**The perimeter of the square is 32**

*Exercise 2:* Add two constructors and a destructor to the class and create the implementation of each. One constructor is the default constructor that sets the side to 1. The other constructor will allow the user to initialize the side at the definition of the object. The destructor does not have to do anything but reclaim memory space. Create an object called box1 that gives the value of 9 to the constructor at the definition. Add output statements so that the following is printed in addition to what is printed in Exercise 1.

**The area of box1 is 81**
**The perimeter of box1 is 36**

## Lab 13.2 Circles as a Class

Retrieve program `circles.cpp` from the Lab 13 folder. The code is as follows:

```cpp
#include <iostream>
using namespace std;
//_____
// This program declares a class for a circle that will have
// member functions that set the center, find the area, find
// the circumference and display these attributes.
// The program as written does not allow the user to input data, but
// rather has the radii and center coordinates of the circles
// (spheres in the program) initialized at definition or set by a function.

//class declaration section    (header file)

class Circles
{
public:
   void setCenter(int x, int y);
   double findArea();
   double findCircumference();
   void printCircleStats(); // This outputs the radius and center of the circle.
   Circles (float r);       // Constructor
   Circles();               // Default constructor
private:
   float   radius;
   int     center_x;
   int     center_y;
};

const double PI = 3.14;

//Client section

int main()
{
   Circles sphere(8);
   sphere.setCenter(9,10);
   sphere.printCircleStats();

   cout << "The area of the circle is " << sphere.findArea() << endl;
   cout << "The circumference of the circle is "
        << sphere.findCircumference() << endl;

   return 0;
}

//_____
```

*continues*

```
//Implementation section     Member function implementation

Circles::Circles()
{
    radius = 1;
}
```

**// Fill in the code to implement the non-default constructor**

**// Fill in the code to implement the findArea member function**

**// Fill in the code to implement the findCircumference member function**

```
void Circles::printCircleStats()
// This procedure prints out the radius and center coordinates of the circle
// object that calls it.

{
    cout << "The radius of the circle is " << radius << endl;
    cout << "The center of the circle is (" << center_x
         << "'" << center_y << ")" << endl;
}


void Circles::setCenter(int x, int y)
// This procedure will take the coordinates of the center of the circle from
// the user and place them in the appropriate member data.

{
    center_x = x;
    center_y = y;
}
```

*Exercise 1*: Alter the code so that setting the center of the circle is also done during the object definition. This means that the constructors will also take care of this initialization. Make the default center at point (0, 0) and keep the default radius as 1. Have sphere defined with initial values of 8 for the radius and (9, 10) for the center. How does this affect existing functions and code in the main function?

The following output should be produced:

**The radius of the circle is 8**
**The center of the circle is (9, 10)**
**The area of the circle is 200.96**
**The circumference of the circle if 50.24**

*Exercise 2*: There can be several constructors as long as they differ in number of parameters or data type. Alter the program so that the user can enter either just the radius, the radius and the center, or nothing at the time the object is defined. Whatever the user does NOT include (radius or center) must be initialized somewhere. There is no setRadius function and there will no longer be a setCenter function. You can continue to assume that the default radius is 1 and the default center is (0, 0). Alter the client portion (main) of the program by defining an object sphere1, giving just the radius of 2 and the default center, and `sphere2` by giving neither the radius nor the center (it uses all the default values). Be sure to print out the vital statistics for these new objects (area and circumference).

In addition to the output in Exercise 1, the following output should be included:

**The radius of the circle is 2**
**The center of the circle is (0, 0)**
**The area of the circle is 12.56**
**The circumference of the circle is 12.56**

**The radius of the circle is 1**
**The center of the circle is (0, 0)**
**The area of the circle is 3.14**
**The circumference of the circle is 6.28**

*Exercise 3*: Alter the program you generated in Exercise 2 so that the user will be allowed to enter either nothing, just the radius, just the center, or both the center and radius at the time the object is defined. Add to the client portion of the code an object called `sphere3` that, when defined, will have the center at (15, 16) and the default radius. Be sure to print out this new object's vital statistics (area and circumference).

In addition to the output in Exercise 1 and 2, the following output should be printed:

**The radius of the circle is 1**
**The center of the circle is (15, 16)**
**The area of the circle is 3.14**
**The circumference of the circle is 6.28**

*Exercise 4*: Add a destructor to the code. It should print the message **This concludes the Circles class** for each object that is destroyed. How many times is this printed? Why?

# LESSON 13B

## Lab 13.3   Arrays as Data Members of Classes

Retrieve program `floatarray.cpp` and `temperatures.txt` from the Lab 13 folder. The code is as follows:

```
// This program reads floating point data from a data file and places those
// values into the private data member called values (a floating point array)
// of the FloatList class. Those values are then printed to the screen.
// The input is done by a member function called GetList. The output
// is done by a member function called PrintList. The amount of data read in
// is stored in the private data member called length. The member function
// GetList is called first so that length can be initialized to zero.

#include <iostream>
#include <fstream>
#include <iomanip>
```

*continues*

```
using namespace std;

const int MAX_LENGTH = 50;   // MAX_LENGTH contains the maximum length of our list
class FloatList              // Declares a class that contains an array of
                             // floating point numbers
{
public:
    void getList(ifstream&);   // Member function that gets data from a file
    void printList() const;    // Member function that prints data from that
                               // file to the screen.
    FloatList();               // constructor that sets length to 0.
    ~FloatList();              // destructor

private:
    int length;                // Holds the number of elements in the array
    float values[MAX_LENGTH];  // The array of values

};

int main()
{
    ifstream tempData;         // Defines a data file

    // Fill in the code to define an object called list of the class FloatList

    cout << fixed << showpoint;
    cout << setprecision(2);

    tempData.open("temperatures.txt");

    // Fill in the code that calls the getList function.
    // Fill in the code that calls the printList function.

return 0;
}
 FloatList::FloatList()
 {
    // Fill in the code to complete this constructor that
    // sets the private data member length to 0
 }

// Fill in the entire code for the getList function
// The getList function reads the data values from a data file
// into the values array of the class FloatList

// Fill in the entire code for the printList function
// The printList function prints to the screen the data in
// the values array of the class FloatList

// Fill in the code for the implementation of the destructor
```

This program has an array of floating point numbers as a private data member of a class. The data file contains floating point temperatures which are read by a member function of the class and stored in the array.

*Exercise 1*:  Why does the member function `printList` have a `const` after its name but `getList` does not?

*Exercise 2*:  Fill in the code so that the program reads in the data values from the temperature file and prints them to the screen with the following output:

**78.90**
**87.40**
**60.80**
**70.40**
**75.60**

*Exercise 3*:  Add code (member function, call and function implementation) to print the average of the numbers to the screen so that the output will look like the output from Exercise 2 plus the following:

**The average temperature is 74.62**

## Lab 13.4    Arrays of Objects

Retrieve program `inventory.cpp` and `inventory.dat` from the Lab 13 folder. The code is as follows:

```
#include <iostream>
#include <fstream>
using namespace std;

// This program declares a class called Inventory that has itemnNumber (which
// contains the id number of a product) and numOfItem (which contains the
// quantity on hand of the corresponding product)as private data members.
// The program will read these values from a file and store them in an
// array of objects (of type Inventory).  It will then print these values
// to the screen.

// Example: Given the following data file:
//     986 8
//     432 24
// This program reads these values into an array of objects and prints the
// following:
//     Item number 986 has 8 items in stock
//     Item number 432 has 24 items in stock


const NUMOFPROD = 10;    // This holds the number of products a store sells

class Inventory
{
public:
```

*continues*

```
            void getId(int item);      // This puts item in the private data member
                                       // itemNumber of the object that calls it.
            void getAmount(int num);   // This puts num in the private data member
                                       // numOfItem of the object that calls it.
            void display();            // This prints to the screen
                                       // the value of itemNumber and numOfItem of the
                                       // object that calls it.


    private:

        int   itemNumber;          // This is an id number of the product
        int   numOfItem;           // This is the number of items in stock

    };



    int main()
    {

        ifstream infile;           // Input file to read values into array
        infile.open("Inventory.dat");

        // Fill in the code that defines an array of objects of class Inventory
        // called products. The array should be of size NUMOFPROD

        int pos;                   // loop counter
        int id;                    // variable holding the id number
        int total;                 // variable holding the total for each id number

        // Fill in the code that will read inventory numbers and number of items
        // from a file into the array of objects. There should be calls to both
        // getId and getAmount member functions somewhere in this code.
        // Example: products[pos].getId(id); will be somewhere in this code

        // Fill in the code to print out the values (itemNumber and numOfItem) for
        // each object in the array products.
        // This should be done by calling the member function display within a loop

        return 0;

    }


    // Write the implementations for all the member functions of the class.
```

---

*Exercise 1*: Complete the program by giving the code explained in the commands in bold.  The data file is as follows:

```
986  8
432  24
132  100
```

123  89
329  50
503  30
783  78
822  32
233  56
322  74

**The output should be as follows:**

**Item number 986 has 8 items in stock**
**Item number 432 has 24 items in stock**
**Item number 132 has 100 items in stock**
**Item number 123 has 89 items in stock**
**Item number 329 has 50 items in stock**
**Item number 503 has 30 items in stock**
**Item number 783 has 78 items in stock**
**Item number 822 has 32 items in stock**
**Item number 233 has 56 items in stock**
**Item number 322 has 74 items in stock**

## LAB 13.5 Student Generated Code Assignments

*Exercise 1:* Give a C++ class declaration called `SavingsAccount` with the following information:

*Operations* (Member Functions)

1.  Open account (with an initial deposit). This is called to put initial values in `dollars` and `cents`.

2.  Make a deposit. A function that will add value to `dollars` and `cents`

3.  Make a withdrawal. A function that will subtract values from `dollars` and `cents`.

4.  Show current balance. A function that will print `dollars` and `cents`.

*Data* (Member Data)

1.  `dollars`

2.  `cents`

Give the implementation code for all the member functions.

NOTE: You must perform normalization on `cents`. This means that if `cents` is 100 or more, it must increment `dollars` by the appropriate amount. Example: if cents is 234, then dollars must be increased by 2 and cents reduced to 34.

Write code that will create an object called `bank1`. The code will then initially place $200.50 in the account. The code will deposit $40.50 and then withdraw $100.98. It will print out the final value of `dollars` and `cents`.

The following output should be produced:

`Dollars = 140    cents = 2.`

Part 2: Change the program to allow the user to input the initial values, deposit and withdrawal.

*Example:*

```
Please input the initial dollars
402

Please input the initial cents
78


Would you like to make a deposit? Y or y for yes
y
Please input the dollars to be deposited
35
Please input the cents to be deposited
67
Would you like to make a deposit? Y or y for yes
y
Please input the dollars to be deposited
35
Please input the cents to be deposited
67
Would you like to make a deposit? Y or y for yes
n
Would you like to make a withdrawal Y or y for yes
y
Please input the dollars to be withdrawn
28
Please input the cents to be withdrawn
08
Would you like to make a withdrawal Y or y for yes
y
Please input the dollars to be withdrawn
75
Please input the cents to be withdrawn
78
Would you like to make a withdrawal Y or y for yes
n


Dollars = 370 Cents = 26
```

*Exercise 2*: Replace the initial member function by two constructors. One constructor is the default constructor that sets both dollars and cents to 0. The other constructor has 2 parameters that set dollars and cents to the indicated values.

Have the code generate two objects: bank1 (which has its values set during definition by the user) and bank2 that uses the default constructor. Have the code input deposits and withdrawals for both bank1 and bank2.

# Visual C++ Environment

In this first lab, you will become acquainted with a software package that will allow you to create, compile and run C++ programs. Visual C++ is a product of Microsoft and is one component of Visual Studio (a complete set of programming language environments). The following steps walk you through most of the commands needed for this course.

## I. Pre-lab Assignment

1. Be sure to read Lesson Set 1 Pre-lab Reading Assignment and do the Pre-lab Writing Assignment before coming to class.

2. Make sure you have a working password or some means of logging on to your particular computer system. Check with your instructor.

## II. Visual C++ environment

1. Make sure you are logged on the system.

2. Select Start→Programs→Microsoft visual Studio 6.1→Microsoft Visual C++6.0 (Your particular system may have an alternative way of accessing Visual C++, check with your instructor).

3. After opening any source file, you must save it to your hard or zip drive before you will be able to compile and run it.

4. Once you are in the Visual C++ package you are ready to open or create files. All files are stored in a workspace.

## III. Opening an Existing File

1. Click on the File Menu (top left corner) then select open.

    (The above step could be done by just clicking on the open folder icon).

2. You now see a window that says open. In the `Look in` box at the top there is a down arrow button. Selecting this helps you browse the drives to find where the files are.

3. Your instructor will tell you where and how to access the programs stored for this lab course, hereafter called the lesson folder.

4. We are going to open the first program. Double click on the `firstprog.cpp`.

5. This brings the file into the workspace; however, we must save it to our own disk space (hard drive or zip drive). Click on File→Save As→ and now use the browse feature to go to your hard drive and save the file there.

6. Your window should say something like `C:\firstprog.cpp`.

7. You can now compile this program by going to the **Build menu** and selecting **compile** (the first choice of the menu).

8. A message pops up that says the file requires an active project workspace. All Visual C++ files are stored in a workspace and must have a project created in that workspace. Just click **yes** to this message.

9. You should see some words at a bottom window that says no errors. When this occurs you are ready to run the program.

10. Click on build and then execute (it has a **red exclamation point**). This exclamation point may also be found somewhere on your screen.

11. Another message appears that asks if you want to build a file. Again just click on **yes.**

12. The program runs and shows an output display window. What is printed on the screen?

13. Hit any key and the message disappears.

14. After completing each lesson you MUST purge the Visual C++ workspace before opening a new source file. Do this by selecting File→Close Workspace. Select Yes when prompted about closing all document windows.

15. All programs brought in from the lesson folder must be saved to your hard or zip drive before compiling or running.

16. You can also create your own file from scratch by selecting File→New→Files then highlight C++ source file (if your are creating a program file) or text file (if you are creating a data file). On the right side, type in the name of the file in the box labeled file name, and determine where you want it saved by giving the drive in the box labeled location.

17. We do not explain at this point how to create a project. This is done for you when you compile a program you wrote or brought in from a lesson folder.

18. You have now completed Lab 1.1 and are ready to begin Lab 1.2.

# UNIX

In this first lab you will learn how to create, compile, and run C++ programs using the UNIX operating system.

## I. Pre-lab Assignment

1. Be sure to read the Lesson Set 1 Pre-lab Reading Assignment and then do the Pre-lab Writing Assignment before coming to class.

2. Make sure you have a login name and a working password to logon to a UNIX system. Your instructor, along with the UNIX administrator, will help you obtain an account and learn how to login.

## II. The UNIX Operating System

UNIX is a very powerful operating system. However, for some users it is not quite as easy to learn as the Windows environment. UNIX requires some extra knowledge on the part of the user. This appendix should help you learn some of the basics of this operating system. Nevertheless, you will most likely need additional information from your instructor or other sources to be a successful UNIX user. This appendix is a terse, but in no way complete, introduction to UNIX.

The UNIX system organizes files in a hierarchical structure. The top of this structure is called the root directory identified by (/). Major directories are located under the root directory. For example, /home indicates the user home directory and /bin is the binary directory for executables. A directory called programs under /home is identified by /home/programs. The *path* /home/programs/program1.cpp shows the location of the C++ program program1.cpp in the /programs directory.

## III. The UNIX Reference Manual

There is a UNIX reference manual that can be accessed during your UNIX session as long as your system has the man program. To get information regarding a particular command type man at the shell prompt followed by the desired command. For example,

```
man mkdir
```

provides you information about the mkdir (make directory) command. A list of useful commands that you may wish to explore as follows:

cd      changes directory
cp      copy file
find    find files
grep    locate text within a file
ls      displays contents of current directory

| man | UNIX reference manual |
| mkdir | makes new directory |
| mv | move and rename a file |
| pwd | display name of current directory with path |
| rm | remove (delete) files |
| rmdir | removes directory |
| vi | begin a vi (visual interpreter) editor session |

Of course, there are many other useful UNIX commands. To learn more about these commands and other important information, visit the UNIX resources at your library and local bookstore.

### IV. Editing with vi

You can create and edit files during a UNIX session using the vi (visual interpreter) editor. First choose the desired subdirectory for your file. For example, if you are in the /home directory, enter cd programs. To start the editor enter vi at the shell prompt followed by the name of your file:

```
vi program1.cpp
```

There are two modes for vi: the text-entry mode and the command mode. First select the text-entry mode by typing the character **a** for append. Now you are ready to enter text.

Type the following:

```
#include <iostream>
using namespace std;

int main()
{
    cout << "Welcome to the UNIX operating system" << endl;
    return 0;

}
```

You do not need to worry about what the code means at this point. Just make sure you can enter this using the vi editor. To exit the text-entry mode, press the Escape key. This will return you to the command mode. Editing commands can be entered from this mode.

A simple example of a vi editing command is the command to delete a character. If you want to delete a single character, move the cursor to the desired character and type **x**. To delete multiple successive characters, move the cursor to the first character and type the desired number followed by **x**. For example, **9x** deletes the next 9 characters. Other editing commands are the following:

| dw | deletes a word |
| dW | deletes a word that contains punctuation |
| ndw | (or ndW) for deleting successive words |
| i | inserts new text (changes to text-entry mode) |
| O | opens a new line above (changes to text-entry mode) |
| o | opens a new line below (changes to text-entry mode) |

For more information on these and other editing commands use the man command described above or some other resource on the vi editor.

To save the program you just entered, make sure you are in command mode and type `:w` and then press ENTER. Your work should now be saved in program1.cpp.

Finally, you will need to exit the `vi` editor before you can compile and run your program. To do this, type `:q` and then press ENTER. The shell prompt should now appear on your screen.

### V. Compiling and Executing a C++ Program

Possible commands to compile your C++ program will depend on your particular system. Many UNIX systems have GNU C/C++ compile. In this case you may type

**g++ program1.cpp**

to compile your program. Assuming you typed everything correctly, there should be no errors and an executable will be created. A shell prompt will appear without any messages. Now type `ls` and then press ENTER. You should see a new file listed named a.out. To execute your program, type **a.out** and then press ENTER. The following should appear on your screen:

```
"Welcome to the UNIX operating system"
```

This indicates that you have executed your program. If `g++` does not successfully compile your program, see your instructor to find out the command necessary for your particular system.

Often, you will want to bring in an existing C++ program from a floppy disk or some other source. Your instructor will show you how to retrieve existing files from other locations.

### VI. Logging Off

To log out upon completion of your UNIX session, type `logout` and then press ENTER. Make sure that you do not misspell `logout`—otherwise you may be leaving your files open to the next user!

# Index